KT-226-499

GERMAN
Phrase book

Carol Stanley and Philippa Goodrich

BBC Books

BBC Books publishes courses on the following languages:

ARABIC	ITALIAN
CHINESE	JAPANESE
FRENCH	PORTUGUESE
GERMAN	RUSSIAN
GREEK	SPANISH
HINDI URDU	TURKISH

For further information write to:
BBC Books
Language Enquiry Service
Room A3116
Woodlands
80 Wood Lane
London
W12 0TT

Consultant: Julia Bueno

Published by BBC Books
A division of BBC Enterprises Ltd
Woodlands, 80 Wood Lane, London W12 0TT

ISBN 0 563 21515-1
First published 1991
© Carol Stanley and Philippa Goodrich 1991
Reprinted 1991, 1992

Set in Times Roman by Ace Filmsetting Ltd, Frome
Text and Cover printed in England by
Clays Ltd, St Ives plc

Published on consultation with the
BBC Continuing Education Advisory Council

CONTENTS

How to use this book	5
Pronunciation	7
The German alphabet	10
General conversation	11
Arriving in the country	21
Directions	24
Road travel	31
Taxis	46
Air travel	49
Travelling by train	55
Buses and coaches	64
Underground travel	69
Boats and ferries	71
At the tourist office	76
Accommodation	80
Telephones	92
Changing money	97
Eating and drinking	101
Menu reader	113
Shopping	127
Business trips	137
Sightseeing	142
Entertainments	146
Sports and activities	152
Health	158
Problems and complaints	170
Basic grammar	178
Days, months, dates	189
Time	193
Countries and nationalities	197
General signs and notices	201
Conversion tables	203
National holidays	207

Useful addresses 208
Numbers 211
Dictionary
German/English 213
English/German 239
Emergencies 285
Emergency telephone numbers 288

HOW TO USE THIS BOOK

Communicating in a foreign language doesn't have to be difficult – you can convey a lot with just a few words (plus a few gestures and a bit of mime). Just remember: keep it simple. Don't try to come out with long, grammatically perfect sentences when one or two words will get your meaning across.

Inside the front and back cover of this book is a list of all-purpose phrases. Some will help you to make contact – greetings, 'please' and 'thank you', 'yes' and 'no'. Some are to get people to help you understand what they're saying to you. And some are questions like 'do you have . . . ?' and 'where is . . . ?', to which you can add words from the Dictionary at the back of the book.

The book is divided into sections for different situations, such as Road travel, Shopping, Health and so on. In each section you'll find

- Words and phrases that you'll see on signs or in print
- Useful tips and information
- Phrases you are likely to want to say
- Things that people may say to you

Many of the phrases can be adapted by simply using another word from the Dictionary. For instance, take the question **Ist der Flughafen weit?** (Is the airport far away?) – if you want to know if the *station* is far away, just substitute **der Bahnhof** (the station) for **der Flughafen** to give **Ist der Bahnhof weit?** You can use the blank bits of pages to make a note of words that are particularly useful to you.

All the phrases have a simple pronunciation guide underneath based on English sounds – this is explained in Pronunciation (page 7).

If you want some guidance on how the German language works, see Basic grammar (page 178).

There's a handy reference section (starts page 189) which contains lists of days and months, countries and nationalities, general signs and notices that you'll see, conversion tables, national holidays and useful addresses. Numbers appear on pages 211–12.

The 5000-word Dictionary (page 213) comes in two sections – German–English and English–German.

At the end of the book (page 285) is an Emergencies section (which we hope you *won't* have to use).

Wherever possible, work out in advance what you want to say – if you're going shopping, for instance, write out a shopping list in German. If you're buying travel tickets, work out how to say where you want to go, how many tickets you want, single or return, etc.

Practise saying things out loud – the cassette that goes with this book will help you get used to the sounds of German.

Above all – don't be shy! It'll be appreciated if you try to say a few words, even if it's only 'good morning' and 'goodbye' – and in fact those are the very sorts of phrases that are worth learning as you'll hear them and need to use them all the time.

If you would like to learn more German, BBC Books also publish *Get by in German*, *Deutsch Direkt* and *Deutsch Express*.

BBC phrase books are also available for the following languages: French, Spanish and Italian. Future titles will include Arabic, Greek, Portuguese and Turkish.

The authors would welcome any suggestions or comments about this book, but in the meantime: Have a good trip! – **Gute Reise!**

PRONUNCIATION

You don't need perfect pronunciation to be able to communicate – it's enough to get the sounds approximately right and stress words in the correct place. If you want to hear real German voices and to practise trying to sound like them, then listen to the cassette.

German pronunciation is very regular – you can tell how a word is pronounced from the way it's written, once you know what each letter (or group of letters) represents. Long words in German are often a combination of several shorter words, so it may help with pronunciation to split the long word into its individual parts. A pronunciation guide is given with the phrases in this book – the system is based on English sounds, as described below.

Many German consonants are pronounced in a similar way to English.

The final 'e' on a word is always pronounced.

For the German alphabet, see page 10.

Stress

In this book, a stressed syllable is shown in the pronunciation guide by bold type:
*prob**laym**, kilo**mayter**.*

Vowels

	Approx. English equivalent	Shown in book as	Example	
a	a in 'cat'	**a**	**danke**	***dan**ke*
or	a in 'car'	**aa**	**abend**	***aa**bent*
ai and **ay**	i in 'pile'	**iy**	**Kaiser**	***kiy**zer*
au	ow in 'cow'	**ow**	**Raucher**	***row**ker*
ä	e in 'let'	**e**	**Geschäft**	*ge**sheft***
or	ay in 'pay'	**ay**	**spät**	*shpayt*
äu	oy in 'boy'	**oy**	**Kohlensäure**	***koh**lenzoyre*
e	e in 'let'	**e**	**essen**	***ess**en*
or	ay in 'pay'	**ay**	**gehen**	***gay**en*
ei and **ey**	i in 'pile'	**iy**	**Bein**	*biyn*
eu	oy in 'boy'	**oy**	**heute**	***hoy**te*
i	i in 'hit'	**i**	**bitte**	***bi**tte*
or	ee in 'meet'	**ee**	**ihn**	*een*
ie	ee in 'meet'	**ee**	**dieser**	***dee**zer*
o	o in 'lot'	**o**	**Woche**	***vo**ke*
or	o in 'bone'	**oh**	**Monat**	***moh**naat*
ö	er in 'fern'	**er**	**können**	***ker**nnen*
u	oo in 'room'	**oo**	**gut**	*goot*
ü	ew in 'dew'	**ew**	**für**	*fewr*
y	ew in 'dew'	**ew**	**typisch**	***tew**pish*

Consonants

	Approx. English equivalent	Shown in book as	Example	
b	b in 'but'	**b**	**Bad**	*baat*
c	c in 'can'	**k**	**Café**	***ka**fay*
ch	k in 'kit'	**k**	**brauche**	***brow**ke*
or	sh in 'shut'	**sh**	**ich**	*ish*
or	c in 'can'	**k**	**Charakter**	*kara**k**ter*
d	d in 'dog'	**d**	**Dame**	***daa**me*
f	f in 'feet'	**f**	**fünf**	*fewnf*
g	g in 'got'	**g**	**grün**	*grewn*
h	h in 'hard'	**h**	**Hand**	*hant*
j	y in 'you'	**y**	**ja**	*yaa*
l	l in 'look'	**l**	**lang**	*lang*
m	m in 'mat'	**m**	**Mutter**	***moot**ter*
n	n in 'not'	**n**	**Name**	***naa**me*
p	p in 'pack'	**p**	**Person**	*perz**ohn***
qu	k + v	**kv**	**Quittung**	***kvitt**oong*
r	rolled at the back of the mouth	**r**	**Rücken**	***rewk**en*
s	s in 'set'	**s**	**es**	*es*
or	z in 'zoo'	**z**	**Sie**	*zee*
or	sh in 'shut'	**sh**	**Stunde**	***shtoon**de*
sch	sh in 'shut'	**sh**	**schnell**	*shnell*
ß	ss in 'press'	**ss**	**heiß**	*hiyss*
t	t in 'tin'	**t**	**Tag**	*taag*
tsch	ch in 'church'	**ch**	**Deutsch**	*doych*
v	f in 'feet'	**f**	**vier**	*feer*
or sometimes	v in 'voice'	**v**	**Ventil**	*vent**il***
w	v in 'voice'	**v**	**wo**	*voh*
x	x in 'taxi'	**ks**	**taxi**	***tak**see*
z	ts in 'hits'	**ts**	**zeigen**	***tsiy**gen*

THE GERMAN ALPHABET

The **umlaut** means that there are three extra vowels in German: 'a' umlaut, 'o' umlaut' and 'u' umlaut.

The **ß** symbol represents a double 's' and is called 's,z' or 'scharfes s'.

Spelling

How is it spelt?
Wie schreibt man das?
vee shriybt man das

Letter	Pronounced	Letter	Pronounced
A	*aa*	**O**	*oh*
Ä	*ay*	**Ö**	*er*
B	*bay*	**P**	*pay*
C	*tsay*	**Q**	*koo*
D	*day*	**R**	*ayr*
E	*ay*	**S**	*es*
F	*ef*	**ß**	*es tset/sharfes es*
G	*gay*	**T**	*tay*
H	*haa*	**U**	*oo*
I	*ee*	**Ü**	*ew*
J	*yot*	**V**	*fow*
K	*kaa*	**W**	*vay*
L	*el*	**X**	*iks*
M	*em*	**Y**	*ewpsilon*
N	*en*	**Z**	*tset*

GENERAL CONVERSATION

• The Germans shake hands on meeting people and greeting friends much more than the British do.

• **Guten Tag** is a general greeting that can be used throughout the day. In Southern Germany and Austria you are much more likely to be greeted with **Grüß Gott!** You'll also hear **Servus!** in the south and in Austria which means hello and goodbye. You may also hear **Pfüeti!** or **Pfüetsi!** in Bavaria and Austria which literally means **Gott behüte dich/Sie** (God look after you) and is another way of saying goodbye. **Guten Morgen** and **Guten Abend** are both used to greet people at the appropriate time of the day and **Gute Nacht** is the equivalent of saying 'good night'.

• There are two ways of saying you – the formal and the informal way. **Sie** (always written with a capital letter) is formal and is used between people who are meeting for the first time or don't know each other well or between younger and older people. **Du** is informal and used between members of a family, friends, young people and to children. The form of the verb changes depending on whether you are addressing someone as **Sie** or **du**; where both forms are given in the phrases, the **Sie** form is given first. If in doubt about which form to use, stick to **Sie**.

Greetings

Hello
Hallo
hallo

Hello/goodbye
Servus! *(S. Germany & Austria)*
servoos

Good morning
Guten Morgen
gooten morgen

Good day/afternoon
Guten Tag/Grüß Gott!
(S. Germany & Austria)
gooten taag/grewss gott

Good night
Gute Nacht
goote naakt

Good evening
Guten Abend
gooten aabent

Goodbye
Auf Wiedersehen
owf veederzayen

'Bye
Tschüß
chewss

See you later
Bis später
bis shpayter

(Hello), how are things?
Hallo, wie geht's?
hallo vee gayts

Fine, thanks
Gut, danke
goot danke

And you?
Und Ihnen? *(formal)*
oont eenen
Und dir? *(informal)*
oont deer

12 Introductions

My name is . . .
Ich heiße . . .
ish hiysse . . .

This is . . .
Das ist . . .
das ist . . .

This is Mr Brown
Das ist Herr Brown
das ist herr brown

This is Mrs Clark
Das ist Frau Clark
das ist frow klark

This my husband/son
Das ist mein Mann/Sohn
das ist miyn mann/zohn

This is my wife/daughter
Das ist meine Frau/Tochter
das ist miyne frow/toshter

Pleased to meet you
Sehr angenehm
zayr angenaym

Talking about yourself and your family

(see Countries and nationalities, *page197)*

I am English
Ich bin Engländer *(male)*
*ish bin **en**glender*
Ich bin Engländerin *(female)*
*ish bin **en**glenderin*

I come from Scotland
Ich komme aus Schottland
*ish **komme** ows **shott**lant*

I come from Ireland
Ich komme aus Irland
*ish **komme** ows **eer**lant*

I come from Wales
Ich komme aus Wales
ish komme ows vales

We live in Newcastle
Wir wohnen in Newcastle
*veer **vohn**en in newkasel*

I am a student
Ich bin Student *(male)*
*ish bin shtoo**dent***
Ich bin Studentin *(female)*
*ish bin shtoo**dent**in*

I am a nurse
Ich bin Krankenschwester
*ish bin **krank**enshvester*

I work in/for . . .
Ich arbeite bei . . .
*ish **arbiyte** biy . . .*

I work in a bank
Ich arbeite bei einer Bank
*ish **arbiyte** biy **iyner** bank*

I work for a computer firm
Ich arbeite bei einer Computerfirma
*ish **arbiyte** biy **iyner** kom**pew**terfirma*

I work in an office/factory
Ich arbeite in einem Büro/in einer Fabrik
*ish **arbiyte** in **iyn**em bew**roh**/in **iyner** fa**breek***

I am unemployed
Ich bin arbeitslos
*ish bin **arbiyt**slohs*

I am (not) married
Ich bin (nicht) verheiratet
*ish bin (nisht) fer**hiy**raatet*

I am separated
Ich lebe getrennt
*ish **laybe** ge**trennt***

I am divorced
Ich bin geschieden
*ish bin ge**sheeden***

I am a widower/widow
Ich bin ein Witwer/eine Witwe
*ish bin iyn **vitver**/**iyne vitve***

I have a son/a daughter
Ich habe einen Sohn/eine Tochter
*ish **haa**be **iy**nen zohn/**iy**ne **tosh**ter*

I have three children
Ich habe drei Kinder
*ish **haa**be driy **kin**der*

I don't have any children
Ich habe keine Kinder
*ish **haa**be **kiy**ne **kin**der*

I have one brother
Ich habe einen Bruder
*ish **haa**be **iy**nen **broo**der*

I have three sisters
Ich habe drei Schwestern
*ish **haa**be driy **shves**tern*

I'm on holiday here
Ich bin im Urlaub hier
*ish bin im **oor**lowp heer*

I'm here on business
Ich bin auf Geschäftsreise hier
*ish bin owf ge**shefts**riyze heer*

I'm here with my husband/wife
Ich bin mit meinem Mann/meiner Frau hier
*ish bin mit **miy**nem man/**miy**ner frow heer*

I'm here with my family
Ich bin mit meiner Familie hier
*ish bin mit **miy**ner fa**mee**lye heer*

I only speak a little German
Ich kann nur ein bißchen Deutsch sprechen
*ish kan noor iyn **bis**syen doych **shpre**ken*

My husband/wife is . . .
Mein Mann/meine Frau ist . . .
*miyn man/**miy**ne frow ist . . .*

My husband is a bus-driver
Mein Mann ist Busfahrer
*miyn man ist **boos**faarer*

My wife is an accountant
Meine Frau ist Buchhalterin
*miyne frow ist **book**halterin*

My husband/wife works in . . .
Mein Mann/meine Frau arbeitet in . . .
*miyn man/**miy**ne frow **ar**biytet in . . .*

My son is five years old
Mein Sohn ist fünf
miyn zohn ist fewnf

My daughter is eight years old
Meine Tochter ist acht
*miyne **tosh**ter ist aakt*

You may hear

Woher kommen Sie?
*voher **kommen** zee*
Where do you come from?

Wie heißen Sie?
*vee **hiy**ssen zee*
What are you called?

Was sind Sie von Beruf?
*vas zint zee fon be**roof***
What do you do?

Sind Sie verheiratet?
*zint zee fer**hiy**raatet*
Are you married?

Haben Sie Kinder?
***haa**ben zee **kin**der*
Do you have children?

Haben Sie Geschwister?
***haa**ben zee **geshvis**ter*
Do you have brothers and sisters?

Wie alt sind sie?
vee alt zint zee
How old are they?

Wie alt sind Sie/bist du?
vee alt zint zee/bist doo
How old are you?

Ist das Ihr Mann/Freund?
ist das eer man/froynd
Is this your husband/boyfriend?

Ist das Ihre Frau/Freundin?
*ist das **eere** frow/**froyn**din*
Is this your wife/girlfriend?

Er/Sie sieht sehr nett aus
er/zee zeet zayr nett ows
He/She looks very nice

Wohin fahren Sie?
***vohin faa**ren zee*
Where are you going?

Wo wohnen Sie?
*voh **voh**nen zee*
Where are you staying?

Wo wohnen Sie in Großbritannien?
*voh **voh**nen zee in grohssbrit**ann**yen*
Where do you live in Great Britain?

Talking about Germany, Austria or Switzerland and your own country

Germany is very beautiful
Deutschland ist sehr schön
doychlant ist zayr shern

It's the first time I have been to Germany
Ich bin zum ersten Mal in Deutschland
ish bin tsoom ersten mal in doychlant

I come to Austria often
Ich komme oft nach Österreich
ish komme oft naak ersterriysh

Do you live here?
Wohnen Sie hier?
vohnen zee heer

Have you ever been to England/Scotland/Ireland/Wales?
Waren Sie schon in England/Schottland/Irland/Wales?
varen zee shon in englant/shottlant/eerlant/vales

Did you like it?
Hat es Ihnen/dir gefallen?
hat es eenen/deer gefallen

You may hear

Gefällt Ihnen Deutschland/Österreich/die Schweiz?
gefellt eenen doychlant/ersterriysh/dee shviyts
Do you like Germany/Austria/Switzerland?

Waren Sie schon in Deutschland?
varen zee shon in doychlant
Have you been to Germany before?

Wie lange bleiben Sie hier?
vee lange bliyben zee heer
How long are you here for?

Was halten Sie von . . . ?
vas halten zee fon . . .
What do you think of . . . ?

Was halten Sie von Österreich?
vas halten zee fon ersterriysh
What do you think of Austria?

Ihr Deutsch ist sehr gut
eer doych ist zayr goot
Your German is very good

Likes and dislikes: food and people

I like . . .
Ich mag . . .
ish maag . . .

I like it . . .
Ich mag es . . .
ish maag es . . .

I like strawberries
Ich mag Erdbeeren
*ish maag **ert**beeren*

I like her
Ich mag sie
ish maag zee

I don't like . . .
Ich mag . . . nicht
ish maag . . . nisht

I don't like it
Ich mag es nicht
ish maag es nisht

I don't like beer
Ich mag Bier nicht
ish maag beer nisht

Do you like it?
Mögen Sie's?/Magst du's?
***mer**gen zeez/maagst dooz*

Do you like ice cream?
Mögen Sie Eis?/Magst du Eis?
***mer**gen zee iys/maagst doo iys*

Likes and dislikes: activities

I like playing football
Ich spiele gern Fußball
*ish **shpee**le gern **foos**sball*

I like swimming
Ich schwimme gern
*ish **shvi**mme gern*

I don't like sailing
Ich segele nicht gern
*ish **zay**gele nisht gern*

Do you like travelling?
Reisen Sie gern?
***riy**zen zee gern*

Invitations and replies

Would you like a drink?
Möchten Sie etwas trinken?
mershten zee etvas trinken

Would you like something to eat?
Möchten Sie etwas essen?
mershten zee etvas essen

Yes, please
Ja bitte
yaa bitte

No, thank you
Nein danke
niyn danke

That's very kind of you
das ist nett von Ihnen
das ist nett fon eenen

Please go away
Bitte gehen Sie weg!
bitte gayen zee vek

You may hear

Möchten Sie . . .
mershten zee . . .
Would you like . . .

Möchten Sie etwas trinken?
mershten zee etvas trinken
Would you like something to drink?

Möchten Sie etwas essen?
mershten zee etvas essen
Would you like something to eat?

Möchten Sie mitkommen?
mershten zee mitkommen
Would you like to come with us?

Was machen Sie heute abend?
vas maaken zee hoyte aabent
What are you doing tonight?

Möchten Sie tanzen gehen?
mershten zee tantsen gayen
Would you like to go dancing?

Möchten Sie essen gehen?
mershten zee essen gayen
Would you like to go for a mea

Für wieviel Uhr sollen wir uns verabreden?
fewr veefeel oor zollen veer oons ferapraydeu
What time shall we meet?

Wo sollen wir uns verabreden?
voh zollen veer oons ferapraydeu
Where shall we meet?

Good wishes and exclamations

Congratulations!
Herzlichen Glückwunsch!
hertslishen glewkvoonsh

Happy Birthday!
Herzlichen Glückwunsch zum Geburtstag!
hertslishen glewkvoonsh tsoom geboortstaag

Happy Christmas!
Frohe Weihnachten!
frohe viynaakten

Happy New Year!
Guten Rutsch ins Neue Jahr!
gooten rootsh ins noye yaar

Good luck!
Viel Glück!
feel glewk

All the best!
Alles Gute!
alles goote

What a pity!
Schade!
shaade

Have a good evening!
Schön' Abend!
shern aabent

Have a good journey!
Gute Reise!
goote riyze

Safe journey home!
Kommen Sie gut nach Hause!
kommen zee goot naak howze

Enjoy your meal!
Guten Appetit!
gooten appeteet

Thank you, same to you
Danke, gleichfalls
danke gliyshfalls

Cheers!
Prost!/Zum Wohl!
prost/tsoom vohl

Talking about the weather

The weather's very good/ bad
Das Wetter ist sehr schön/ schlecht
*das **vetter** ist zayr shern/ shlesht*

It's very hot/cold
Est ist sehr warm/kalt
es ist zayr varm/kalt

It's good/bad
Es ist gut/schlecht
es ist goot/shlesht

It's a wonderful day
Es ist ein herrlicher Tag
*es ist iyn **herr**lisher taag*

I don't like the heat
Ich mag die Hitze nicht
*ish maag dee **hit**tse nisht*

It's very windy
Es ist sehr windig
*es ist zayr **vin**dig*

Is it going to rain?
Wird es regnen?
*vird es **ray**gnen*

ARRIVING IN THE COUNTRY

• Whether you arrive by air, road or sea, the formalities (passport control and Customs) are quite straightforward; the only document you need is a valid passport.

• You will probably not need to say anything in German unless you are asked the purpose of your visit, or have something to declare at Customs. If you need to say what you have to declare (rather than just showing it), look up the words you need in the dictionary. EC duty-free allowances apply in West Germany – you can get a leaflet with the details at your point of departure.

• Duty-free allowances for Austria and Switzerland follow the EC pattern; details from the Swiss and Austrian National Tourist Offices.

You may see

Anmeldefreie Waren	Nothing to declare
Anmeldepflichtige Waren	Goods to declare
EG	EC
Grenze	Border
Grenzpolizei	Border police
Paßkontrolle	Passport control
Willkommen	Welcome
Zoll	Customs

I am here on holiday
Ich bin auf Urlaub hier
*ish bin owf **oor**lowp heer*

I am here on business
Ich bin auf einer Geschäftsreise hier
*ish bin owf **iyner** ge**sheftsr**iyze heer*

It's a joint passport
Es ist ein Familienpaß
*es ist iyn fa**meel**yenpass*

I have something to declare
Ich habe etwas zu verzollen
*ish **haa**be **et**vas tsoo fer**tsol**len*

I have this
Ich habe das
*ish **haa**be das*

I have two bottles of whisky
Ich habe zwei Flaschen Whisky
*ish **haa**be tsviy **flash**en **vis**kee*

I have two cartons of cigarettes
Ich habe zwei Stangen Zigaretten
*ish **haa**be tsviy **shtang**en tsi**garret**ten*

I have a receipt for this
Ich habe eine Quittung dafür
*ish **haa**be **iy**ne **kvit**toong daa**fewr***

You may hear

Ihren Paß, bitte
eeren pass bitte
Your passport, please

Ihre Papiere, bitte
eere papeere bitte
Your documents, please

Was is der Zweck Ihres Besuchs?
vas ist der tsvek eeres bezooks
What is the purpose of your visit?

Sind Sie im Urlaub oder auf Geschäftsreise hier?
zint zee im oorlowp ohder owf gesheftsriyze heer
Are you here on holiday or business?

Wie lange bleiben Sie hier?
vee lange bliyben zee heer
How long are you going to stay here?

Wo fahren Sie hin?
voh faaren zee hin
Where are you going?

Bitte öffnen Sie diese Tasche/diesen Koffer
bitte erffnen zee deeze tashe/ deezen koffer
Please open this bag/ suitcase

Bitte öffnen Sie den Kofferraum
bitte erffnen zee dayn kofferrowm
Please open the boot

Wir müssen das Auto durchsuchen
veer mewssen das owto doorshzooken
We have to search the car

Haben Sie noch andere Gepäckstücke?
haaben zee nok andere gepekshtewke
Do you have any other luggage?

Sie müssen Zoll darauf zahlen
zee mewssen tsoll darowf tsaalen
There is duty to pay on this

Kommen Sie bitte mit mir/ mit uns
kommen zee bitte mit meer/mit oons
Come along with me/with us, please

DIRECTIONS

• Some general maps are available from the German National Tourist Office (address, page 208). A wide range of road maps and some more specialised maps, e.g. for walkers, are obtainable from bookshops and specialist mapsellers. Local tourist offices can provide town plans and regional maps.

• When you need to ask the way somewhere, the easiest thing is just to name the place you're looking for and add 'please', e.g. **Kurfürstendamm, bitte?** Or you can start with 'where is . . . ?' **Wo ist . . . ?**

• If you're looking for a particular address, have it written down. In Germany, addresses are written with the street name first and the number afterwards, e.g. **Hamburgerstraße 23**. The name of the town and postcode may be written before the street name.

• When you're being given directions, listen out for the important bits (such as whether to turn left or right), and try to repeat each bit to make sure you've understood it correctly. If you can't understand something, ask the person to say it again more slowly, prompting with **Wie bitte?** ('pardon?') if necessary.

You may see

Allee	Avenue
Bahnhof	Station
Burg	Castle, fortress
Bushaltestelle	Bus stop
Dom	Cathedral
Fußgänger	Pedestrians
Fußgängerüberweg	Pedestrian crossing
Fußgängerzone	Pedestrian precinct
Gasse	Alley
Hauptbahnhof	Main station
Hof	Court
Kirche	Church
Kunsthalle	Art gallery
Marktplatz	Market-place
Museum	Museum
Palast	Palace
Platz	Square
Privat	Private
Radweg	Cycle path
S-Bahn	Express underground or overground
Schloß	Castle, palace
Straße	Street
Straßenbahnhaltestelle	Tram stop
U-Bahn	Underground
Unbefügtes Betreten verboten	Trespassers will be prosecuted
Weg	Way
Zebrastreifen	Zebra crossing

You may want to say

Excuse me (please)
Entschuldigen Sie, bitte
*ent**shool**digen zee **bi**tte*

Pardon?
Wie bitte?
*vee **bi**tte*

Can you repeat that, please?
Noch einmal, bitte
*nok **iyn**mal **bi**tte*

More slowly, please
Langsamer, bitte
*lang**zaa**mer **bi**tte*

Where are we?
Wo sind wir?
voh zint veer

Where does this road/street lead to?
Wo führt diese Straße hin?
*voh fewrt **dee**ze **shtraa**sse hin*

Is this the right way to Worpsweder?
Ist das die Straße nach Worpsweder?
*ist das dee **shtraa**sse naak vorps**vay**der*

Is this the footpath for Seefeld?
Ist das der Fußweg nach Seefeld?
*ist das der **foos**vayg naak **zay**felt*

Can you show me on the map?
Können Sir mir das auf der Karte zeigen?
*ker**nn**en zee meer das owf der **kar**te **tsiy**gen*

The station, please?
Der Bahnhof, bitte?
*der **baan**hof **bi**tte*

The (town) centre, please?
Das Stadtzentrum, bitte?
*das **stat**tsentroom **bi**tte*

The road to Berchtesgaden?
Die Straße nach Berchtesgaden?
*dee **shtraa**sse naak **bersh**tesgaaden*

How do I/we get to. . . ?
Wie kommt man nach/zu . . . ?
vee kommt man naak/tsoo

How do I/we get to Freiburg?
Wie kommt man nach Freiburg?
*vee kommt man naak **friy**boorg*

How do I/we get to the airport?
Wie kommt man zum Flughafen?
*vee kommt man tsoom **floog**haafen*

How do I/we get to the beach?
Wie kommt man zum Strand?
vee kommt man tsoom shtrant

Where is . . . ?
Wo ist . . . ?
voh ist

Where is this? *(if you've got an address written down)*
Wo ist das?
voh ist das

Where is the tourist office?
Wo ist das Fremdenverkehrsbüro?
*voh ist das fremdenfer**kayrz**bewroh*

Where is the Post Office?
Wo ist die Post?
voh ist dee post

Where is this office/room?
Wo ist dieses Büro/Zimmer?
*voh ist **dee**zes bew**roh/tsimm**er*

Where are the toilets?
Wo sind die Toiletten?
*voh zint dee toy**letten***

Is it far?
Ist es weit?
ist es viyt

Is the airport far away?
Ist der Flughafen weit?
*ist der **floog**haafen viyt*

How many kilometres?
Wie viele Kilometer?
*vee **feele** kilo**may**ter*

How long does it take (on foot/by car)?
Wie lange dauert es (zu Fuß/ mit dem Auto)?
*vee **lange** **dow**ert es tsoo fooss/ mit daym **ow**to*

Is there a bus/train?
Gibt es einen Bus/einen Zug?
*gipt es **iy**nen boos/**iy**nen tsoog*

Can I/we get there on foot?
Kann man zu Fuß dorthinkommen?
*kan man tsoo fooss dort-**hin**kommen*

Can I/we get there by car?
Kann man mit dem Auto dorthinkommen?
*kan man mit daym **ow**to dort-**hin**kommen*

Is there . . . ?
Gibt es . . . ?
gipt es

Is there a bank around here?
Gibt es eine Bank hier in der Nähe?
*gipt es **iy**ne bank heer in der **naye***

Is there a supermarket in the village?
Gibt es einen Supermarkt im Dorf?
*gipt es **iy**nen **zoo**permarkt im dorf*

Where is the nearest service station?
Wo ist die nächste Tankstelle?
*voh ist dee **nek**ste **tank**shtelle*

Where is the nearest bar?
Wo ist die nächste Bar?
*voh ist dee **nek**ste bar*

You may hear

Sie haben sich geirrt
*zee **haa**ben zish ge-**eert***
You've made a mistake

Wir sind hier
veer zint heer
We are here

Hier
heer
Here

Da, dort
daa, dort
There

Hier entlang
*heer ent**lang***
This way, Along here

Da entlang
*daa ent**lang***
That way, Along there

Rechts
reshts
(To the) right

Links
links
(To the) left

(Immer) geradeaus
*immer **geraa**deows*
Straight on

Die erste (Straße)
*dee **erste** **shtraa**sse*
The first (street/turning)

Die zweite (Straße)
*dee **tsviyte** **shtraa**sse*
The second (street/turning)

Die dritte (Straße)
*dee **dritte** **shtraa**sse*
The third (street/turning)

Am Ende der Straße
*am **ende** der **shtraa**sse*
At the end/bottom of the street

Auf der anderen Seite des Platzes
*owf der **an**deren **ziyte** des **plat**tses*
On the other side of the square

An der Ecke
*an der **eke***
On the corner

Unten
***oon**ten*
Down, Downstairs

Oben
***oh**ben*
Up, Upstairs

Dort unten
*dort **oon**ten*
Down there

Da oben
*daa **oh**ben*
Up there

Da hinten
*daa **hin**ten*
Behind there

Unter
*oon**ter***
Under

Über
*ew**ber***
Over

Vor der Ampel
*for der **am**pel*
Before the traffic lights

Nach dem Dom
naak daym dohm
After/Past the cathedral

Gegenüber
*gegen**ew**ber*
Opposite

Vor
for
In front of

Hinter
*hin**ter***
Behind

In der Nähe von . . .
*in der **naye** fon*
Near, Close to . . .

Es ist auf dem Platz
es ist owf daym platts
It's in the square

An der Siemensallee
*an der **zee**menzal**lay***
At (When you get to) Siemensallee

Richtung Stadtzentrum
***rish**toong **shtat**tsentroom*
Towards the town centre

Bis zur Kreuzung
*bis tsoor **kroy**tsoong*
As far as the crossroads

Es ist im dritten Stock
*es ist im **drit**ten shtock*
It's on the third floor

Die erste/zweite Tür
*dee **erste/tsviy**te tewr*
The first/second door

Es ist (nicht) weit
es ist (nisht) viyt
It's (not) far away

Sehr weit, ziemlich weit
*zayr viyt, **tseem**lish viyt*
Very far, Quite far

Es ist in der Nähe
*es ist in der **naye***
It's close by

Sehr nah, ziemlich nah
*zayr naa, **tseem**lish naa*
Very close, Quite close

Es ist fünf Minuten von hier
*es ist fewnf min**oo**ten fon heer*
It's five minutes away

Es ist zwanzig Kilometer von hier
*es ist **tsvantsig** kilo**mayter** fon heer*
It's twenty kilometres away

Sie müssen den Bus/den Zug nehmen
*zee **mewssen** dayn boos/dayn tsoog **naymen***
You have to catch the bus/train

You may also hear phrases like these:

Gehen Sie . . .
gayen zee
Go . . .

Fahren Sie . . .
faaren zee
Drive . . .

Fahren Sie dort entlang
*faaren zee dort ent**lang***
Drive along there

Fahren Sie die Straße entlang
*faaren zee dee **shtraasse** ent**lang***
Drive along the street

Fahren Sie dort hinüber
*faaren zee dort hin**ewber***
Drive over there

Fahren Sie über die Brücke
*faaren zee **ewber** dee **brewke***
Drive over the bridge

Nehmen Sie . . .
naymen zee
Take . . .

Nehmen Sie die dritte Ausfahrt
*naymen zee dee **dritte** **owsfaart***
Take the third exit

Biegen Sie an der Ampel ab
*beegen zee an der **ampel** ap*
Turn off at the traffic lights

ROAD TRAVEL

• Consult the motoring organisations for information on driving in Germany. The German motoring organisations include **ADAC (Allgemeiner Deutscher Automobil Club)** and **AvD (Automobil Club von Deutschland)**.

• To take a car to Germany you need a valid driving licence and the green international insurance card. Drivers without this must take out short-term third party insurance. Insurance policies can be renewed at any **ADAC** office.

• You drive on the right in Germany. Traffic from the right has priority on roads, even on roundabouts, unless otherwise indicated. Seatbelts are compulsory, both in the front and the back (if you have them). Crash helmets are compulsory for both drivers and passengers of motorbikes and scooters.

• Speed limits are generally: 50 km per hour in towns and 100 km per hour on ordinary roads. There is no speed limit on motorways but 130 km per hour is the recommended speed.

• Main roads are as follows:
Autobahn – motorway
Bundesstraße – main 'A' road
Landstraße – 'B' road

• There are no tolls on German motorways.

• The main grade of petrol is **Super** (4-star). Unleaded petrol (**bleifreies Benzin**) is very widely available. Diesel is easily obtainable.

• Service stations are open on motorways round the clock and many have very good toilet and restaurant facilities. They normally take credit cards as do service stations in big cities. It's always best to check, though. Self-service garages are indicated by the sign **Selbsttanken** or **Selbstbedienung**.

• Parking within towns and cities is allowed on the right-hand side of the road unless otherwise indicated by 'no parking' signs. Some car parks have an attendant, and there are meters, underground car parks and multi-storey car parks in most cities.

In a Blue Zone (**Blaue Zone**) parking time is limited and you must display a parking disc or ticket to show the time you parked. Discs are available from newsagents.

If you park illegally you are likely to be fined on the spot or have your car towed away.

• You can arrange car hire in Britain with the large international car hire firms. They also have offices at airports and elsewhere in Germany (and there will often be someone who speaks English). There are local companies too in most towns and cities – look for the sign **Autovermietung**. You may be able to hire bicycles, especially in tourist areas.

• If you have to tell a mechanic what's wrong with your vehicle, the easiest way is to indicate the part affected and say 'This isn't working': **Das funktioniert nicht**, or **Das ist kaputt**. Otherwise, look up the word for the appropriate part.

ADAC and **AvD** run a patrol service on motorways and main roads. There are emergency telephones every 2 km on the motorways. When you get through, ask for the **Straßenwachthilfe**. This recovery service is free of charge, motorists only pay for the materials used in repairs. Both organisations have offices in major cities to ring in an emergency for repairs. The German National Tourist Office has a list of numbers. Don't hang up if you don't get through as the calls are stored. **ADAC** operates an urban breakdown service too.

Accidents

Accidents involving injury must be reported to the police. If a third party is involved, the insurance company of the appropriate country must be informed.

• Many drivers in Germany take part in the **Mitfahrgelegenheit** system and offer lifts to people going to the same destination as they are. The system is a cheap and reliable way of getting round the country if you are travelling without a car and is coordinated by a **Mitfahrzentrale** ('lift centre'). Passengers pay a small fee to the centre to organise a lift for them and then split the petrol costs with the driver. There are **Mitfahrzentralen** in most big towns and in some places there are women-only centres, **Frauenmitfahrzentralen**.

Austria and Switzerland

The rules and regulations are much the same as for Germany. A green card is recommended for both countries.

• The speed limits for both countries are:
Austria: 50 km/h in built-up areas, 100 km/h on normal roads and 130 km/h on motorways.
Switzerland: 50 km/h in built-up areas, 80 km/h on normal roads and 120 km/h on motorways.

• There is no leaded two-star petrol, **Normal**, available in Switzerland or in Austria. **Eurosuper** or **Euro-95** is four-star unleaded petrol available in some service stations in Austria.

• Take care on mountain roads. In Switzerland a yellow posthorn on a blue rectangle on some mountain roads indicates that post vans have precedence. You must switch your headlights on in mountain road tunnels.

• A motorway sticker, a **vignette**, is required to travel on Swiss motorways. You can buy these at the border from the **ACS** (**Automobil Club der Schweiz**) or from motoring organisations in this country. There are tolls on mountain passes and tunnels in Switzerland and Austria.

• In Austria the **ÖAMTC** (**Österreichischer Automobil und Motorräder Touring Club**) operates a 24-hour recovery service. The number to dial is **120**. The Austrian motoring organisations also rent out snow chains for use in the winter.

You may see

Achtung	Caution
Anlieger frei	Access to residents only
Ausfahrt	Exit
Autobahn	Motorway
Autovermietung	Car hire
Bahnübergang	Level crossing
Bewachte/Tiefgarage	Supervised/underground car park
Blaue Zone	Blue Zone
DB	German Railways
Durchfahrt verboten	No through traffic
Durchgangsverkehr	Through traffic
Einbahnstraße	One-way street
Einfahrt freihalten	Allow free access
Einordnen	Get in lane
Ende der Autobahn	End of motorway
Erste Hilfe	First Aid
Frostschäden	Frost damage
Fußgänger	Pedestrians
Fußgängerzone	Pedestrian precinct
Fußgängerüberweg	Pedestrian crossing
Gefahr	Danger
Gefährliche Kurve	Dangerous bend
Gegenverkehr	Two-way traffic
Geschwindigkeitsgrenze	Speed limit

Glatteisgefahr	Black ice
Halt	Stop
Halten verboten	No stopping
Hochgarage/Parkhaus	Multi-storey car park
Höchstgeschwindigkeit	Maximum speed
Hupen verboten	No hooting
Kein Durchgang für Fußgänger	No pedestrians
Langsam	Slow
Letzte Tankstelle vor der Autobahn	Last petrol station before the motorway
Links fahren/Rechts fahren	Drive on the left/right
Mautgebühr	Toll
Messegelände	Exhibition centre
Motor abschalten	Switch your engine off
Notrufsäule	Emergency telephone (on motorway)
P	Parking
Parken verboten/beschränkt	Parking prohibited/limited
Paß geschlossen	(Mountain) pass closed
Radweg	Cycle path
Radweg kreuzt	Cycle path crossing
Reparaturwerkstatt	Car repairs/Garage
Rollsplit	Loose grit
Sackgasse	Cul-de-sac, no through road
Scheinwerfer anschalten (im Tunnel)	Use headlights (in tunnel)
Schleudengefahr bei Nässe	Slippery surface in damp weather
Schritttempo	Dead slow
Schule	School
Stadtzentrum	Town/city centre
Straße gesperrt	Road closed
Straßenbauarbeiten	Road works
Straßenschäden	Uneven road surface
Steinschlag	Falling rocks
Tankstelle	Service/petrol station
Überholen verboten	No overtaking

Umleitung	Diversion
Unbeschränkter Bahnübergang	Unguarded level crossing
Viehpfad	Cattle track
Vorfahrt achten	Give way
Vorsicht	Caution
Vorsicht vor den Zügen	Beware of trains
Zollamt	Customs
Zutritt verboten	No entry

You may want to say

Petrol

Where is the nearest petrol station?
Wo ist die nächste Tankstelle?
*voh ist dee **nekste tank**shtelle*

4-star
Super
zooper

Unleaded petrol
Bleifreies Benzin
bliyfriyes bentseen

Diesel
Diesel
deezel

20 litres of 4-star, please
Zwanzig Liter Super, bitte
tsvantsig leeter zooper bitte

30 marks' worth of unleaded, please
Dreißig Mark bleifreies Benzin, bitte
driyssig mark bliyfriyes bentseen bitte

Fill it up with 4-star please
Volltanken mit Super bitte
folltanken mit zooper bitte

A (litre) can of oil, please
Einen Kanister Öl, bitte
iynen kanister erl bitte

A (half-litre) can of oil, please
Eine Dose Öl, bitte
iyne dohze erl bitte

A can of petrol, please
Einen Reservekanister Benzin, bitte
iynen reservekanister bentseen bitte

Water, please
Wasser, bitte
vasser bitte

Can you check the pressure in the tyres?
Können Sie den Reifendruck prüfen?
kernnen zee dayn riyfendrook prewfen

Can you change the tyre?
Können Sie den Reifen wechseln?
*kernnen zee dayn **riyfen vek**seln*

Can you clean the windscreen?
Können Sie die Windschutzscheibe waschen?
*kernnen zee dee **vint**shootsshiybe **va**shen*

Where is the air, please?
Wo ist die Luft, bitte?
*voh ist dee looft **bi**tte*

How does the car wash work?
Wie funktioniert die Autowäsche?
*vee foonktsyo**neert** dee **ow**toveshe*

How much is it?
Was kostet das?
*vas **kos**tet das*

Parking

Where can I/we park?
Wo kann man parken?
*voh kann man **par**ken*

Can I/we park here?
Kann man hier parken?
*kan man heer **par**ken*

How long can I/we park here?
Wie lange kann man hier parken?
*vee **lange** kan man heer **par**ken*

How much is it per hour?
Was kostet es die Stunde?
*vas **kos**tet es dee **shtoon**de*

A parking disc, please
Eine Parkscheibe, bitte
*iyne **park**shiybe **bi**tte*

Hiring a car

(see Days, months, dates, *page 189)*

I want to hire a car
Ich möchte ein Auto mieten
*ish **mersh**te iyn **owto mee**ten*

A small car, please
Ein kleines Auto, bitte
*iyn **kliy**nes **owto bit**te*

A medium-sized car, please
Ein mittelgroßes Auto, bitte
*iyn **mit**telgrohsses **owto bit**te*

A large car, please
Ein großes Auto, bitte
*iyn **grohs**ses **owto bit**te*

An automatic car, please
Ein Auto mit Automatik, bitte
*iyn **owto** mit owto**maa**tik **bit**te*

For three days
Für drei Tage
*fewr driy **taa**ge*

For a week
Für eine Woche
*fewr **iy**ne **vo**ke*

For two weeks
Für zwei Wochen
*fewr tsviy **vo**ken*

From . . . to . . .
Von . . . bis . . .
fon . . . bis

From Monday to Friday
Von montag bis freitag
*fon **mohn**taag bis **friy**taag*

From 10 to 17 August
Vom zehnten bis zum siebzehnten August
*fom **tsayn**ten bis tsoom **zeeb**tsaynten ow**goost***

How much is it?
Was kostet das?
*vas **kost**et das*

Per day
Pro Tag
proh taag

Per week
Pro Woche
*proh **vo**ke*

Per kilometre
Pro Kilometer
*proh kilo**may**ter*

Is mileage (kilometrage) included?
Ist die Kilometerzahl inbegriffen?
*ist dee kilo**may**tertsaal **in**begriffen*

Is petrol included?
Ist das Benzin inbegriffen?
*ist das ben**tseen** **in**begriffen*

Is insurance included?
Ist die Versicherung inbegriffen
*ist dee fer**zish**eroong **in**begriffen*

Comprehensive insurance cover
Vollkasko(versicherung)
follkaskoh(verzisheroong)

My husband/wife is driving too
Mein Mann/Meine Frau fährt auch
miyn mann/miyne frow fayrt owk

Is there a deposit?
Muß ich Geld hinterlegen?
mooss ish gelt hinterlaygen

Do you take credit cards?
Nehmen Sie Kreditkarten?
naymen zee kredeetkarten

Do you take traveller's cheques?
Nehmen Sie Reiseschecks?
naymen zee riyzeshecks

Can I leave the car in Hamburg?
Kann ich das Auto in Hamburg lassen?
kan ish das owto in Hamboorg lassen

Can I leave the car at the airport?
Kann ich das Auto am Flughafen lassen?
kan ish das owto am flooghaafen lassen

How do the . . . work?
Wie funktionieren die . . . ?
vee foonktsyoneeren dee

How do the gears work?
Wie funktionieren die Gänge?
vee foonktsyoneeren dee genge

Breakdowns and repairs

(*See also list of* car parts *on page 43.*)

My car has broken down
Ich habe eine Panne
ish haabe iyne panne

Can you telephone a garage?
Können Sie eine Reparaturwerkstatt anrufen?
kernnen zee iyne reparatoorverkshtatt anroofen

I've run out of petrol
Der Tank ist leer
der tank ist layr

Where is the nearest garage?
Wo ist die nächste Reparaturwerkstatt?
voh ist dee nekste reparatoorverkshtatt

Can you send a mechanic?
Können Sie einen Mechaniker schicken?
kernnen zee iynen mekaniker shiken

Do you do repairs?
Nehmen Sie Reparaturen vor?
naymen zee reparatooren for

I don't know what's wrong
Ich weiß nicht, was los ist
ish viyss nisht was lohs ist

I think . . .
Ich glaube . . .
ish glowbe

It's the clutch
Es ist die Kupplung
es ist dee kooploong

It's the radiator
Es ist der Kühler
es ist der kewler

It's the brakes
Es sind die Bremsen
es zint dee bremzen

The car won't start
Das Auto startet nicht
das owto shtartet nisht

The battery is flat
Die Batterie ist leer
dee batteree ist layr

The engine is overheating
Das Motor überhitzt
das mohtor ewberhitzt

It's losing water/oil
Es verliert Wasser/Öl
es ferleert vasser/erl

I have a puncture
Ich habe einen Platten
ish haabe iynen platten

The . . . doesn't work
Der/die/das . . . funktioniert nicht
der/dee/das . . . foonktsyoneert nisht

I need . . . *(for other car parts, see page 43)*
Ich brauche . . .
ish browke

Is it serious?
Ist es schlimm?
ist es shlimm

Can you repair it (today)?
Können Sie es (heute) reparieren?
kernnen zee es hoyte repareeren

When will it be ready?
Wann wird es fertig sein?
van virt es fertig ziyn

How much will it cost?
Was wird es kosten?
vas virt es kosten

Petrol

Was möchten Sie?
*vas **mersh**ten zee*
What would you like?

Wieviel möchten Sie?
*vee**feel** **mersh**ten zee*
How much do you want?

Den Schlüssel, bitte
*dayn **shlew**ssel **bi**tte*
The key, please

Parking

Sie können hier nicht parken
*zee **kern**nen heer nisht **parken***
You can't park here

Es kostet zehn Mark die Stunde
*es **kos**tet tsayn mark dee **shtoon**de*
It's DM 10 an hour

Es kostet nichts
*es **kos**tet nishts*
You don't pay

Es ist umsonst/gratis
*es ist oom**zonst/graa**tis*
It's free

Es gibt dort drüben einen Parkplatz
*es gipt dort **drew**ben **iy**nen **park**platts*
There's a car park over there

Hiring a car

Was für ein Auto möchten Sie?
*vas fewr iyn **ow**to **mersh**ten zee*
What kind of car do you want?

Für wie lange?
*fewr vee **lange***
For how long?

Für wie viele Tage?
*fewr vee **feele** **taage***
For how many days?

Wer fährt?
ver fayrt
Who is driving?

Wer ist der Hauptmieter?
*ver ist der **howptmeeter***
Who is the main driver?

Es gibt eine Anzahlung von hundert Mark
*es gipt **iyne antsaaloong fon hoondert** mark*
There is a deposit of DM 100

Haben Sie eine Kreditkarte?
*haaben zee **iyne kredeetkarte***
Have you got a credit card?

Es kostet siebzig Mark/ zweihundertfünfzig Mark
*es **kostet zeebtsig** mark/ tsviyhoondert**fewnftsig** mark*
It costs DM 70/250

Pro Tag
proh taag
Per day

Pro Woche
*proh **voke***
Per week

Ihr Führerschein, bitte
*eer **fewrershiyn bitte***
Your driving licence, please

Was ist Ihre Adresse?
*vas ist **eere adresse***
What is your address?

Hier ist der Schlüssel
*heer ist der **shlewssel***
Here is the key

Bitte bringen Sie das Auto mit vollem Tank zurück
*bitte **bringen** zee das **owto** mit **vollem** tank tsoo**rewk***
Please return the car with a full tank

Bitte bringen Sie das Auto vor sechs Uhr zurück
*bitte **bringen** zee das **owto** for zeks oor tsoo**rewk***
Please return the car before six o'clock

Wenn das Büro geschlossen ist, können Sie den Schlüssel im Briefkasten lassen
*venn das bew**roh geshlossen** ist, **kernnen** zee dayn **shlewssel** im **breefkasten** lassen*
If the office is closed, you can leave the key in the letterbox

Breakdowns and repairs

Was ist los?
vas ist lohs
What's wrong with it?

Ich habe die nötigen Ersatzteile nicht
*ish **haa**be dee **ner**tigen **erzats**tiyle nisht*
I don't have the necessary parts

Ich muß die Ersatzteile bestellen
*ish mooss dee **erzats**tiyle **beshtellen***
I will have to order the parts

Kommen Sie nächsten Dienstag zurück
*kommen zee **nek**sten **deen**ztaag tsoo**rewk***
Come back next Tuesday

Es wird bis Montag fertig sein
*es virt bis **mohn**taag **fer**tig ziyn*
It will be ready on Monday

Es wird fünfundvierzig Mark kosten
*es virt fewnfoont**feer**tsig mark **kos**ten*
It will cost DM 45

Car and bicycle parts

Accelerator	**das Gaspedal**	*gaspay**daal***
Air filter	**der Luftfilter**	***looft**filter*
Alternator	**die Lichtmaschine**	***lisht**masheene*
Battery	**die Batterie**	*batte**ree***
Bonnet	**die Motorhaube**	*moh**tor**howbe*
Boot	**der Kofferraum**	***kof**ferrowm*
Brakes	**die Bremsen**	***brem**zen*
Front wheel brake	**die Vorderrad-bremse**	***for**derraatbremze*
Rear wheel brake	**die Hinterrad-bremse**	***hin**terraatbremze*
Brake cable	**der Bremskabel**	***brem**zkaabel*
Brake fluid	**die Bremsflüssigkeit**	***brem**zflewssigkiyt*
Brake hose	**der Bremsschlauch**	***brem**zshlowk*
Disc brakes	**die Scheiben-bremsen**	***shiy**benbremzen*
Carburettor	**der Vergaser**	*fer**gaa**zer*

Chain	**die Kette**	*kette*
Choke	**der Choke**	*chohke*
Clutch	**die Kupplung**	*koopploong*
Distributor	**der Zündverteiler**	*tsewndfertiyler*
Electrical system	**die Electric**	*elayktrik*
Engine	**der Motor**	*mohtor*
Exhaust pipe	**der Auspuff**	*owspoof*
Fanbelt	**der Keilriemen**	*kiylreemen*
Frame	**der Rahmen**	*raamen*
Fuel gauge	**die Tankanzeige**	*tankantsiyge*
Fuel pump	**die Benzinpumpe**	*bentseenpoompe*
Fuses	**die Sicherungen**	*zisheroongen*
Gears	**die Gänge**	*genge*
Gearbox	**das Getriebe**	*getreebe*
Gear lever	**der Schalthebel**	*shalthaybel*
Handbrake	**die Handbremse**	*hantbremze*
Handlebars	**die Lenkstange**	*lenkshtange*
Headlights	**die Scheinwerfer**	*shiynverfer*
Heater	**die Heizung**	*hiytsoong*
Horn	**die Hupe**	*hoope*
Ignition	**die Zündung**	*tsewndoong*
Ignition key	**der Zündschlüssel**	*tsewndshlewssel*
Indicators	**die Blinker**	*blinker*
Inner tube	**der Schlauch**	*shlowk*
Lights	**das Licht**	*lisht*
Front lights	**das Vorderlicht**	*forderlisht*
Rear lights	**das Rücklicht**	*rewklisht*
Side lights	**das Standlicht**	*shtantlisht*
Lock	**das Schloß**	*shloss*
Oil filter	**der Ölfilter**	*erlfilter*
Oil gauge	**die Ölanzeige**	*erlantsiyge*
Pedal	**das Pedal**	*paydaal*
Points	**die Unterbrecher-kontakte**	*oonterbresher-kontakte*
Pump	**die Pumpe**	*poompe*
Radiator	**der Kühler**	*kewler*

Radiator hose (top/bottom)	**der Kühlerschlauch (oberer/unterer)**	*kewlershlowk (ohberer/oonterer)*
Reversing lights	**die Rückfahrschein-werfer**	*rewkfaarshiyn-verfer*
Rotor arm	**der Verteilerfinger**	*fertiylerfinger*
Saddle	**der Sattel**	*sattel*
Silencer	**der Schalldämpfer**	*shaaldempfer*
Spare wheel	**der Ersatzreifen**	*erzattsriyfen*
Spark plugs	**die Zündkerzen**	*tsewndkertsen*
Speedometer	**der Tachometer**	*takohmayter*
Spokes	**die Speichen**	*shpiyken*
Starter motor	**der Anlasser**	*anlasser*
Steering	**die Lenkung**	*lenkoong*
Steering wheel	**das Lenkrad**	*lenkraat*
Transmission (automatic)	**das Schaltgetriebe**	*shaltgetreebe*
Tyre	**der Reifen**	*riyfen*
Front tyre	**der Vorderreifen**	*forderriyfen*
Back tyre	**der Rückreifen**	*rewkriyfen*
Valve	**das Ventil**	*venteel*
Warning light	**das Blinklicht**	*blinklisht*
Wheel (front/rear)	**das Rad**	*raat*
Front wheel	**das Vorderrad**	*forderraat*
Back wheel	**das Rückrad**	*rewkraat*
Wheel rim	**der Radkranz**	*raatkrants*
Window	**das Fenster**	*fenster*
Windscreen	**die Windschutz-scheibe**	*vintshootsshiybe*
Windscreen washer	**Der Scheibenspül-apparat**	*shiybenshpewl-apparaat*
Windscreen wipers	**die Scheibenwischer**	*shiybenvisher*

TAXIS

- It's not usual in Germany to hail a taxi in the street. Go to a taxi rank or phone a **Taxizentrale**, taxi centre, the number will be in the telephone book. If a taxi is free the sign on top of the car will be lit up.

- All taxis have meters and the driver usually rounds the fare up so a tip isn't obligatory. There is a basic starting fare and supplements may be added for luggage or journeys to the airport.

- Write down clearly the address of your destination if it's at all complicated so that you can show it to the taxi driver.

- Taxis are beige in most German cities.

- **Swiss** taxi drivers expect a tip.

- In **Austria** taxis are metered in the larger cities. In smaller towns there are fixed charges for certain destinations. In Vienna a supplement is added for trips to the airport. Tips are at your discretion.

You may want to say

(see also Directions, *page 24)*

Is there a taxi rank around here?
Gibt es einen Taxistand in der Nähe?
*gipt es **iynen taksishtant** in der **naye***

I need a taxi
Ich brauche ein Taxi
*ish **browke** iyn **taksi***

Can you call me a taxi?
Können Sie ein Taxi für mich bestellen?
*kernnen zee iyn **taksi** fewr mish **beshtellen***

Immediately
Bitte jetzt gleich
bitte yettst gliysh

For tomorrow at nine o'clock
Für morgen um neun Uhr
*fewr **morgen** oom noyn oor*

I'm going to the airport
Ich möchte zum Flughafen
*ish **mershte** tsoom **flooghaafen***

Can I order a taxi, please
Kann ich ein Taxi bitte bestellen
*kan ish iyn **taksi bitte** beshtellen*

My address is . . .
Meine Adresse ist . . .
miyne adresse ist . . .

The airport, please
Zum Flughafen, bitte
*tsoom **flooghaafen bitte***

The station, please
Zum Bahnhof, bitte
*tsoom **baanhof bitte***

The Hotel Bellevue, please
Hotel Bellevue, bitte
hotel bellvew bitte

To this address, please
Zu dieser Adresse, bitte
tsoo deezer adresse bitte

Is it far?
Ist es weit?
ist es viyt

How much will it cost?
Wieviel wird es kosten?
veefeel virt es kosten

I am in a hurry
Ich bin in Eile
ish bin in iyle

Stop here, please
Halten Sie bitte hier
halten zee bitte heer

That's fine here, thanks
Das geht hier schon
das gayt heer shon

Can you wait (a few minutes), please?
Können Sie bitte (ein paar Minuten) warten?
kernnen zee bitte (iyn paar minooten) varten

How much is it?
Was macht das?
vas maakt das

I think there is a mistake
Ich glaube, hier stimmt etwas nicht
ish glowbe heer shtimmt etvas nisht

On the meter it's DM 7,50
Es ist sieben Mark fünfzig auf dem Zähler
es ist zeeben mark fewnftsig owf daym tsayler

Keep the change
Behalten Sie den Rest
behalten zee dayn rest

That's all right
Ist gut so/Es stimmt so
ist goot zoh/es shtimmt zoh

Can you give me a receipt?
Können Sie mir eine Quittung geben?
kernnen zee meer iyne kvittoong gayben

For DM 9
Für Neun Mark
fewr noyn mark

You may hear

Es ist zehn Kilometer von hier
es ist tsayn kilomayter fon heer
It's ten kilometres away

Es wird ungefähr fünfzehn Mark kosten
es virt oongefayr fewnftsayn mark kosten
It will cost approximately DM 15

(Das macht) achtzehn Mark
(das maakt) aakttsayn mark
(It's) DM 18

Dazu kommt ein Zuschlag
daatsoo kommt iyn tsooshlaag
There is a supplement

Für das Gepäck
fewr das gepek
For the luggage

Für jeden Koffer
fewr yayden koffer
For each suitcase

Für die Fahrt zum Flughafen
fewr dee faart tsoom flooghaafen
For the journey to the airport

AIR TRAVEL

- There are regular shuttle services between all the big German cities. The major German airport is Frankfurt.

- At airports and airline offices you'll generally find someone who speaks English, but be prepared to say a few things in German.

- Signs at major airports will be in English and German.

- Approximate flight times from Frankfurt to some other main cities:

Hamburg - 55 minutes
Hanover - 50 minutes
Cologne/Bonn - 40 minutes
Munich - 55 minutes
Düsseldorf - 45 minutes
Berlin - 55 minutes
Stuttgart - 45 minutes

Frankfurt is an hour and 35 minutes from London.

- There are more than 20 flights a day from Frankfurt and Hamburg to Berlin and flights from all other airports. All flights land at Tegel airport, 5 miles from the city centre. There is a regular and direct bus link to the centre.

- Frankfurt airport has its own station with connecting trains to the Inter City Network and regular services into the centre of the city. All German airports have good connections to the local transport system.

- There are **DB** offices at all airports from which luggage can be sent to any station.

- The international car hire firms have offices at major airports where you can arrange to hire or pick up cars.

• The main airports in **Switzerland** are Zürich and Geneva. There are good links between the airports and the city centre. Zürich airport has its own station with through services to many major towns.

• There are airports in **Austria** in Vienna, Salzburg, Graz, Linz and Klagenfurt with regular shuttle services between them.

You may see

Abflughalle	Departure lounge
Abflug	Departures
Anmeldefreie Waren	Nothing to declare
Ankunft	Arrivals
Anmeldepflichtige Waren	Goods to declare
Ausgang	Exit
Auskunft	Information
Ausland	International departures
Autovermietung	Car hire
Bitte anschnallen	Fasten seatbelts
Bus (zum Stadtzentrum)	Buses (to the town/city centre)
EG	EC
Eingang	Entrance
Filmsicher	Film safe
Gepäckausgabe	Luggage reclaim
Inland	Domestic departures
Paßkontrolle	Passport control
Rauchen verboten	No smoking
Toiletten	Toilets
Taxis	Taxis
Wechselstube	Bureau de change
Zoll	Customs

You may want to say

(see Numbers, *page 211;* Days, months, dates, *page 189;* Time, *page 193)*

Is there a flight (from Frankfurt) to Hamburg?
Gibt es einen Flug (von Frankfurt) nach Hamburg?
*gipt es **iy**nen floog (fon **frank**foort) naak **ham**boorg*

Today
Heute
***hoy**te*

This morning/afternoon
Heute morgen/Heute nachmittag
***hoy**te **morg**en/**hoy**te **naak**mittag*

Tomorrow (morning/afternoon)
Morgen (früh/nachmittag)
***morg**en (frew/**naak**mittag)*

Do you have a timetable of flights to Hanover?
Haben Sie einen Flugplan für Hannover?
***haa**ben zee **iy**nen **floog**plaan fewr han**noh**ver*

What time is the first flight to Berlin?
Um wieviel Uhr ist der erste Flug nach Berlin?
*oom **veefeel** oor ist der **er**ste floog naak ber**leen***

The next flight
Der nächste Flug
*der **nek**ste floog*

The last flight
Der letzte Flug
*der **lett**ste floog*

What time does it arrive (at Berlin)?
Um wieviel Uhr kommt es (in Berlin) an?
*oom **veefeel** oor kommt es (in ber**leen**) an*

A ticket/Two tickets to Stuttgart, please
Eine Fahrkarte/Zwei Fahrkarten nach Stuttgart, bitte
*iyne **faar**karte/tsviy **faar**karten naak **shtoottgart** **bitte***

Single
Ein Hinflug
*iyn **hinfloog***

Return
Ein Hin- und Rückflug
*iyn hin oont **rewkfloog***

First class/Business class
Erste Klasse/Business Klasse
*erste **klasse/bizness** **klasse***

For the eleven o'clock flight
Für den Flug um elf Uhr
fewr dayn floog oom elf oor

I want to change/cancel my reservation
Ich möchte meine Reservierung ändern/stornieren
*ish **mershte** **miyne** rezerveeroong **endern**/shtor**neeren***

What is the number of the flight?
Was ist die Flugnummer?
*vas ist dee **floog**noommer*

What time do I/we have to check in?
Um wieviel Uhr muß man einchecken?
*oom **veefeel** oor mooss man **iyn**cheken*

Which gate is it?
Welcher Flugsteig ist es?
***velsher** **floog**shtiyg ist es*

Is there a delay?
Ist es verspätet?
*ist es fer**shpay**tet*

I don't want to put my camera/bag through the machine
Ich möchte meinen Photoapparat/meine Tasche nicht durchleuchten lassen
*ish **mershte miynen fohtoapparaat/miyne tashe** nisht **doorsh**loyshten **lassen***

You can hand search it
Sie können es bei Hand durchsuchen
*zee **kernnen** es biy hant **doorsh**zooken*

Where is the luggage from the flight to London?
Wo ist das Gepäck vom Flug aus London?
*voh ist das **gepek** fom floog ows **lon**don*

My luggage is not here
Mein Gepäck ist nicht da
*miyn **gepek** ist nisht da*

Is there a bus to the centre of town?
Gibt es einen Bus zum Stadtzentrum?
*gipt es **iynen** boos tsoom **shtatt**sentroom*

You may hear

Möchten Sie einen Fensterplatz?
mershten zee iynen fensterplatts
Would you like a seat by the window?

Möchten Sie einen Gangplatz?
mershten zee iynen gangplatts
Would you like a seat on the aisle?

Raucher oder Nichtraucher?
rowker ohder nishtrowker
Smoking or non-smoking?

Der Flug wird um . . . aufgerufen
der floog virt oom . . . owfgeroofen
The flight will be called/board at . . (time)

Flugsteig Nummer sieben
floogshtiyg noommer zeeben
Gate number seven

Ihre Flugticket, bitte
eere floogticket bitte
Your ticket, please

Ihren Paß, bitte
eeren pass bitte
Your passport, please

Ihre Bordkarte, bitte
eere bordkarte bitte
Your boarding card, please

Wie sieht Ihr Gepäck aus?
vee zeet eer gepek ows
What does your luggage look li

Haben Sie das Gepäcketikett?
haaben zee das gepeketikett
Do you have the reclaim tag?

Words to listen out for

Aufruf	*owfroof*	Call
Flug	*floog*	Flight
Flugsteig	*floogshtiyg*	Gate
Letzter Aufruf	*lettster owfroof*	Last call
Verspätung	*fershpaytoong*	Delay

TRAVELLING BY TRAIN

- The German State Railway is the **Deutsche Bundesbahn**.

- There are various types of train, including, in reverse order of speed:

Nahverkehrszug – short-distance, suburban train
Personenzug – slow, local train which stops at every station
Eilzug – stops at stations in bigger towns
D-Zug
Schnellzug
Express
Inter City
} All fast trains, often travelling between countries, only stopping at principal stations
TEE – Trans-European Express. Luxury, high-speed train with first-class accommodation only

- Sleepers and couchettes must be booked in advance. Tourists can opt for either 2- or 3-berth sleeper compartments – many of which are equipped with showers.

- You can send bicycles in advance by train and pick them up at your destination. There are bicycles for hire at many **DB** stations.

- Single tickets for distances up to 100 km are only valid for a day. For longer distances, single tickets are valid for four days and returns for a month.

- Holders of standard single and return tickets travelling 51 km or over can go on express and Inter City trains without paying the supplement.

- There are also various types of tickets available to tourists:

Tourist cards are recommended for tourists who are undertaking extensive train travel in Germany. They are available for periods of 4, 9 or 16 days or for young people for 9 or 16 days. The card entitles the holder to unlimited travel in first-

or second-class accommodation. (Young Persons' cards are second class only.) Tourist cards are also valid on some bus routes and on boats of the **Deutsche Rheinschiffahrt** on the Rhine and Moselle. The cards are obtainable from British Rail Travel Centres and from travel agents which deal with train travel. It's best to buy the card before you go.

Other discounts include:
Reductions for families, young people and senior citizens.
'Saver' and 'Super Saver' tickets.
Details from British Rail Travel Centres.

- Children under 4 travel free on the German railways (though they are not entitled to a seat at peak times) and children between 4 and 11 travel for half price.

- Refreshments are available in the buffet car or 'minibar' on long journeys.

- Information centres at large stations may be able to book accommodation for you. You can also change money at large stations, though the exchange rate may not be as good as in a bank.

- There is an extensive Motorail service within Germany. Further details from the German National Tourist Office.

- The **Swiss** railways offer various concessions to rail travellers. These include the **Swiss Pass** which operates along the same lines as the German tourist card (see above) and regional passes which are valid for 15 days for tourists visiting a particular region during the summer.

- The Austrian State Railway is the **Österreichische Bahn** (**ÖB**). Their special offers include the **Rabbitkarte** which is valid for ten days, four of which can be travelled on.

You may see

Abfahrt	Departure
Ankunft	Arrival
Ausgang	Exit
Auskunft	Information
Bahnsteig	Platform
Bahnhof	Railway station
Bahnhofsmission	Travellers' Aid
Damen	Ladies
Deutsche Bundesbahn (DB)	German State Railway
Eingang	Entrance
Fahrkarten	Tickets
Fahrkartenschalter	Ticket office
Fahrplan	Train timetable
Fundbüro	Lost property office
Geldwechsel	Change office
Gepäckabfertigung/ Gepäckannahme	Luggage office
Gepäckaufbewahrung	Left luggage
Gleise	Platforms, Tracks
Herren	Gentlemen
Kein Zutritt	No access
Liegewagen	Couchettes
Nicht hinauslehnen	Do not lean out
Reiseziel	Destination
Reservierungen	Reservations
Schlafwagen	Sleeping-car
Schliessfächer	Luggage lockers
Speisewagen	Dining-car
Täglich	Daily
Toiletten	Toilets
Wartesaal	Waiting room
Zimmernachweis	Accommodation information
Zu den Bahnsteigen	To the platforms

Information

(see Time, *page 193)*

Is there a train to Hanover?
Gibt es einen Zug nach Hannover?
*gipt es **iy**nen tsoog naak han**noh**ver*

Do you have a timetable of trains to Regensburg?
Haben Sie einen Fahrplan für Züge nach Regensburg?
*haaben zee **iy**nen **faar**plan fewr **tsoo**ge naak **ray**genzboorg*

What time . . . ?
Um wieviel Uhr . . . ?
*oom **vee**feel oor*

What time is the train to Munich?
Um wieviel Uhr fährt der Zug nach München?
*oom **vee**feel oor fayrt der tsoog naak **mewn**chen*

What time is the first train to Salzburg?
Um wieviel Uhr fährt der erste Zug nach Salzburg?
*oom **vee**feel oor fayrt der **er**ste tsoog naak **salts**boorg*

The next train
Der nächste Zug
*der **nek**ste tsoog*

The last train
Der letzte Zug
*der **lett**ste tsoog*

What time does it arrive (in Bremen)?
Um wieviel Uhr kommt er (in Bremen) an?
*oom **vee**feel oor kommt er (in **bray**men) an*

What time does the train from Stuttgart arrive?
Um wieviel Uhr kommt der Zug von Stuttgart an?
*oom **vee**feel oor kommt der tsoog fon **shtoott**gart an*

Which platform (for Freiburg)?
Von welchem Gleis fährt der Zug (nach Freiburg)?
*fon **vel**shem gliys fayrt der tsoog (naak **friy**boorg)*

Does this train go to Augsburg?
Fährt dieser Zug nach Augsburg?
*fayrt **dee**zer tsoog naak **owks**boorg*

Is this right for Constance?
Ist das hier der Zug nach Konstanz?
*ist das heer der tsoog naak **kon**stants*

Do I have to change trains?
Muß ich umsteigen?
*mooss ish **oom**shtiygen*

Where?
Wo?
voh

Tickets

(see Time, *page 193;* Numbers, *page 211)*

One/two tickets to Vienna, please
Eine Fahrkarte/Zwei Fahrkarten nach Wien, bitte
*iyne **faar**karte/tsviy **faar**karten naak veen, **bi**tte*

Single
Einfach
*iyn**faak***

Return
Hin und zurück
*hin oont tsoo**rewk***

For one adult/two adults
Für einen Erwachsenen/zwei Erwachsene
*fewr **iy**nen **ervaks**enen/tsviy **ervaks**ene*

(And) one child/two children
(Und) ein Kind/zwei Kinder
*oont iyn kint/tsviy **kinder***

First/second class
Erste Klasse/zweite Klasse
erste klasse/tsviyte klasse

For the 10.00 train to Düsseldorf
Für den Zug um zehn nach Düsseldorf
*fewr dayn tsoog oom tsayn naak **dewsseldorf***

For the Inter City to Cologne
Für den Inter City nach Köln
fewr dayn inter city naak kerln

I want to reserve a seat/two seats
Ich möchte einen Platz/zwei Plätze buchen
*ish **mershte** iynen platts/tsviy **plettse** **booken***

I want to reserve a sleeper
Ich möchte einen Platz im Schlafwagen buchen
*ish **mershte** iynen platts im **shlaaf**vaagen **booken***

I want to reserve a couchette
Ich möchte einen Platz im Liegewagen buchen
*ish **mershte** iynen platts im **leegevaagen** **booken***

I want to book tickets on the car-train to Geneva
Ich möchte Plätze auf dem Autozug nach Genf buchen
*ish **mershte** **plettse** owf daym **owtotsoog** naak genf **booken***

For the car and two passengers
Für ein Auto und zwei Passagiere
*fewr ein **owto** oont tsviy **passajeere***

The car is a Volkswagen Beetle
Das Auto ist ein Käfer
*das **owto** ist iyn **kayfer***

Can I send my bicycle on to Nuremberg?
Kann ich mein Fahrrad nach Nürnberg aufgeben?
*kan ish miyn **faarr**aat naak **newrn**berg **owf**gayben*

How much is it?
Was kostet das?
*vas **kos**tet das*

Is there a supplement?
Muß ich einen Zuschlag bezahlen?
*mooss ish **iy**nen **tsoo**shlaag **betsaa**len*

Left luggage

Can I leave this?
Kann ich das hinterlassen?
*kan ish das hinter**lassen***

Can I leave these two suitcases?
Kann ich diese zwei Koffer hier lassen?
*kan ish **dee**ze tsviy **ko**ffer heer **lassen***

Until three o'clock
Bis drei Uhr
bis driy oor

What time do you close?
Um wieviel Uhr schließen Sie?
*oom **vee**feel oor **shlee**ssen zee*

How much is it?
Was kostet das?
*vas **kos**tet das*

On the train

I have reserved a seat
Ich habe einen Platz gebucht
*ish **haa**be **iy**nen platts **gebookt***

I have reserved a sleeper/couchette
Ich habe einen Platz im Schlafwagen/Liegewagen gebucht
*ish **haa**be **iy**nen platts im **shlaaf**vaagen/**lee**gevaagen **gebookt***

Is this seat taken?
Ist dieser Platz frei?
*ist **dee**zer platts friy*

Excuse me, may I get by?
Entschuldigung/Pardon
*ent**shool**digoong/par**don***

Where is the dining-car?
Wo ist der Speisewagen?
*voh ist der **shpiy**zevaagen*

Where is the sleeping-car?
Wo ist der Schlafwagen?
*voh ist der **shlaaf**vaagen*

May I open the window?
Darf ich das Fenster öffnen?
*darf ish das **fen**ster **erf**fnen*

May I smoke?
Darf ich rauchen?
*darf ish **row**ken*

Where are we?
Wo sind wir?
voh zint veer

Are we at Basel?
Sind wir in Basel?
*zint veer in **baa**zel*

How long does the train stop here?
Wie lange bleibt der Zug hier?
*vee **lange** bliypt der tsoog heer*

Can you tell me when we get to Kaiserslauten?
Können Sie mir bitte sagen, wenn wir in Kaiserslauten ankommen?
*kernnen zee meer **bi**tte **zaa**gen ven veer in **ki**yzerslowten **an**kommen*

You may hear

Information

(see Time, *page 193;* Numbers, *page 211)*

Er fährt um zehn Uhr dreißig ab
*er fayrt oom tsayn oor **driy**ssig ap*
It leaves at 10.30

Er kommt um zehn nach vier an
er kommt oom tsayn naak feer an
It arrives at ten past four

Sie müssen in Trier umsteigen
*zee **moos**sen in **tree**-er **oom**shtiygen*
You have to change trains at Trier

Es ist Gleis vier
es ist gliys feer
It's platform number four

Tickets

Für wann möchten Sie die Fahrkarte?
*fewr van **mersh**ten zee dee **faar**karte*
When do you want the ticket for?

Wann wollen Sie fahren?
*van **vollen** zee **faaren***
When do you want to travel?

Einfach oder hin und zurück?
iyn**faak oder hin oont tsoo**rewk
Single or return?

Wann möchten Sie zurückkommen?
*van **mersh**ten zee tsoo**rewk**kommen*
When do you want to return?

Raucher oder Nichtraucher?
***rowk**er oder **nisht**rowker*
Smoking or non-smoking?

(Das macht) dreißig Mark
*das maakt **driy**ssig mark*
(It's) DM 30

Dazu kommt ein Zuschlag von fünf Mark
*daa**tsoo** kommt iyn **tsoo**shlaag fon fewnf mark*
There is a supplement of DM 5

Der Zug hat nur erste Klasse
*der tsoog hat noor **erste** **klas**se*
That train's first class only

BUSES AND COACHES

• You usually pay as you enter on buses in towns and cities. There may be automatic ticket machines at bus stops. Tickets for some long-distance services can be bought at bus station ticket offices.

• If you intend to use the buses a lot in a town or city, you can buy **eine Tageskarte**, a day card, which is valid on buses, trams and the underground. You can buy them from machines in underground stations or from kiosks. Most cities are divided into zones; make sure all the zones you want to travel in are stamped on your ticket.

• You can also buy tickets which are valid for shorter periods such as two hours.

• There are on-the-spot fines for travelling without a valid ticket.

• A good way to see Germany by coach is to go on one of the **DB**'s (German Railways) coach tours. There are excursions in the Rhine area and in the Alps. More information from the German National Tourist Office or the main railway station in any big city.

• **Switzerland** has several Postbus routes. Further information on Postbus services, including the Alpine services, and excursions is available from local tourist offices. A **Swiss Pass** ticket is valid for buses as well as trains.

• **Austria** There are plenty of local bus services operating throughout the country to take tourists on excursions and between towns and cities.

You may see

Bedarfhaltestelle	Request stop
Busbahnhof	Bus station
Bushaltestelle	Bus stop
Eingang	Entrance
Hinten einsteigen	Enter by the back door
Kein Ausstieg	No exit
Kein Einstieg	No entry
(Not)ausgang	(Emergency) exit
Rauchen verboten	No smoking
Während der Fahrt nicht mit dem Fahrer sprechen	Do not talk to the driver
Vorne aussteigen	Exit by the front door

You may want to say

(for sightseeing bus tours, see Sightseeing, *page 142)*

Where is the bus stop?
Wo ist die Bushaltestelle?
*voh ist dee **boos**halteshtelle*

Where is the bus station?
Wo is der Busbahnhof?
*voh ist der **boos**baanhof*

Is there a bus to the lake?
Gibt es einen Bus zum See?
*gipt es **iy**nen boos tsoom zay*

What number is the bus to the station?
Welche Buslinie fährt zum Bahnhof?
***velshe boos**leenye fayrt tsoom **baan**hof*

Do they go often?
Fahren sie oft?
faaren zee oft

What time is the bus to Berlin?
Um wieviel Uhr fährt der Bus nach Berlin?
oom veefeel oor fayrt der boos naak berleen

What time is the first bus to Celle?
Um wieviel Uhr fährt der erste Bus nach Celle?
oom veefeel oor fayrt der erste boos naak zelle

The next bus
Der nächste Bus
der nekste boos

The last bus
Der letzte Bus
der lettste boos

What time does it arrive?
Um wieviel Uhr kommt er an?
oom veefeel oor kommt er an

Where can I buy tickets?
Wo kann ich Fahrkarten kaufen?
voh kan ish faarkarten kowfen

Where can I get a day ticket?
Wo kann ich eine Tageskarte kaufen?
voh kan ish iyne taageskarte kowfen

Where does the bus to the town centre leave from?
Wo fährt der Bus zum Stadtzentrum ab?
voh fayrt der boos tsoom shtattsentroom ap

Does the bus to the airport leave from here?
Fährt der Bus zum Flughafen von hier ab?
fayrt der boos tsoom flooghaafen fon heer ap

Does this bus go to Blankenese?
Fährt dieser Bus nach Blankenese?
fayrt deezer boos naak blankeneze

Can you tell me where to get off?
Können Sie mir sagen, wo ich aussteigen muß?
kernnen zee meer zaagen voh ish owsshtiygen mooss

The next stop, please
Die nächste Haltestelle, bitte
dee nekste halteshtelle bitte

Can you open the door, please?
Bitte die Tür öffnen!
bitte dee tewr erffnen

Excuse me, may I get by?
Pardon
pardon

Tickets

One/two to the centre, please
Eins/zwei zum Zentrum, bitte
iyns/tsviy tsoom tsentroom bitte

A day card, please
Eine Tageskarte, bitte
iyne taageskarte bitte

How much is it?
Was kostet das?
vas kostet das

You may hear

Der Bus zum Stadtzentrum fährt von dieser Haltestelle da ab
*der boos tsoom **shtatt**sentroom fayrt fon **dee**zer **hal**teshtelle daa ap*
The bus to the town centre leaves from that stop there

Der siebenundfünfziger fährt zum Bahnhof
*der zeebenoond**fewnf**tsiger fayrt tsoom **baan**hof*
The 57 goes to the station

Sie fahren alle zehn Minuten
*zee **faa**ren **al**le tsayn mi**noo**ten*
They go every ten minutes

Sie können eine Tageskarte bei einem Kiosk kaufen
*zee **ker**nnen **iy**ne **taa**geskarte biy **iy**nem **kee**osk **kow**fen*
You can buy a day ticket from a kiosk

Wie viele Zonen möchten Sie?
*vee **fee**le **tsoh**nen **mersh**ten zee*
How many zones do you want?

Sie zahlen beim Fahrer
*zee **tsaa**len biym **faa**rer*
You pay the driver

Steigen Sie hier aus?
***shtiy**gen zee heer ows*
Are you getting off here?

Sie müssen an der nächsten Haltestelle aussteigen
*zee **mew**ssen an der **nek**sten **hal**teshtelle **ows**shtiygen*
You have to get off at the next stop

Sie haben die Haltestelle verpaßt
*zee **haa**ben dee **hal**teshtelle fer**passt***
You've missed the stop

UNDERGROUND TRAVEL

• The underground is called the **U-Bahn**, and there are systems in most large cities. The **S-Bahn** is an express underground, or overground, which goes further afield. You can buy tickets for your journey at an automatic machine in the station. In most large cities tickets for the bus (and tram) are also valid on the **U-Bahn**, though not always on the **S-Bahn**.

• Children under 4 travel free, and there are concessions for children under 14.

• In **Austria** tourists can buy a **Wochenkarte**, weekly card, for the underground and buses.

You may see

Ausgang	Exit
Eingang	Entrance
Hinweis	Information
S-Bahn	Express underground or overground
Rauchen verboten	No smoking
U-Bahn	Underground

You may want to say

Do you have a map of the underground?
Haben Sie einen Zonenplan?
haaben zee iynen tsohnenplaan

One/Two, please
Eins/Zwei, bitte
iyns/tsviy bitte

Which line is it for Dammtor station?
Welche Linie fährt zum Dammtor?
velshe leenye fayrt tsoom dammtor

Which stop is it for the Theresienwiesen?
Wo muß ich für die Theresienwiesen aussteigen?
voh mooss ish fewr dee terayzyenveezen owsshtiygen

Where are we?
Wo sind wir?
voh zint veer

Is this the right stop for the Fish Market?
Ist das hier richtig für den Fischmarkt?
ist das heer rishtig fewr dayn fishmarkt

Does this train go to the Rathaus?
Fährt dieser Zug zum Rathaus?
fayrt deezer tsoog tsoom raathows

You may hear

Es ist die Linie S zwei
es ist dee leenye s tsviy
It's line number S2

Es ist die nächste Station
es ist dee nekste shtatsyon
It's the next stop

Es war die letzte Station
es vaar dee lettste shtatsyon
It was the last stop

BOATS AND FERRIES

• The **Rheinschiffahrt** company organises long- and short-distance cruises on the Rhine and the Moselle and there are boat trips and cruises on all the major German rivers. There are cruises and excursions on Lake Constance (**der Bodensee**) and also a car ferry service. If you have a Lake Constance pass you are entitled to concessions.

• If you want to visit the German North Sea Islands or the Baltic island of Fehmarn, one rail ticket will cover you for travel to the coast, the ferry across and transport the other side. There are also motorail services to the islands.

• There are steam cruises on the Danube (**Donau**) and on the larger Austrian and Swiss lakes all through the summer. Further information is available from local tourist offices.

Signs you may see

Anlegestelle	Pier, embarkation point
Autodeck	Car deck
Bootfahrten	Cruises
Bootrundfahrt	Round trip
Dampfer	Steamer
Dampferfahrten	Steam cruises
Fähre	Ferry
Flußfahrten	River trips
Hafen	Port, harbour
Kabinen	Cabins
Luftkissenfahrzeug	Hovercraft
Rettungsring	Lifebelt
Rheinfahrten	Rhine cruises

Information

(see Time, *page 193)*

Is there a boat to Weltenburg (today)?
Fährt (heute) ein Schiff nach Weltenburg?
*fayrt **hoyte** iyn shiff naak **veltenboorg***

Is there a car ferry to Constance?
Fährt eine Fähre nach Konstanz?
*fayrt **iyne fayre** naak **konstants***

Are there any boat trips?
Gibt es Schiffahrten?
*gipt es **shiffaarten***

What time is the boat to Passau?
Um wieviel Uhr fährt das Schiff nach Passau ab?
*oom **veefeel** oor fayrt das shiff naak **passow** ap*

What time is the first boat?
Um wieviel Uhr fährt das erste Schiff?
*oom **veefeel** oor fayrt das **erste** shiff*

The next boat
Das nächste Schiff
*das **nekste** shiff*

The last boat
Das letzte Schiff
*das **lettste** shiff*

What time does it arrive?
Um wieviel Uhr kommt es an?
*oom **veefeel** oor kommt es an*

What time does it return?
Um wieviel Uhr kommt es zurück?
oom veefeel oor kommt es tsoorewk

How long is the cruise?
Wie lange dauert die Fahrt?
vee lange dowert dee faart

Where does the boat to Koblenz leave from?
Wo fährt das Schiff nach Koblenz ab?
voh fayrt das shiff naak koblents ap

Where can I buy tickets?
Wo kann ich Karten kaufen?
voh kan ish karten kowfen

What is the lake like today?
Wie ist der See heute?
vee ist der zay hoyte

Tickets

(see Numbers, *page 211)*

Four tickets to Mainz, please
Vier Fahrkarten nach Mainz, bitte
feer faarkarten naak miynts bitte

Two adults and two children
Zwei Erwachsene und zwei Kinder
tsviy ervaksene oont tsviy kinder

Single
Einfach
iynfaak

Return
Hin und zurück
hin oont tsoorewk

I want to book tickets for the ferry to Fehmarn
Ich möchte Fahrkarten für die Fähre nach Fehmarn buchen
ish mershte faarkarten fewr dee fayre naak faymarn booken

For a car and two passengers
Für ein Auto und zwei Passagiere
fewr iyn owto oont tsviy passajeere

I want to book a cabin
Ich möchte eine Kabine buchen
*ish **mershte iyne** kabeene **booken***

For one person
Für eine Person
*fewr **iyne perzohn***

For two people
Für zwei Personen
*fewr tsviy **perzohnen***

How much is it?
Was kostet das?
*vas **kostet** das*

On board

I have reserved a cabin
Ich habe eine Kabine gebucht
*ish **haabe iyne** kabeene **gebookt***

I have reserved a two-berth cabin
Ich habe eine Zweierkabine gebucht
*ish **haabe iyne tsviyerkabeene gebookt***

Where are the cabins?
Wo sind die Kabinen?
*voh zint dee **kabeenen***

Where is cabin number 20?
Wo ist Kabine Nummer zwanzig?
*voh ist **kabeene noommer tsvantsig***

Can I/we go out on deck?
Kann man auf das Deck gehen?
*kan man owf das deck **gayen***

You may hear

Schiffe fahren dienstags und freitags
shiffe faaren deenstaags oond friytaags
There are boats on Tuesdays and Fridays

Das Schiff nach Konstanz fährt um neun Uhr ab
das shiff naak konstants fayrt oom noyn oor ap
The boat to Constance leaves at nine o'clock

Es kommt um halb fünf zurück
es kommt oom halp fewnf tsoorewk
It returns at half past four

Das Schiff nach Mainz fährt von Anlegestelle zwei ab
das shiff naak miynts fayrt fon anlaygeshtelle tsviy ap
The boat to Mainz leaves from pier number two

Der See ist still
der zay ist shtil
The lake is calm

Der See ist stürmisch
der zay ist shtewrmish
The lake is rough

AT THE TOURIST OFFICE

• There are tourist information offices in most towns and cities – look for any of the words listed below. There will usually be someone who speaks English.

• Tourist offices have leaflets about sights worth seeing, lists of hotels, town plans and regional maps, and can supply information about opening times and local transport. They can also book hotel rooms for you for a small fee.

• Tourist offices have the same sort of opening hours as shops (*see page 127*).

You may see

Any of these signs means tourist information:

Fremdenverkehrsamt
Fremdenverkehrsbüro
Fremdenverkehrsverein
Verkehrsamt
Verkehrsverein

You may want to say

(see Directions, *page 24;* Sightseeing, *page 142;* Time, *page 193)*

Where is the tourist office?
Wo ist das Fremdenverkehrsbüro?
*voh ist das fremdenferkayrzbew**roh***

Do you have . . . ?
Haben Sie . . . ?
***haa**ben zee . . .*

Do you have a plan of the town?
Haben Sie einen Stadtplan?
***haa**ben zee **iy**nen **shtat**plaan*

Do you have a map of the town/village and surrounding area?
Haben Sie einen Plan von der Stadt/dem Dorf und der Umgebung?
***haa**ben zee **iy**nen plaan fon der shtat/daym dorf oont der oom**gay**boong*

Do you have a list of hotels?
Haben Sie eine Hotelliste?
***haa**ben zee **iy**ne **hotel**liste*

Do you have a list of campsites?
Haben Sie eine Liste von Campingplätzen?
***haa**ben zee **iy**ne **liste** fon **kam**pingplettsen*

Can you recommend a cheap hotel?
Können Sie ein preiswertes Hotel empfehlen?
***ker**nnen zee iyn **priys**vertes **hotel** emp**fay**len*

Can you book a hotel room for me, please?
Können Sie für mich ein Hotelzimmer bitte buchen?
***ker**nnen zee fewr mish iyn **hotel**tsimmer **bit**te **book**en*

Can you recommend a traditional restaurant?
Können Sie mir ein typisches Restaurant empfehlen?
***ker**nnen zee meer iyn **too**pishes **resto**ron emp**fay**len*

Where can I/we hire a car?
Wo kann man ein Auto mieten?
*voh kan man iyn **owto** **mee**ten*

What is there to see here?
Was gibt es hier für Sehenswürdigkeiten?
*vas gipt es heer fewr **zay**enzvewrdigkiyten*

Do you have any leaflets?
Haben Sie irgendwelche Prospekte?
***haa**ben zee irgent**vel**she pros**pek**te*

Where is the city art gallery?
Wo ist die Kunsthalle?
*voh ist dee **koonst**halle*

Can you show me that on the map?
Können Sie mir das auf dem Stadtplan zeigen?
***ker**nnen zee meer das owf daym **shtat**plaan **tsiy**gen*

When is the museum open?
Wann ist das Museum offen?
*van ist das moo**zay**oom **offen***

Are there any excursions?
Gibt es irgendwelche Ausflüge?
*gipt es irgent**vel**she **ows**flewge*

You may hear

Kann ich Ihnen helfen?
*kan ish **eenen helfen***
Can I help you?

Sind Sie Englisch?
*zint zee **english***
Are you English?

Französisch?
*frant**serzish***
French?

Wie lange ist Ihr Aufenthalt?
*vee **lange** ist eer **owfenthalt***
How long are you going to be here?

Wo wohnen Sie?
*voh **vohnen** zee*
Where are you staying?

Was für ein Hotel möchten Sie?
*vas fewr iyn **hotel mershten** zee*
What kind of hotel do you want?

Was für ein Zimmer möchten Sie?
*vas fewr iyn **tsimmer mershten** zee*
What kind of room do you want?

Es ist in der Altstadt
*es ist in der **altshtat***
It's in the old part of town

ACCOMMODATION

• There is a wide range of hotels, inns and guest houses in West Germany.

• **Hotels** are not officially graded but standards conform to the usual European star system. Prices are always displayed in the rooms.

• A **Hotel garni** offers bed and breakfast. A **Pension** is a guest house and a **Gasthof** is like a country inn and offers good food and a limited amount of accommodation. The sign **Zimmer frei** indicates rooms to let in a private house.

• There are motels along major routes. The 'International Motel Guide', available in Germany from **ADAC** (the German motoring organisation) offices, has a list.

• The German National Tourist Office has information about accommodation in castles and stately homes. The organisation that runs these hotels is **Gast im Schloss**.

• Some hotels in **Switzerland** offer special facilities for convalescence, rest and relaxation. A list is available from the Swiss National Tourist Office.

• There are plenty of campsites all over Germany, including special winter campsites. Further information and a list of sites is available from the German National Tourist Office. It is best to book in good time during the busy summer season. There are reductions at **DCC** (**Deutscher Camping Club**) sites for holders of international carnets. The same applies to many campsites in **Austria**, where there are also reductions for children. Wild camping is allowed with the landowner's permission.

• There are over 600 Youth Hostels, **Jugendherbergen**, in Germany which are open to members of any organisation affiliated to the IYHF. The YHA in London has further information and the International Youth Hostel Handbook. In **Switzerland** hostels are open to young people under 25 and to the over-25s if there is room. Foreign visitors must have a membership card of an organisation affiliated to the International Youth Hostelling Federation for hostels in Switzerland and Austria.

• When you book in somewhere you will usually be asked for your passport. In a hotel, you may have to fill in a registration card, **ein Anmeldeschein**, which will usually have an English translation. You may also have to leave your passport at reception overnight.

• There are plenty of chalets, villas and apartments for rent throughout the year - some of them in holiday villages. The German National Tourist Office has a brochure and you can make bookings through regional tourist offices in Germany and travel agents too. Many farms, **Bauernhöfe**, offer accommodation and holidays to tourists.

Information requested on a registration card

Vorname	First name
Familienname	Surname
Wohnort/Straße/Nr.	Home address/Street/Number
Nationalität	Nationality
Beruf	Occupation
Geburtsdatum	Date of birth
Geburtsort	Place of birth
Paßnummer	Passport number
Letzter Aufenthaltsort/ Reiseziel	Coming from/going to
Ausgestellt	Issued at
Datum	Date
Unterschrift	Signature

You may see

Aufenthaltsraum	Lounge
Ausgebucht	Full up
Bitte läuten	Please ring the bell
Campingplatz/Zeltplatz	Campsite
Camping verboten	No camping
Chemische Toilette hier abladen	Empty chemical toilets here
Duschen	Showers
Das Abladen von Abfällen ist untersagt	Do not dump rubbish
Empfang/Rezeption	Reception
Erdgeschoß	Ground floor
Erster Stock	First floor
Eßzimmer	Dining-room
Fahrstuhl	Lift
Fernsehraum	Television room
Frühstücksbüffet	Breakfast bar
Garage	Garage
Gasthof	Inn, hotel
Gaststätte	Restaurant
Halbpension	Half board
Hotel	Hotel
Hotel garni	Bed and breakfast
Jugendherberge	Youth hostel
Keine Lagerfeuer anzünden	Do not light fires
Luxus Hotel	Five-star, luxury hotel
Müll	Rubbish
(Not)ausgang	(Emergency) exit
Pension	Guest house
Strom	Electricity
Toiletten	Toilets
Trinkwasser	Drinking water
Vollpension	Full board
Wäscherei	Laundry

Wohnwagen verboten	No caravans
Zimmerservice	Room service
Zimmer frei	Rooms vacant (often in a private house)
Zweiter Stock	Second floor

You may want to say

Booking in and out

I've reserved a room
Ich habe ein Zimmer reservieren lassen
*ish **haabe** iyn **tsimmer** rezerveeren **lassen***

I've reserved two rooms
Ich habe zwei Zimmer reservieren lassen
*ish **haabe** tsviy **tsimmer** rezerveeren **lassen***

I've reserved a place
Ich habe einen Platz reservieren lassen
*ish **haabe iynen** platts rezerveeren **lassen***

My name is . . .
Mein Name ist . . .
*miyn **naame** ist*

Do you have a room?
Haben Sie ein Zimmer?
haaben** zee iyn **tsimmer

A single room
Ein Einzelzimmer
*iyn **iyntseltsimmer***

A double room
Ein Doppelzimmer
*iyn **doppeltsimmer***

A twin-bedded room
Ein Zimmer mit zwei Einzelbetten
*iyn **tsimmer** mit tsviy **iyn**tselbetten*

For one night
Für eine Nacht
*fewr **iyne** naakt*

For two nights
Für zwei Nächte
*fewr tsviy **nekte***

With bath/shower
Mit Bad/Dusche
*mit baat/**dooshe***

Do you have space for a tent?
Haben Sie Platz für ein Zelt?
***haa**ben zee platts fewr iyn tselt*

Do you have space for a caravan?
Haben Sie Platz für einen Wohnwagen?
***haa**ben zee platts fewr **iyn**en **vohn**vaagen*

How much is it?
Was kostet das?
*vas **kost**et das*

Per night
Pro Nacht
proh naakt

Per week
Pro Woche
*proh **voke***

Is there a reduction for children?
Gibt es eine Ermäßigung für Kinder?
*gipt es **iyne** er**may**sigoong fewr **kin**der*

Is breakfast included?
Ist das Frühstück inbegriffen?
*ist das **frew**shtewk **in**begriffen*

It's too expensive
Es ist zu teuer
*es ist tsoo **toyer***

Do you have anything cheaper?
Haben Sie etwas Billigeres?
***haa**ben zee **et**vas **bil**ligeres*

Do you have anything bigger/smaller?
Haben Sie etwas Größeres/Kleineres?
***haa**ben zee **et**vas **grer**sseres/**kliy**neres*

I'd like to stay another night
Ich möchte noch eine Nacht bleiben
*ish **mersh**te nok **iy**ne naakt **bliy**ben*

I am leaving tomorrow morning
Ich fahre morgen früh ab
*ish **faa**re **mor**gen frew ap*

Thank you, it's been very nice here
Vielen Dank, es hat uns hier gut gefallen
*feelen dank es hat oons heer goot ge**fal**len*

The bill, please
Die Rechnung, bitte
*dee **resh**noong **bi**tte*

Do you take credit cards?
Nehmen Sie Kreditkarten?
***nay**men zee kre**deet**karten*

Do you take traveller's cheques?
Nehmen Sie Reiseschecks?
***nay**men zee **riy**zeshecks*

Can you recommend a hotel in Würzburg?
Können Sie ein Hotel in Würzburg empfehlen?
kernnen zee iyn hotel in vertsboorg empfaylen

Can you book a room for me there, please?
Können Sie bitte ein Zimmer für mich dort buchen?
kernnen zee bitte iyn tsimmer fewr mish dort booken

In hotels

(see Problems and complaints, *page 170;* Time, *page 193)*

Where can I/we park?
Wo kann man parken?
voh kan man parken

Do you have a cot for the baby?
Haben Sie ein Kinderbett für das Baby?
haaben zee iyn kinderbett fewr das baybee

Is there room service?
Gibt es Zimmerservice?
gipt es tsimmerservis

Do you have facilities for the disabled?
Bieten Sie Möglichkeiten für Behinderte?
beeten zee merglishkiyten fewr behinderte

A room with a view, please
Ein Zimmer mit Aussicht, bitte
iyn tsimmer mit owssisht bitte

Can I see the room, please?
Kann ich das Zimmer bitte sehen?
kan ish das tsimmer bitte zayen

What time is breakfast?
Um wieviel Uhr ist das Frühstück?
oom veefeel oor ist das frewshtewk

Can I/we have breakfast in the room?
Kann man im Zimmer frühstücken?
*kan man im **tsimmer** **frew**shtewken*

What time is dinner?
Um wieviel Uhr ist das Abendessen?
*oom **veefeel** oor ist das **aa**bentessen*

What time does the hotel close?
Wann schließen Sie das Hotel ab?
*van **shlee**ssen zee das **hotel** ap*

I'll be back very late
Ich komme sehr spät zurück
*ish **komme** zayr shpayt tsoo**rewk***

Where is the bathroom?
Wo ist das Badezimmer?
*voh ist das **baa**detsimmer*

Where is the dining-room?
Wo ist das Eßzimmer?
*voh ist das **esstsimmer***

(Key) number 42, please
(Schlüssel) Nummer zweiundvierzig, bitte
*(**shloo**ssel) **noomm**er tsviyoont**feer**tsig **bi**tte*

Are there any messages for me?
Hat jemand für mich angerufen?
*hat **yay**mant fewr mish **an**geroofen*

Can I leave this in the safe?
Kann ich das im Safe lassen?
*kan ish das im sayf **lassen***

Can you give me my things from the safe?
Können Sie mir meine Sachen vom Safe geben?
*kernnen zee meer **miyne** **zaa**ken vom sayf **gay**ben*

Can you call me at eight o'clock?
Können Sie mich um acht Uhr wecken?
kernnen zee mish oom aakt oor veken

Can you order me a taxi?
Können Sie bitte ein Taxi bestellen?
kernnen zee bitte iyn taksi beshtellen

For right now
Gleich
gliysh

For tomorrow at nine o'clock
Für morgen um acht Uhr
fewr morgen oom aakt oor

Can you clean this jacket for me?
Können Sie diese Jacke für mich reinigen lassen?
kernnen zee deeze yake fewr mish riynigen lassen

Can you find me a babysitter?
Können Sie mir einen Babysitter besorgen?
kernnen zee meer iynen baybeesitter bezorgen

Can you put it on the bill, please?
Schreiben Sie es mir auf die Rechnung, bitte
shriyben zee es meer owf dee reshnoong bitte

Room number 21
Zimmer Nummer einundzwanzig
tsimmer noommer iynoonttsvantsig

I need another pillow
Ich brauche noch ein Kopfkissen
ish browke nok iyn kopfkissen

I need a towel
Ich brauche ein Handtuch
ish browke iyn hanttook

At campsites

Is there a campsite around here?
Gibt es einen Zeltplatz hier in der Nähe?
*gipt es **iy**nen **tselt**platts heer in der **naye***

Where are the toilets?
Wo sind die Toiletten?
*voh zint dee toy**letten***

Do we pay extra for the showers?
Müssen wir extra für die Duschen bezahlen?
***mew**ssen veer **ek**stra fewr dee **doosh**en bet**saa**len*

Can we camp here?
Können wir hier zelten?
***ker**nnen veer heer **tsel**ten*

Where are the showers?
Wo sind die Duschen?
*voh zint dee **doosh**en*

Is the water drinkable?
Ist das Wasser trinkbar?
*ist das **vasser trink**bar*

Where is there an electric point?
Wo ist der Stromanschluß?
*voh ist der **shtrom**anshloos*

Where are the dustbins?
Wo sind die Mülleimer?
*voh zint dee **mewll**iymer*

Self-catering accommodation

(see Directions, *page 24;* Problems and complaints, *page 170)*

I have rented a chalet
Ich habe ein Chalet gemietet
*ish **haa**be iyn **sha**lay **gemee**tet*

I have rented an apartment
Ich habe eine Ferienwohnung gemietet
*ish **haa**be **iy**ne **fay**ree-envohnoong **gemee**tet*

We're in number 11
Wir sind in Nummer elf
*veer zint in **noomm**er elf*

My name is . . .
Mein Name ist . . .
*miyn **naa**me ist . . .*

What is the address?
Was ist die Adresse?
*vas ist dee **adresse***

How do we get there?
Wie kommen wir dahin?
*vee **komm**en veer daa**hin***

Can you give me the key, please?
Können Sie mir bitte den Schlüssel geben?
kernnen zee meer bitte dayn shloossel gayben

Where is . . . ?
Wo ist . . . ?
voh ist

Where is the stopcock?
Wo ist der Abstellhahn?
voh ist der apshtellhaan

Where is the fusebox?
Wo ist der Sicherungskasten?
voh ist der zisheroongskasten

Are there any shops around here?
Gibt es irgendwelche Geschäfte hier in der Nähe?
gipt es irgentvelshe geshefte heer in der naye

How does the cooker work?
Wie funktioniert der Herd?
vee foonktsyoneert der hert

How does the water-heater work?
Wie funktioniert der Warmwasserbereiter?
vee foonktsyoneert der varmvasserberiyter

Is there air conditioning?
Gibt es eine Klimaanlaage?
gipt es iyne kleema-anlaage

Is there another gas bottle?
Gibt es eine andere Flasche Ga
gipt es iyne andere flashe gas

Are there any more blankets?
Gibt es noch Bettdecken?
gipt es nok bettdeken

When does the cleaning lady come?
Wann kommt die Putzfrau?
van kommt dee poottsfrow

Where do I/we put the rubbish?
Wo stelle ich/stellen wir den Müll hin?
voh shtelle ish/shtellen veer dayn mewll hin

When do they collect the rubbish?
Wann kommt die Müllabfuhr?
van kommt dee mewllapfoor

Where can I contact you?
Wo kann ich Sie erreichen?
voh kan ish zee erriyshen

You may hear

Kann ich Ihnen helfen?
*kan ish **eenen helfen***
Can I help you?

Wie heißen Sie, bitte?
*vee **hiy**ssen zee **bi**tte*
What's your name, please?

Für wie viele Nächte?
*fewr vee **feele nek**te*
For how many nights?

Für wie viele Personen?
*fewr vee **feele perzoh**nen*
For how many people?

Mit oder ohne Bad?
*mit **oh**der **oh**ne baat*
With bath or without bath

Haben Sie ein großes oder ein kleines Zelt?
*haaben zee iyn **grohsses oh**der iyn **kliy**nes tselt*
Have you got a big or a small tent?

Es tut mir leid, wir sind voll
es toot meer liyt veer zint foll
I'm sorry, we're full

Ihren Paß, bitte
*eeren pass **bi**tte*
Your passport, please

Können Sie bitte hier unterschreiben?
*kernnen zee **bi**tte heer oonter**shriy**ben*
Can you sign here, please?

Die Putzfrau kommt jeden (zweiten) Tag
*dee **poottsfrow** kommt **yay**den (**tsviy**ten) taag*
The cleaning lady comes every (other) day

Sie kommen freitags
*zee **kommen friy**taags*
They come on Fridays

TELEPHONES

• National and international calls can be made in phone boxes with the sign **Ausland** and from post offices with coin-operated phones. Lift the receiver first and then put the money in; there are usually pictures giving operating instructions in the phone box.

• German speakers usually start a formal or business call by saying 'Here is Mr/Mrs. . .', **Hier ist Herr/Frau . . .** They answer the phone by simply giving their surname.

• The number for the police is **110** and for the other emergency services, **112**. (See Emergency telephone numbers, page 288.)

• To call abroad, first dial **00**, then the code for the country – for the UK it's **44** from Germany, Austria and Switzerland. Follow this with the town code minus the 0, and then the number you want. For example: for a central London number, dial **00 44 71**, then the number.

• The numbers for directory enquiries are:
118 (for numbers within Germany)
00118 (for international numbers)

• The numbers for the emergency services in **Austria** are:
Police **133**
Fire **122**
Ambulance **144**

• It's cheaper to make calls after 6 pm and at weekends.

• If you make a call from a public telephone in Austria you may have to press an extra button, **der Zahlknopf**, to complete the connection.

• Useful telephone numbers in **Switzerland** are:
Police **117**
Fire **118**
Ambulance **144**
International Directory Enquiries **191**
Directory Enquiries **111**
Tourist Information and snow bulletin **120**
Avalanche bulletin **187**
International operator **114**

• Phone cards are available in both Austria and Switzerland from newsagents, post offices and kiosks.

You may see

Ferngespräch	Long-distance
Inland/Ausland	Local and international calls
International	International calls
Bundespost	Telephone company
Telefon	Telephone

You may want to say

Is there a telephone?
Ist hier ein Telefon?
ist heer iyn telefohn

Where is the telephone?
Wo ist das Telefon?
voh ist das telefohn

May I use your telephone, please?
Kann ich Ihr Telefon bitte benutzen?
kan ish eer telefohn bitte benootsen

Do you have change for the telephone, please?
Haben Sie bitte Kleingeld fürs Telefon?
haaben zee bitte kliyngelt fewrz telefohn

A phone card, please
Eine Telefonkarte, bitte
*iyne tele**fohn**karte **bi**tte*

Do you have the Bonn telephone directory?
Haben Sie das Bonner Telefonbuch?
*haaben zee das **bonner** tele**fohn**book*

I want to call England
Ich möchte ein Gespräch nach England machen
*ish **mershte** iyn **geshprek** naak **englant** **maaken***

I want to make a reverse charge call
Ich möchte ein Rückgespräch machen
*ish **mershte** iyn **rewk**geshprek **maaken***

Mr Reimann, please
Herr Reimann, bitte
*herr **riymann** **bi**tte*

Extension number 121, please
Apparat eins, zwei, eins, bitte
*appa**raat** iyns tsviy iyns **bi**tte*

It's Mrs Stanley speaking
Hier ist Frau Stanley
heer ist frow stanley

It's Robert speaking
Hier ist Robert
*heer ist **roh**bert*

My name is . . .
Mein Name ist . . .
*miyn **naame** ist*

When will he/she be back?
Wann kommt er/sie zurück?
*van kommt er/zee tsoo**rewk***

I'll call later
Ich werde später zurückrufen
*ish **verde** **shpay**ter tsoo**rewk**roofen*

Can I leave a message?
Können Sie etwas für mich ausrichten?
*ker**n**nen zee **et**vas fewr mish **ows**rishten*

Please tell him/her that . . . called
Bitte, sagen Sie ihm/ihr, *(your name)* **hat angerufen**
*bitte **zaa**gen zee eem/eer, . . . hat **an**geroofen*

I am in the Hotel Bellevue
Ich wohne bei Hotel Bellevue
*ish **vohne** biy ho**tel** bell**vew***

My telephone number is . . .
Meine Telefonnummer ist . . .
*mi**yne** tele**fohn**noommer ist*

Can he/she call me?
Kann er/sie mich anrufen?
*kan er/zee mish **an**roofen*

I beg your pardon?
Wie bitte?
*vee **bitte***

More slowly, please
Langsamer, bitte
*lang**zamer** **bitte***

We were cut off
Wir sind unterbrochen worden
*veer zint oonter**broken** **vorden***

How much is the call?
Was kostet der Anruf?
*vas **kostet** der **an**roof*

Can you give me a number to call a taxi?
Können Sie mir eine Nummer für ein Taxi geben?
kernnen zee meer iyne noommer fewr iyn taksi gayben

You may hear

Hallo
hallo
Hello?

Reimann
riymann
Herr/Frau Reimann speaking

(Ja, ich bin) am Apparat
(yaa ish bin) am apparaat
Speaking

Wer spricht?
ver shprikt
Who's calling?

Augenblick, bitte
owgenblick bitte
One moment, please

Er/Sie ist nicht hier
er/zee ist nisht heer
He/She is not in

Bitte warten Sie einen Moment
bitte varten zee iynen mohment
Please wait

Ich verbinde Sie
ish ferbinde zee
I'm putting you through

Es ist besetzt
es ist bezettst
The line's engaged

Möchten Sie warten?
mershten zee varten
Do you want to hold?

Es meldet sich niemand
es meldet zish neemant
There's no answer

Sie haben sich verwählt
zee haaben zish fervaylt
You've got the wrong number

CHANGING MONEY

• The German unit of currency is the **Deutschmark** (abbreviated as **DM**). There are coins of 1, 2, 5, 10 and 50 **Pfennige** (**Pf**) and 1, 2 and 5 **DM**. There are 100 **Pfennige** in a **Deutschmark**. There are notes of 5, 10, 20, 50, 100, 500 and 1000 **DM**.

• You can change money, travellers' cheques or Eurocheques into Deutschmarks at banks and other places (hotels, travel agencies, main railway stations and airports) where you see a **Wechsel** sign. You'll probably get the best rate in a bank.

• Banks are open from 8.30 am – 12.30 pm and 2 pm – 4 pm on Mondays to Fridays. On Thursdays they stay open until 5.30 pm. They are closed on Saturdays.

• In banks you go first to the **Wechsel** desk where a form is filled in for you to sign. You then get your money from the cashier (**Kasse**). You'll need your passport to change any money.

• You can get money from banks on credit cards.

• The currency in **Austria** is the Austrian **Schilling** (**Sch**). There are coins of 1, 5, 10, 20, 25, 50, 100, 500 and 1000 **Schillings** and notes of 20, 50, 100, 500 and 1000 **Schillings**. There are also 2, 5, 10 and 50 **Groschen** coins. There are 100 **Groschen** in a **Schilling**. Banks are open from 8 am to midday and from 1.30 pm – 3 pm Mondays to Fridays with late opening to 5.30 pm on Thursdays.

• The currency in **Switzerland** is the Swiss **franc**. There are coins of 5, 10, 20 and 50 **centimes**, and 1, 2 and 5 **francs**, and banknotes of 10, 20, 50, 100, 500 and 1000 **francs**. There are 100 **centimes** in a **franc**. Check locally, but normal opening times for banks are Mondays to Fridays from 7.30 am to midday and 1.45 pm – 6 pm. On Saturdays they are generally open from 7.30 am – 11 am.

You may see

Ausgang	Exit
Bank	Bank
Drücken	Press
Eingang	Entrance
EC Automat	Cash dispenser
Geöffnet	Open
Geschäftszeiten	Business hours
Geschlossen	Closed
Sparkasse	Savings bank
Wechsel	Exchange
Wechselstube	Exchange office
Ziehen	Pull

You may want to say

I'd like to change some pounds sterling
Ich möchte Sterling wechseln
*ish **mershte** sterling **vek**seln*

I'd like to change some travellers' cheques
Ich möchte Reiseschecks wechseln
*ish **mershte** **riy**zeshecks **vek**seln*

I'd like to change a Eurocheque
Ich möchte einen Euroscheck wechseln
*ish **mershte** **iy**nen **oy**rosheck **vek**seln*

I'd like to get some money with my credit card
Ich möchte mit meiner Kreditkarte Geld abheben
*ish **mershte** mit **miy**ner kre**deet**karte gelt **ap**-hayben*

What's the exchange rate today, please?
Wie ist heute der Wechselkurs, bitte?
*vee ist **hoy**te der **vek**selkoors **bi**tte*

Can you give me some change, please?
Können Sie mir bitte Kleingeld geben
kernnen zee meer bitte kliyngelt gayben

Can you give me two ten-Mark notes?
Können Sie mir bitte zwei zehn Mark Scheine geben?
kernnen zee meer bitte tsviy tsayn mark shiyne gayben

I'm at the Vierjahreszeiten
Ich wohne im Hotelvierjahreszeiten
ish vohne im hotelfeerjaarestsiyten

I'm staying with friends
Ich wohne bei Freunden
ish vohne biy froynden

The address is Steinstraße 23
Die Adresse ist Steinstraße dreiundzwanzig
dee adresse ist shtiynshtraasse driyoondtsvantsig

Here's the address
Hier ist die Adresse
heer ist dee adresse

You may hear

Ihren Paß, bitte
eeren pass bitte
Your passport, please

Wieviel möchten Sie wechseln?
veefeel mershten zee vekseln
How much do you want to change?

Ihre Adresse, bitte?
eere adresse bitte
Your address, please

Der Name Ihres Hotels, bitte?
der naame eeres hotels bitte
The name of your hotel, please

Bitte hier unterschreiben
bitte heer oontershriyben
Please sign here

Bitte zur Kasse gehen
bitte tsoor kasse gayen
Please go to the cashier

EATING AND DRINKING

• To order something, all you need do is name it, and say 'please', adding 'for me', 'for him' or 'for her' if you're ordering for several people to show who wants what.

• In bars and cafés you often pay for all your drinks and so on when you leave, though in the larger, busy bars you will probably have to pay for each round. There is always waiter service in cafés, pubs and wine bars and even though service is included in your bill, it's usual to leave a tip for your waiter or waitress. It's cheaper to drink at the bar in a pub. In restaurants service at 10 or 15 per cent is usually included, but again a tip is normal practice.

• Cafés usually open early in the morning and close at about 6.00 pm unless they're a **Bistro** as well in which case they stay open until ten or eleven at night. Restaurants serve hot meals from around midday to 2.00 pm and from 6.00 pm to nine or ten at night. Some are open all the way through the afternoon too.

• Meal times in all three countries are roughly the same as in Britain. Lunch, **Mittagessen**, is the largest meal of the day. Many Germans only have a light supper, **Abendbrot**, in the evening, unless they are eating out.

• Bars and cafés serve all kinds of drinks – alcohol, soft drinks, coffee and tea etc. Cafés usually serve cakes or flans and perhaps omelettes in the way of food. Sandwiches and rolls are often sold to take away at a **Metzgerei**, a **Feinkostgeschäft** or a **Bäckerei**. (See Shopping, page 127.)

• **Schnellimbiß, Imbißstube, Würstchenbude**: all offer a cheap but filling hot meal which might mean a plate of chips with mayonnaise, a sausage such as a **Bratwurst** or **Currywurst**, soup, omelette or potato salad. You can also get tea, coffee, bottled and canned beer and soft drinks in any of them. You can often get similar snacks in a **Kneipe** or **Wirtschaft**, including **Bratkartoffeln**, fried potatoes. In Switzerland these are known as **Rösti**. A **Weinstube** usually serves more up-market food.

• Most restaurants have waiter service. The menu should be displayed outside or in the window to give you some idea of prices before you go in. They will often provide children's portions, look for **Kinderteller** on the menu. Many of them do a special set menu, **Touristen-Menü**, and they may offer late night snacks, ask for the **kleine Karte**.

• The Germans drink excellent black and white coffee, **schwarzer Kaffee** or **Kaffee mit Sahne** (cream or tinned milk). **Cappuccinos** are popular too. In **Switzerland** coffee is usually served with warm, fresh milk.

• **Vienna** is the coffee house capital of Europe and there is such a wide selection of coffee on the menu that you need to specify when you make your order. An **Einspänner** comes in a glass with **Schlagobers** (whipped cream - known as **Schlagsahne** in Germany.) **Mokka** is strong and black, **Großer Brauner** and **Kleiner Brauner** both come with a dash of milk or cream. **Melange** is half coffee and half warm milk.

• If you ask for tea with milk, **Tee mit Milch**, you'll probably be given a little pot of long-life milk. Herbal teas such as **Kamillentee** (camomile tea), **Hagebutten** (rose-hip tea), and **Pfefferminztee** (peppermint tea) are common.

• **Heiße Schokolade**, hot chocolate, with or without whipped cream is delicious, especially in Southern Germany and Austria.

• All three countries produce their own wines. German wines include **Rheinhessen** and **Rheinpfalz**, sweet and white, and **Badischer Wein**, which is dry and white. **Veltliner** is a red or white Austrian wine.

• The German equivalent to Champagne is **Sekt**.

• **Heurigenlokale** are peculiar to Vienna and are wine bars or gardens where you can drink the year's wine harvest. Most Heurigenlokale only serve cold snacks, but you can bring your own food.

• There are all sorts of different beers and lagers in Germany. **Dunkles Bier** is dark and like brown ale. **Altbier** is like bitter; **Weizenbier** is a bitter made from barley and **Malzbier** is a dark, sweet malt beer. Draught beer is **Bier vom Faß**. The best-known lagers are probably **Pilsener**, which has quite a bitter taste, and **Export**. **Berliner Weisser** is light Berlin ale with raspberry juice and makes a very refreshing drink.

Swiss and Austrian beer are more of the lager type.

• All three countries have a wide range of fiery spirits. **Schnapps** and **Korn** are both distilled from grain and there are various different flavours. **Kirschwasser** is Black Forest brandy distilled from cherries.

• Regional food specialities vary from country to country and region to region within the different countries. **Swiss** specialities include **Raclette** and **Fondue**, both cheese dishes, and delicious pastries and cakes. **Austria** has inherited its cuisine from its once vast Empire and this is reflected in the variety of dishes on the menus. **Wiener Schnitzel** is escalope of veal in breadcrumbs. Desserts include a good choice of pancakes, **Palatschinken**, and cakes include the delicious, chocolate **Sachertorte**. **Sauerkraut**, pickled white cabbage, is eaten all over Germany and fish is popular in the north. **Aalsuppe**, eel soup, is a Hamburg speciality.

You may see

Wir nehmen Kreditkarten	We accept credit cards
Selbstbedienung	Self-service
Bar	Bar
Beisel	Pub (*Austria*)
Biergarten	Beer garden
Bierkeller	Beer cellar
Café	Café
Eisdiele	Ice-cream café
Fischrestaurant	Fish restaurant
Garderobe	Cloakroom
Gasthof	Inn
Gaststätte	Restaurant/Pub
Gastwirtschaft	Inn, guest house
Grillstube	Steak house
Hähnchen-Grill	Roast chicken takeaway
Heurigenlokal	Wine bar, garden (*Austria*)
Imbißstube	Snack bar
Kneipe	Pub
Lokal	Pub
Kaffeehaus	Café
Pizzeria	Pizzeria, eat in or takeaway
Rasthof	Motorway rest area and café
Ratskeller	Restaurant (often in basement of local town hall)
Rastplatz	Open-air snack bar; picnic area
Restaurant	Restaurant
Schnellimbiß	Snack bar
Toiletten	Toilets
Touristen-Menü	Tourist menu/set meal
Weinstube	Wine bar
Wirtschaft	Pub
Würstchenbude	Sausage and burger stand

General phrases

Is there an inexpensive restaurant around here?
(*see* Directions, *page 24*)
Gibt es ein preiswertes Restaurant in der Nähe?
*gipt es iyn **priysvertes resteron** in der **naye***

A (one) . . ., please
Ein/Eine . . ., bitte
*iyn/iyne . . . **bitte***

Another . . ., please
Noch ein/eine . . ., bitte
*nok iyn/iyne . . . **bitte***

A little more . . ., please
Ein bißchen mehr, bitte
*iyn **bissyen** mayr **bitte***

A little less . . .
Ein bißchen weniger . . ., bitte
*iyn **bissyen vayniger**, **bitte***

For me
Für mich
fewr mish

For him
Für ihn
fewr een

For her
Für sie
fewr zee

For them
Für sie
fewr zee

This, please
Das, bitte
*das **bitte***

Two of these, please
Zwei davon, bitte
*tsviy **daafon**, **bitte***

Do you have . . .?
Haben Sie . . .?
***haaben** zee*

Is/Are there any . . .?
Gibt es . . .?
gipt es

What do you have for . . ./ what kind of . . . do you have?
Was für . . . haben Sie?
*vas fewr **haaben** zee*

What do you have for dessert?
Was für Nachspeisen haben Sie?
*vas fewr **naakshpiyzen haaben** zee*

What kind of soups do you have?
Was für Suppen haben Sie ?
*vas fewr **zooppen haaben** zee*

What do you recommend?
Was können Sie mir empfehlen?
*vas **kern**nen zee meer emp**fay**len*

Do you have any typical local dishes?
Haben Sie irgendwelche Spezialitäten?
*haaben zee irgend**vel**she shpetsee-ali**tay**ten*

What is this?
Was ist das?
vas ist das?

How do you eat this?
Wie ißt man das?
vee isst man das

Cheers!
Prost!/Zum Wohl!
prost/tsoom vohl

Enjoy your meal!
Guten Appetit!
*goo**ten** appe**teet***

Thank you, same to you
Danke gleichfalls
*dan**ke** gliy**sh**falls*

Where are the toilets?
Wo sind die Toiletten?
*voh zint dee toy**letten***

Nothing else, thanks
Sonst nichts, danke
*zonzt nishts **danke***

The bill, please
Die Rechnung, bitte
*dee **resh**noong **bi**tte*

Bars, cafés and snack bars

A black coffee, please
Einen schwarzen Kaffee, bitte
*iynen **shvartsen** kaffay **bi**tte*

Two cappuccinos, please
Zwei Cappuccinos, bitte
*tsviy kappoo**cheenos** **bi**tte*

A tea with milk/lemon, please
Einen Tee mit Milch/ Zitrone, bitte
*iynen tay mit milsh/tsi**trohne** **bi**tte*

A coffee with cream, please
Einen Kaffee mit Sahne, bitte
*iynen kaffay mit **zaane** **bi**tte*

A hot chocolate, please
Eine heiße Schokolade, bitte
*iyne **hiy**sse shoko**laa**de **bi**tte*

Mineral water, please
Ein Mineralwasser, bitte
*iyn mine**raal**vasser **bi**tte*

Fizzy or still?
Mit oder ohne Kohlensäure?
*mit **ohder ohne kohlenzoyre***

A lemonade, please
Eine Limonade, bitte
*iyne limo**naade** bitte*

What fruit juices do you have?
Was für Säfte haben Sie?
*vas fewr **zefte haaben** zee*

An orange juice, please
Einen Orangensaft, bitte
*iynen **oronjenzaft** bitte*

A milk shake, please
Ein Milchshake, bitte
*iyn **milsh**shake bitte*

A coke and lemonade, please
Ein Spezi, bitte
*iyn **shpay**tsee bitte*

A beer, please
Ein Bier, bitte
iyn beer bitte

A glass of red wine, please
Ein Glas Rotwein, bitte
*iyn glas **roht**viyn bitte*

A gin and tonic, please
Ein Gin-Tonik, bitte
*iyn gin-**ton**ik bitte*

With ice
Mit Eis
mit iys

A glass of water, please
Ein Glas Wasser, bitte
*iyn glas **vasser bitte***

A cake, please
Einen Kuchen, bitte
*iynen **kooken bitte***

A piece of cheesecake, please
Ein Stück Käsekuchen, bitte
*iyn shtewk **kay**zekooken bitte*

A piece of Black Forest gateau, please
Ein Stück Schwarzwälder Kirschtorte, bitte
*iyn shtewk **shwartsvelder kirsh**torte, bitte*

A Bratwurst (spicy sausage), please
Eine Bratwurst, bitte
*iyne **braat**voorst bitte*

A Frankfurter, please
Eine Bockwurst, bitte
*iyne **bok**voorst bitte*

Chips with mayonnaise and ketchup, please
Pommes Rot-Weiß, bitte
pomm es roht viyss bitte

What sandwiches do you have?
Was für Brötchen haben Sie?
*vas fewr **brertyen haaben** zee*

A ham roll, please
Ein Schinkenbrötchen, bitte
*iyn **shin**kenbrertyen bitte*

Two cheese rolls, please
Zwei Käsebrötchen, bitte
*tsviy **kay**zebrertyen **bi**tte*

Do you have ice-creams?
Haben Sie Eis?
***haa**ben zee ys*

Two chocolate ice creams, please
Zwei Schokoladeneis, bitte
*tsviy shoko**laa**deniys **bi**tte*

Booking a table

I want to reserve a table for two people
Ich möchte einen Tisch für zwei Personen reservieren lassen
*ish **mersh**te **iy**nen tish fewr tsviy per**zoh**nen rezer**veer**en **la**ssen*

For nine o'clock
Für neun Uhr
fewr noyn oor

For tomorrow evening at half past eight
Für morgen abend um halb neun
*fewr **mor**gen **aa**bent oom halp noyn*

I have booked a table
Ich habe einen Tisch reservieren lassen
*ish **haa**be **iy**nen tish rezer**veer**en **la**ssen*

My name is . . .
Mein Name ist . . .
*miyn **naa**me ist*

In restaurants

A table for four, please
Ein Tisch für vier Personen, bitte
*iyn tish fewr feer per**zoh**nen **bi**tte*

Outside/On the terrace, if possible
Draußen/Auf der Terrasse, wenn's möglich ist
***drow**ssen/owf der ter**ra**sse venns **merg**lish ist*

Excuse me!
Entschuldigen Sie bitte!
entshooldigen zee bitte

The menu, please
Die Speisekarte, bitte
dee shpiyzekarte bitte

The wine list, please
Die Weinkarte, bitte
dee viynkarte bitte

Do you have an à la carte menu?
Haben Sie eine Speisekarte?
haaben zee iyne shpiyzekarte

Do you have vegetarian dishes?
Haben Sie vegetarische Gerichte?
haaben zee vegetarishe gerishte

The tourist menu, please
Das Touristen-Menü, bitte
das tooristen menew bitte

For the starter . . .
Als Vorspeise . . .
als forshpiyze

Onion soup, please
Zwiebelsuppe, bitte
tsveebelzooppe bitte

Pickled herring, please
Rollmops, bitte
rollmops bitte

For the meat/fish course . . .
Als Hauptgericht . . .
als howptgerisht

The Wiener Schnitzel, please
Das Wienerschnitzel, bitte
das veenershnittsel bitte

The trout, please
Die Forelle, bitte
dee forelle bitte

Are vegetables included?
Kommt das mit Gemüse?
kommt das mit gemewze

Is there a salad with it?
Ist da Salat dabei?
ist da zalaat daabiy

With chips
Mit Pommes frites
mit pomme freet

And a mixed/green salad
Und ein gemischter/grüner Salat
oont iyn gemishter/grewner zalaat

For dessert . . .
Als Nachspeise . . .
als naakshpiyze

Pancake with raisins and almonds, please
Kaiserschmarren, bitte
kiyzershmarren bitte

Ice cream with hot raspberries
Vanilleeis mit heißen Himbeeren
*vanilleniys mit **hiy**ssen **him**beeren*

What cheeses are there?
Was für Käse haben Sie ?
*vas fewr **kay**ze **haa**ben zee*

Excuse me, where is my meal?
Entschuldigung, wo bleibt mein Essen?
*ent**shool**digoong voh bliypt miyn **ess**en*

More bread, please
Noch etwas Brot, bitte
*nok etvas broht **bi**tte*

More chips, please
Noch Pommes frites, bitte
*nok pomme freet **bi**tte*

A glass of water
Ein Glas Wasser
*iyn glas **va**sser*

A bottle of red wine
Eine Flasche Rotwein
*iyne **fla**she **roht**viyn*

A bottle of white wine
Eine Flasche Weißwein
*iyne **fla**she **viyss**viyn*

Half a litre of white wine
Einen halben Liter Weißwein
*iynen **hal**ben **lee**ter **viyss**viyn*

A carafe of red wine
Eine Karaffe Rotwein
*iyne ka**raf**fe **roht**viyn*

(*for ordering coffee, see page 106*)

It's very good
Es ist sehr gut
es ist zayr goot

It's really delicious
Es ist ausgezeichnet
*es ist **ows**getsiyshnet*

This is burnt
Es ist angebrannt
*es ist **an**gebrannt*

This is not cooked
Das ist nicht gar
das ist nisht gar

No, I ordered the chicken
Nein, ich habe das Hähnchen bestellt
*niyn ish **haa**be das **hayn**chen be**shtellt***

The bill, please
Die Rechnung, bitte
*dee **resh**noong **bi**tte*

Do you accept credit cards?
Nehmen Sie Kreditkarten?
*nay**men** zee kre**deet**karten*

Do you accept travellers' cheques?
Nehmen Sie Reiseschecks?
naymen zee riyzesheks

Excuse me, there is a mistake here
Entschuldigung, Sie haben sich hier geirrt
entshooldigoong zee haaben zish heer ge-eert

You may hear

Bars, cafés and snack bars

Ja, bitte
yaa bitte
What can I do for you?

Was hätten Sie gern?
vas hetten zee gern
What would you like?

Mit Eis?
mit iys
Would you like ice?

Mit oder ohne Kohlensäure?
mit ohder ohne kohlenzoyre
Fizzy or still?

Groß oder klein?
grohss ohder kliyn
Large or small?

Schoppen oder viertel?
shoppen ohder feertel
Large or small? (*wine*)

Sofort
zohfort
Right away

Wir haben . . .
veer haaben
We have . . .

Welche(r)?
velshe(r)
Which one?

Mit Sahne?
mit zaane
With whipped cream?

Bezahlen Sie zusammen oder getrennt?
betsaalen zee tsoozammen ohder getrennt
Are you paying together or separately?

Restaurants

Für wie viele Personen?
*fewr vee **feele** perzo**hn**en*
For how many people?

Einen Moment
*i**y**nen moh**ment***
Just a moment

Haben Sie einen Tisch reserviert?
haa**ben zee **iy**nen tish rezer**veert
Have you booked a table?

Sie müßten zehn Minuten warten
*zee **mewss**ten tsayn mi**nooten** **varten***
You'd have to wait ten minutes

Möchten Sie warten?
mersh**ten zee **varten
Would you like to wait?

Was hätten Sie gern?
*vas **hetten** zee gern*
What would you like?

Haben Sie sich entschieden?
haa**ben zee zish ent**sheeden
Have you decided?

Wir empfehlen . . .
*veer em**pfaylen***
We recommend . . .

Als Vorspeise
*als **forshpiyze***
For the starter

Als Hauptgericht
*als **howptgerisht***
For the main course

Als Nachspeise
*als **naakshpiyze***
For dessert

Was möchten Sie trinken?
*vas **mersh**ten zee **trin**ken*
To drink?

Für wen war . . .?
fewr vayn var
Who was the . . . for?

Schmeckt es Ihnen?
*shmekt es **eenen***
Are you enjoying your food?

Möchten Sie eine Nachspeise?
***mersh**ten zee **iy**ne **naak**shpiyze*
Would you like a dessert?

Sind Sie fertig?
*zint zee **fertig***
Have you finished?

Sonst noch etwas?
*zonst nok **etvas***
Anything else?

Haben Sie noch einen Wunsch?
***haa**ben zee nok **iy**nen voonsh*
Anything else?

MENU READER

General Phrases

Abendessen	Dinner
Bedienung inbegriffen	Service included
Beilage	Side dish or garnish
Eintopfgerichte	Stews
Eierspeisen	Egg dishes
Eis	Ice cream
Extraaufschlag	Supplementary charge
Fischgerichte	Fish dishes
Fleischgerichte	Meat dishes
Frühstück	Breakfast
Gemüse	Vegetables
Getränke	Drinks
Im Preis inbegriffen	Included in the price
Käse	Cheese
Mehlspeisen	Desserts *(Austria)*
Mehrwertsteuer inklusiv	VAT inclusive
Mittagessen	Lunch
Nachspeisen	Desserts
Nach Wahl	According to choice
Obst	Fruit
Salatteller	Salads
Schoppenkarte	Wine list
Spezialität des Hauses	Speciality of the house
Suppen	Soups
Süßspeisen	Desserts
Vorspeisen	Starters
Tagesgedeck	Set menu
Tagesgericht	Dish of the day
Touristen-Menü	Tourist menu
Weinkarte	Wine list
Wild und Geflügel	Game and poultry

Drinks

Bier	Beer
Alsterwasser	Shandy *(north Germany)*
Altbier	Bitter with high hop content
Altbierbowle	Bitter punch with bits of pineapple
Berliner Weisser	Light Berlin ale with raspberry juice
Bockbier	Strong, malt beer
Doppelbock	Strong, malt Munich beer
dunkles Bier	Dark, strong beer
Kupferbier	Dark, malt beer
Malzbier	Dark, sweet malt beer
Märzen	Strong, malt, Munich beer
Pilsener	Strong, hoppy lager
Radler(maß)	(a litre of) Shandy
Weißbier	Yeasty beer brewed with wheat
Weizenbier	Light beer brewed with wheat
Bommerlunder	Caraway brandy
Danziger Goldwasser	Aniseed liqueur
Dornkaat	German gin
Fruchtsaft	Fruit juice
Apfelsaft	Apple juice
Johannisbeersaft	Red- or blackcurrant juice
Orangensaft	Orange juice
Tomatensaft	Tomato juice
Traubensaft	Grape juice
Eierlikör	Egg nog
Gespritzter Wein (süß oder sauer)	White wine with lemonade (**süß**) or mineral water (**sauer**)
Glühwein	Mulled wine
Heidelbeergeist	Blueberry brandy
Heiße Schokolade	Hot chocolate

Himbeergeist	Raspberry brandy
Kaffee	Coffee
Einspänner	Black coffee with whipped cream
Expresso	Strong, black espresso coffee
großer Brauner	Large black coffee with a dash of milk
großer Schwarzer	Large black coffee
kleiner Brauner	Small black coffee with a dash of milk
koffeinfrei	Decaffeinated
Melange	Half coffee, half warm milk
mit Sahne	With cream (white coffee)
Mokka	Strong black coffee
Kirschwasser	Cherry brandy
Korn	Distilled grain spirit
Weizenkorn	Distilled wheat spirit
Limonade	Lemonade
Milchmixgetränk	Milk shake
Mineralwasser	Mineral water
mit Kohlensäure	Fizzy
ohne Kohlensäure	Still
Orangeade	Orangeade
Pflümliwasser	Plum brandy
Sekt	German equivalent to Champagne
Schnapps	Brandy
Apfelschnapps	Apple brandy
Steinhäger	Juniper berry brandy (like gin)

Tee	Tea
Eistee	Iced tea
Hagebuttentee	Rose-hip tea
Kamillentee	Camomile tea
Kräutertee	Herb tea
mit Milch	With milk (usually condensed milk)
mit Zitrone	With lemon
Wein	
Auslese	Medium dry wine made with late grapes
Beerenauslese	Medium sweet wine made with overripe grapes
herb	Dry
lieblich	Sweet
Rotwein	Red wine
Spätlese	Dry wine made with late grapes
süß	Sweet
trocken	Dry
Trockenbeerenauslese	Sweet dessert wine made with dried grapes
vollmundig	Full bodied
Weißwein	White wine
Schaumwein	Sparkling wine
Weinbrand	Brandy

Food

Aal	Eel
Räucheraal	Smoked eel
Altenburger	Mild goat's cheese
Ananas	Pineapple
Apfel	Apple
Apfelmus	Apple sauce
Apfelsine	Orange

Apfelstrudel	Apple, nuts and raisins sandwiched between thin layers of pastry
Appenzeller	Mild, firm Swiss cheese
Aprikose	Apricot
Artischocke	Artichoke
Aubergine	Aubergine
Auflauf	Soufflé
Aufschnitt	Sliced cold meat and sausage
Austern	Oysters
Backpflaumen	Prunes
Backsteinkäse	Strong, Bavarian cheese
Bananen	Bananas
Barsch	Freshwater perch
Basilikum	Basil
Bauernfrühstück	*(lit. farmer's breakfast)* Egg, bacon and potatoes
Bauernomelett	Bacon and onion omelette
Bauernschmaus	Sauerkraut with bacon, sausages, pork, dumpling and potatoes
Belegtes Brot	Open sandwich
Berliner	Jam doughnut
Berner Platte	Sauerkraut (or green beans) with various cooked meats (pork, beef, sausages, bacon)
Bienenstich	Honey and almond cake
Birne	Pear
Bismarckhering	Pickled herring with onions
Blumenkohl	Cauliflower
Bohnen	Beans
grüne Bohnen	Green (French) beans
Bouillon	Broth, consommé
Bratkartoffeln	Fried potatoes

Braten	Roast meat
Hackbraten	Meatloaf
Jungfernbraten	Roast pork with bacon
Rostbraten	Rump steak
Sauerbraten	Marinated, braised beef
Brombeeren	Blackberries
Brot	Bread
Roggenbrot	Rye bread
Schwarzbrot	Black bread, pumpernickel
Vollkornbrot	Wholemeal bread
Brötchen	Bread roll
Brühe	Broth
Champignons	Button mushrooms
Datteln	Dates
Deutschesbeefsteak	Hamburger
Dorsch	Cod
Eier	Eggs
Rührei	Scrambled egg
Spiegelei	Fried egg
Eintopf	Stew
Eis	Ice cream
Eisbecher	Ice cream sundae
Eisbein	Pig's knuckle
Eisbombe	Ice bomb
Emmentaler	Mild, Swiss cheese
Ente	Duck
Erbsen	Peas
Erdapfel	Potato *(Austria)*
Erdbeeren	Strawberries
Fasan	Pheasant
Feigen	Figs
Fisolen	French beans (*Austria*)
Fondue	Hot melted cheese dip with white wine, kirsch and a touch of garlic (*Switzerland*)

Forelle	Trout
Frikadellen	Meatballs
Froschschenkel	Frogs' legs
Frucht	Fruit
nach Jahreszeit	Seasonal fruit
Gans	Goose
Gedämpft	Steamed
Gedünstet	Steamed
Gefüllt	Stuffed
Geräuchert	Smoked
Gewürzt	Spicy
Götterspeise	*(lit. food of the gods)* Jelly
Granatrührei	Scrambled egg with prawns
Hackfleisch	Mince
Hähnchen	Chicken
Hase	Hare, rabbit
Hausfrauenart	Served with apple, sour cream and onions
Hausgemacht	Homemade
Heilbutt	Halibut
Hendl	Chicken *(Austria)*
Hering	Herring
Himbeeren	Raspberries
Himmel und Erde	*(lit. heaven and earth)* Bacon and meat casserole with apple sauce
Hoppel-Poppel	Scrambled egg with diced bacon and sausage
Hühnchen	Chicken
Hummer	Lobster
Hummerkrabben	King prawns
Ingwer	Ginger
Jägerart	*(lit. hunter's style)* Served in red wine sauce with mushrooms
Jakobsmuscheln	Scallops
Johannisbeeren	Red or Blackcurrants

Kabeljau	Cod
Kaiserschmarren	Shredded sweet pancake with raisins
Kalbfleisch	Veal
Kalbmilch	Veal sweetbreads
Kalbsrolle	Braised stuffed veal roll
Kaninchen	Rabbit
Karfiol	Cauliflower
Karpfen	Carp
Karotten	Carrots
Kartoffeln	Potatoes
Pellkartoffeln	Potatoes boiled in their skins
Petersilienkartoffeln	Boiled potatoes with parsley and butter
Salzkartoffeln	Boiled potatoes
Kartoffelbrei	Mashed potatoes
Kartoffelpuffer mit Apfelmus	Potato pancakes with apple sauce
Käse	Cheese
Käsesahne	Fresh creamy curd cheese gateau
Käseschnitte	Open, melted cheese sandwich
Käseteller	Plate of assorted cheeses, probably including Emmentaler
Käsewähe	Hot cheese tart
Kasseler Rippen	Roast smoked loin of pork
Kastanien	Chestnuts
Kirschen	Cherries
Knoblauch	Garlic
Klöße	Dumplings
Knödel	Dumplings
Kohl	Cabbage
Kohlroulade	Cabbage leaves stuffed with minced meat

Kohlrabi	Kohlrabi (cross between cabbage and turnip)
Kompott	Stewed fruit
Königinpastete	Puff pastry filled with chopped meat and mushrooms
Königsberger Klopse	Meatballs in white caper sauce
Kotelett	Chop
Sülzkotelett	Pork chop in aspic
Krabben	Prawns
Kraftbrühe	Beef consommé
mit Einlage	With a garnish
Kräuter	Herbs
Kräuterbutter	Garlic butter
Krebs	Crab, crayfish
Kren	Horseradish *(Austria)*
Kuchen	Cake
Kümmelkäse	Mild cheese with caraway seeds
Kürbis	Pumpkin
Labskaus	Thick stew of minced meat with mashed potatoes
Lachs	Salmon
Lammfleisch	Lamb
Lammkeule	Leg of lamb
Lauch	Leek
Lende	Loin
Mais	Sweetcorn
Makrele	Mackerel
Mandeln	Almonds
Marillen	Apricots *(Austria)*
Mark	Bone marrow
Matjeshering	Young, salted herring
Meeresfrüchte	Sea food
Meerrettich	Horseradish

Melone	Melon
Möhren	Carrots
Mohrrüben	Carrots
Mus	Puréed stewed fruit
Nelken	Cloves
Nieren	Kidneys
Nockerl	Dumpling
Grießnockerl	Semolina dumpling
Salzburgernockerl	Sweet egg soufflé flavoured with vanilla
Nürnbergerbratwurst	Nuremberg sausage cooked on a charcoal grill
Nudeln	Pasta
Nuß	Nut
Haselnuß	Hazelnut
Muskatnuß	Nutmeg
Walnuß	Walnut
Nußstrudel	Flaky pastry with nuts and honey
Oliven	Olives
Palatschinken	Pancakes *(Austria)*
Pampelmuse	Grapefruit
Paniert	Cooked in egg and breadcrumbs
Paradeiser	Tomatoes
Petersilie	Parsley
Pfannkuchen	Pancakes
Pfeffersteak	Steak covered with half peppercorns
Pfirsich	Peach
Pflaumen	Plums
Pichelsteiner Fleisch	Mixed meat and vegetable stew
Pilze	Mushrooms
Pommes frites	Chips
Porree	Leek
Powidl	Plum

Powidltatschkerln	Pancake with a plum filling
Preiselbeeren	Cranberries
Pudding	Blancmange
Pute	Turkey
Quark	Curd cheese (fromage frais)
Quarkspeise	Dessert made with quark and (usually) fruit
Rahm	Cream
Rebhuhn	Partridge
Reh	Venison
Rehrücken	Saddle of venison
Reis	Rice
Rhabarber	Rhubarb
Rindfleisch	Beef
Rohschinken	Cured ham
Rollmops	Pickled herring wrapped round slices of onion
Rosenkohl	Brussels sprout
Rosinen	Raisins
Rösti	Fried potatoes *(Switzerland)*
Rote Beete	Beetroot
Rote Grütze	Red fruit jelly
Rotkohl	Red cabbage
Rouladen	Slices of rolled beef or veal in gravy
Russische Eier	Hard boiled eggs with mayonnaise
Sahne	Cream
Schlagsahne	Whipped cream
Salat	Salad
gemischter Salat	Mixed salad
grüner Salat	Green salad
Kopfsalat	Lettuce salad
Obstsalat	Fruit salad
russischer Salat	Diced vegetables in mayonnaise

Salbei	Sage
Sardellen	Anchovies
Sauerkraut	Pickled white cabbage
Schinken	Ham
Schlachtplatte	Assorted cold meat and sausages
Schlagobers	Whipped cream *(Austria)*
Schmelzkäse	Soft cheese, used in cooking
Schnitzel	Escalope (usually veal)
Holsteiner Schnitzel	Veal cutlet in breadcrumbs with vegetables and a fried egg on top
Rahmschnitzel	Escalope of veal in cream sauce
Wienerschnitzel	Escalope of veal cooked in egg and breadcrumbs
Schnecken	Snails
Weinbergschnecken	Snails with garlic, herbs and butter
Schnittlauch	Chives
Schokolade	Chocolate
Scholle	Plaice
Schwarzwälderkirschtorte	Black Forest gateau
Schweinefleisch	Pork
Seebarsch	Sea bass
Sellerie	Celery
Semmel	Bread roll *(Austria)*
Soße	Sauce
Spargel	Asparagus
Spargelspitzen	Asparagus tips
Spätzle	Tiny dumplings
Speck	Smoked bacon
Spinat	Spinach
Stachelbeeren	Gooseberries
Steinbutt	Turbot
Stelze	Pig's knuckle *(Austria)*

Stollen	Cake with almonds, nuts and candied and dried fruits (often eaten at Christmas)
Strammer Max	Raw ham and fried eggs served on rye bread
Streuselkuchen	Cake with a butter, sugar, flour and cinammon topping
Suppe	Soup
Aalsuppe	Eel soup
Baselermehlsuppe	Thick soup with grated cheese *(Switzerland)*
Bohnensuppe	Bean soup
Fischbeuschelsuppe	Fish roe and vegetable soup
Frühlingssuppe	Spring vegetable soup
Königinsuppe	Soup with beef, sour cream and almonds
Leberknödelsuppe	Soup with liver dumplings
Linsensuppe	Lentil soup
Ochsenschwanzsuppe	Oxtail soup
Paradeissuppe	Tomato soup
Schildkrötensuppe	Turtle soup
Serbischebohnensuppe	Spicy Serbian bean soup
Tomatensuppe	Tomato soup
Teig	Dough
Teigwaren	Pasta
Thunfisch	Tuna fish
Tomaten	Tomatoes
Topfen	Curd cheese *(Austria)*
Topfenstrudel	Thin layers of pastry filled with curd cheese
Torte	Gateau, flan
Linzertorte	Almond flan with a raspberry topping
Sachertorte	Rich chocolate cake (from Sacher's café in Vienna)
Truthahn	Turkey

Überbacken	Baked
Weintrauben	Grapes
Wildschwein	Wild boar
Windbeutel	Cream puff
Wurst	Sausage
Bierwurst	Smoked pork and beef sausage
Blutwurst	Black pudding
Bockwurst	Frankfurter
Bratwurst	Spicy, fried sausage
Currywurst	Curry sausage
Jagdwurst	Smoked sausage with garlic and mustard
Rauchwurst	Smoked sausage
Weißwurst	Veal, bacon, parsley and onion sausage
Wienerli	Vienna-style frankfurter
Zervelat	Spicy smoked sausage
Zimt	Cinnamon
Zitrone	Lemon
Zucchini	Courgettes
Zwetschken	Plums *(Austria)*
Zwiebel	Onion

SHOPPING

• There are local variations in shop opening times, but in general shops are open from 9.00 am–6.30 pm on Mondays to Fridays, and from 9.00 am–2.00 pm on Saturdays. On the first Saturday of every month, **langer Samstag**, shops stay open until 6.00 pm. Shops in towns and cities don't usually close for lunch.

• Chemists, **Apotheken**, have the same opening hours as shops, though they are closed on Wednesdays. Addresses of emergency and late chemists can be found in the local newspapers or on the door. You need a prescription to get medicines from an **Apotheke**. No prescription is needed in a **Drogerie** which also sells cosmetics, perfumes and health foods. A **Parfümerie** only sells perfume and cosmetics.

• Films can be developed at photo shops, in a **Drogerie** or in large department stores. Films tend to be cheaper in Germany but developing more expensive.

• You can buy stamps at Post Offices or anywhere where you buy postcards. There are sometimes stamp machines next to post boxes.

• There are regular fruit and vegetable markets in most towns. At weekends there are flea markets, **Flohmärkte**, in many of the big cities. You can pick up bargains in the way of clothes, jewellery, antiques, books and memorabilia.

• Shops are open in **Austria** from seven or eight in the morning until six or six-thirty at night. Outside the cities they usually close at lunch times. Saturday opening hours vary but are generally from 8.00 am to midday. Some shops in Austria display a 'tax free' sticker which means that customers are entitled to a VAT refund on goods bought there. To claim the refund, fill in a customs declaration form on leaving the country.

• In **Switzerland** shops are open from 8.00 am to midday and then from 1.30 pm to 6.30 pm or 4.00 pm on Saturdays. Shops may close on Monday afternoons. You can only buy stamps from Post Offices which are open from 7.30 am–midday and from 1.45 pm to 6.30 pm. Most close at 11.00 am on Saturdays. There are stamp machines at railway stations and airports.

You may see

Antiquitäten	Antiques
Andenkenladen	Souvenirs
Ausverkauf	Sale
Bäckerei	Baker's
Bitte nicht berühren	Please do not touch
Boutique	Clothes/Fashions
Buchhandlung	Bookshop
Delikatessen	Delicatessen
Drogerie	Drugstore
Duchgehend geöffnet	Open all day
Eingang	Entrance
Eisenwarenhandlung	Ironmonger's/Hardware
Elektrogeschäft	Electrical goods
Feinkostgeschäft	Delicatessen
Fischladen	Fishmonger's
Fleischerei	Butcher's
Friseursalon	Hairdresser's
Geöffnet	Open
Geschäftszeiten	Business hours
Geschenkartikel	Gift shop/Souvenirs
Geschlossen	Closed
Haushaltswarenhandlung	Hardware
Juwelier	Jeweller's
Im Angebot	On offer
Kasse	Cashier
Kein Ausgang	No exit
Kein Eingang	No entry

Konditorei	Cake shop
Lebensmittelgeschäft	Groceries
Lederwaren	Leather goods
Metzgerei	Butcher's
Möbelgeschäft	Furniture
Modegeschäft	Clothes/Fashions
Nachtdienst/Sontagsdienst	Duty Chemist's (or doctor's)
(Not)ausgang	(Emergency) Exit
Obst- und Gemüsehandlung	Fruit/Fruiterer's
Optiker	Optician's
Parfümerie	Perfumery
Photogeschäft	Photo shop
Postamt	Post Office
Reformhaus	Health foods
Reinigung	Dry-cleaner's
Schallplatten	Records
Schlußverkauf	Sale
Schreibwarengeschäft	Stationer's
Schuhgeschäft	Shoe shop
Selbstbedienungsladen	Self-service shop
Spielwarengeschäft	Toy shop
Sportgeschäft	Sports goods
Supermarkt	Supermarket
Süßwarenladen	Confectioner's
Tabakladen	Tobacconist's
Uhrmacher	Watchmaker's
Umkleidekabine	Fitting rooms
Warenhaus	Department store
Weinhandlung	Wine shop
Zeitungshändler	Newsagent's

General phrases

(*See also* Directions, *page 24*; Problems and complaints, *page 170*; Numbers, *page 211*)

Where is . . .
Wo ist . . .
voh ist

Where is the main shopping area?
Wo ist die Einkaufsstraße?
*voh ist dee **iyn**kowfsshtraasse*

Where is the chemist's?
Wo ist die Apotheke?
*voh ist dee apo**tayke***

Is there a food shop around here?
Gibt es ein Lebensmittelgeschäft in der Nähe?
*gipt es iyn **lay**benzmittelge**sheft** in der **naye***

Where can I buy batteries?
Wo kann ich Batterien kaufen?
*voh kan ish batte**ree**-en **kow**fen*

I'd like . . .
Ich möchte . . .
*ish **mersh**te*

Have you got . . .?
Haben Sie . . .?
***haa**ben zee*

Have you got stamps?
Haben Sie Briefmarken?
***haa**ben zee **bree**fmarken*

How much is it?/How much does it cost?
Was kostet es . . .?
*vas **kos**tet es*

How much do they cost?
Was kosten sie?
*vas **kos**ten zee*

How much does it come to?
Was macht das?
vas maakt das?

I don't understand
Ich verstehe nicht
*ish fer**shtaye** nisht*

Can you write it down please?
Können Sie es bitte aufschreiben?
***ker**nnen zee es **bi**tte **owf**shriyben*

It's too expensive
Es ist zu teuer
*es ist tsoo **toyer***

Have you got anything cheaper?
Haben Sie etwas Billigeres?
haaben zee etvas billigeres

I don't have enough money
Ich habe nicht genug Geld
ish haabe nisht genoog gelt

Can you keep it for me?
Können Sie es für mich zurücklegen?
kernnen zee es fewr mish tsoorewklaygen

When do you open in the morning?
Wann machen Sie morgens auf?
van maaken zee morgenz owf

When do you close?
Wann machen Sie zu?
van maaken zee tsoo

What time . . .?
Um wieviel Uhr . . .?
oom veefeel oor

What time does the Post Office open?
Um wieviel Uhr macht die Post auf?
oom veefeel oor maakt dee post owf

Do you close for lunch?
Schließen Sie mittags?
shleessen zee mittaags

I'm just looking
Ich sehe mich nur um
ish zaye mish noor oom

I'll have to think about it
Ich muß darüber nachdenken
ish muss darewber naakdenken

That one there, please
Das da bitte
das daa bitte

This one here, please
Dies hier bitte
dees heer bitte

Two of those, please
Zwei von denen bitte
tsviy fon daynen bitte

Some of these, please
Einige von diesen bitte
iynige fon deezen bitte

A bit of that, please
Ein bißchen von dem bitte
iyn bissyen fon daym bitte

What is this?
Was ist das?
vas ist das

Can I try it?
Kann ich das probieren?
kan ish das probeeren

Not that one – this one here
Nicht das – dieser hier
nisht das – deezer heer

There's one in the window
Es ist im Schaufenster
*es ist im **showfenster***

A bag please
Eine Tüte bitte
*iyne **tewte bitte***

The receipt please
Die Quittung bitte
*dee **kvittoong bitte***

It's a gift
Es ist ein Geschenk
*es ist iyn **geshenk***

I'm taking it to England
Ich nehme es nach England mit
*ish **nayme** es naak **englant** mit*

Can you wrap it please?
Können Sie es bitte verpacken?
kernnen** zee es **bitte ferpaken

With lots of paper, please
Mit viel Papier bitte
*mit feel pa**peer bitte***

Where is the cash desk?
Wo ist die Kasse?
*voh ist dee **kasse***

Do you take credit cards?
Nehmen Sie Kreditkarten?
***naymen** zee kre**deet**karten*

Do you take travellers' cheques?
Nehmen Sie Reiseschecks?
naymen** zee **riyzesheks

I'm sorry, I don't have any change
Es tut mir leid, ich habe kein Kleingeld
*es toot meer liyt ish **haabe** kiyn **kliyngelt***

That's fine
Das ist in Ordnung
*das ist in **ortnoong***

I'll take it
Ich nehme es
*ish **nayme** es*

Nothing else, thank you
Das ist alles
*das ist **alles***

Buying food and drink

A kilo of . . . please
Ein Kilo . . . bitte
*iyn **keeloh** . . . **bitte***

A kilo of cherries, please
Ein Kilo Kirschen, bitte
*iyn **keeloh keer**shen **bitte***

2 kilos of apples, please
Zwei Kilo Äpfel, bitte
*tsviy **keeloh** **epfel** **bitte***

Half a kilo of courgettes, please
Ein halbes Kilo Zucchini, bitte
*iyn **halbes** **keeloh** tsoo**keenee** **bitte***

A pound of tomatoes, please
Ein Pfund Tomaten, bitte
*iyn pfoont to**maaten** **bitte***

A hundred grams of . . . please
Hundert Gramm . . . bitte
hoondert** gramm . . . **bitte

A hundred grams of olives, please
Hundert Gramm Oliven, bitte
hoondert** gramm **oleeven** **bitte

Two hundred grams of liver sausage, please
Zweihundert Gramm Leberwurst, bitte
tsviyhoondert** gramm **laybervoorst** **bitte

A piece of cheese, please
Ein Stück Käse, bitte
*iyn shtewk **kayze** **bitte***

Five slices of ham, please
Fünf Scheiben Schinken, bitte
*fewnf **shiyben** **shinken** **bitte***

A bottle of water, please
Eine Flasche Wasser, bitte
*iyne **flashe** **vasser** **bitte***

A litre of wine, please
Ein Liter Wein, bitte
*iyn **leeter** viyn **bitte***

Half litre of milk, please
Einen halben Liter Milch, bitte
*iynen **halben** **leeter** milsh **bitte***

A crate of beer, please
Einen Kasten Bier, bitte
*iynen **kasten** beer **bitte***

A bit more, please
Ein bißchen mehr, bitte
*iyn **bissyen** mayr **bitte***

A bit less, please
Ein bißchen weniger, bitte
*iyn **bissyen** **vayniger** **bitte***

That's enough, thank you
Das ist genug, danke
*das ist **genoog** **danke***

That's all, thank you
Das wär's, danke
*das vayrz **danke***

What's this like?
Wie ist das?
vee ist das

What's this made of?
Aus was ist das gemacht?
*ows vas ist das **gemaakt***

At the chemist's

Aspirins/plasters, please
Aspirin/Pflaster, bitte
aspeereen/pflaster, bitte

Have you got something for . . .
Haben Sie etwas für . . .
haaben zee etvas fewr . . .

Have you got something for sunburn?
Haben Sie etwas für Sonnenbrand
haaben zee etvas fewr zonnenbrannt

Have you got something for diarrhoea?
Haben Sie etwas für Durchfall?
haaben zee etvas fewr doorshfall

Have you got something for period pains?
Haben Sie etwas für Regelschmerzen?
haaben zee etvas fewr raygelshmertsen

Buying clothes and shoes

I'd like a skirt
Ich möchte einen Rock
ish mershte iynen rok

I'm looking for a suit
Ich möchte einen Anzug
ish mershte iynen antsoog

My size is . . .
Meine Größe ist . . .
miyne grersse ist

Can I try it on?
Kann ich das anprobieren?
kan ish das anprohbeeren

Can I try them on?
Kann ich sie anprobieren
kan ish zee anprohbeeren

Is there a mirror?
Gibt es einen Spiegel?
gipt es iynen shpeegel

I like it
Es gefällt mir
es gefellt meer

I don't like it
Es gefällt mir nicht
es gefellt meer nisht

It's very nice
Es ist sehr schön
es ist zayr shern

They're very nice
Sie sind sehr schön
zee zint zayr shern

Fine
Sehr gut
zayr goot

It's too big
Es ist zu groß
es ist tsoo grohss

They're too big
Sie sind zu groß
zee zint tsoo grohss

It's too small
Es ist zu klein
es ist tsoo kliyn

They're too small
Sie sind zu klein
zee zint tsoo kliyn

What size is it?
Welche Größe ist es?
velshe grersse ist es

Have you got size 42?
Haben Sie Größe zweiundvierzig?
haaben zee grersse tsviyoontfeertsig

Have you got a smaller size?
Haben Sie es kleiner?
haaben zee es kliyner

Have you got a bigger size?
Haben Sie es größer?
haaben zee es grersser

Have you got another colour?
Haben Sie eine andere Farbe?
haaben zee iyne andere farbe

Can you measure me, please?
Können Sie meine Größe bitte messen?
kernnen zee miyne grersse bitte messen

Miscellaneous

Five stamps for England, please
Fünf Briefmarken für England bitte
fewnf breefmarken fewr englant bitte

For letters/postcards
Für Briefe/Postkarten
fewr breefe/postkarten

Three postcards, please
Drei Postkarten bitte
driy postkarten bitte

Have you got an English newspaper?
Haben Sie eine englische Zeitung?
haaben zee iyne englishe tsiytoong

Matches, please
Streichhölzer bitte
shtriykherltser bitte

A film for this camera, please
Ein Film für diese Kamera bitte
iyn film fewr deeze kamera bitte

You may hear

Darf ich Ihnen helfen?
darf ish eenen helfen
May I help you?

Was möchten Sie?
vas mershten zee
What would you like?

Wieviel möchten Sie?
veefeel mershten zee
How much would you like?

Wie viele möchten Sie?
vee feele mershten zee
How many would you like?

Sonst noch etwas?
zonst nok etvas
Anything else?

Es tut mir leid, wir sind ausverkauft
es toot meer liyt veer zint owsferkowft
I'm sorry, we're sold out

Es tut mir leid, wir sind jetzt zu
es toot meer liyt veer zint jetst tsoo
I'm sorry, we're closed now

Soll ich das verpacken?
zoll ish das ferpaken
Shall I wrap it for you?

Haben Sie Kleingeld?
haaben zee kliyngelt
Have you got any change?

Bezahlen Sie bar?
betsaalen zee bar
Are you paying cash?

Sie brauchen dafür ein Rezept
zee browken daafewr iyn raytsept
You need a prescription for that

Welche Größe haben Sie?
velshe grersse haaben zee
What size are you?

Postkarte oder Brief?
postkarte ohder breef
Postcard or letter?

Was für . . .
vas fewr
What sort of . . .

Was für eine Kamera haben Sie
vas fewr iyne kamera haaben zee
What sort of camera do you have?

Was für einen Film möchten Sie?
vas fewr iynen film mershten zee
What sort of film do you want

BUSINESS TRIPS

• You'll probably be doing business with the help of interpreters or in a language everyone speaks, but you may need a few German phrases to cope at a company's reception desk.

• Women are usually referred to as **Frau** whether they are married or not. If someone has **Doktor** in their title they are referred to as either **Herr Doktor** . . . or **Frau Doktor** . . . . The same applies to **Professor**.

• When you arrive for an appointment, all you need do is say who you've come to see and give your name or hand over your business card. However, if you're not expected you may need to make an appointment or leave a message.

• It is important to be punctual for business appointments in Germany.

You may see

AG (Aktiengesellschaft)	Joint stock company
Außer Betrieb	Out of order
Drücken	Press, push
Eingang	Entrance
Erdgeschoß	Ground floor
Erster Stock	1st floor
Fahrstuhl	Lift
Gesellschaft	Company
G.m.b.H. = Gesellschaft mit beschränkter Haftung	Limited company
Rauchen verboten	No smoking
Treppe	Stairs
Zutritt verboten	No entry
Empfang/Rezeption	Reception
(Not)Ausgang	(Emergency) exit
Ziehen	Pull
Zweiter Stock	2nd floor

You may want to say

(*See also* Days, months, dates, *page 189;* Time, *page 193*)

Mr Kochmann, please
Herr Kochmann, bitte
*herr **kok**mann **bit**te*

Dr Paulick, please
Frau Doktor Paulick, bitte
*frow **dok**tor **pow**lick **bit**te*

Mrs Gromm, please
Frau Gromm, bitte
*frow gromm **bit**te*

The manager, please
Den Geschäftsführer, bitte
*dayn **ge**sheftsfewrer **bit**te*

My name is . . .
Mein Name ist . . .
*miyn **naa**me ist*

I work for . . .
Ich arbeite bei . . .
*ish **ar**biyte biy*

I have an appointment with Mr Dieter Kochmann
Ich habe einen Termin mit Herrn Dieter Kochmann
*ish **haa**be **iy**nen **ter**meen mit herrn **dee**ter **kok**mann*

I don't have an appointment
Ich habe keinen Termin
*ish **haa**be **kiy**nen **ter**meen*

I'd like . . .
Ich möchte . . .
*ish **mersh**te*

I'd like to make an appointment with Mrs Gromm
Ich möchte einen Termin mit Frau Gromm vereinbaren
*ish **mersh**te **iy**nen **ter**meen mit frow gromm **feriyn**baren*

I'd like to talk to the export manager
Ich möchte den Exportmanager sprechen
*ish **mersh**te dayn **eks**portmanager **shpre**ken*

What is his/her name?
Wie heißt er/sie?
vee hiysst er/zee

When will he/she be back?
Wann kommt er/sie zurück?
*van kommt er/zee tsoo**rewk***

I am free this afternoon at five o'clock
Ich bin heute nachmittag um fünf Uhr frei
*ish bin **hoy**te **naak**mittag oom fewnf oor friy*

Can I leave a message?
Können Sie etwas ausrichten?
kernnen zee etvas owsrishten

Can he/she call me?
Kann er/sie mich anrufen?
kan er/zee mish anroofen

My telephone number is . . .
Meine Telefonnummer ist . . .
miyne telefohnnoommer ist

I am staying at the Hotel Excelsior
Ich wohne im Hotel Excelsior
ish vohne im hotel exchelsior

Where is his/her office?
Wo ist sein/ihr Büro?
voh ist ziyn/eer bewroh

I am here for the exhibition
Ich bin für die Ausstellung hier
ish bin fewr dee owsshtelloong heer

I am here for the trade fair
Ich bin für die Messe hier
ish bin fewr dee messe heer

I am attending the conference
Ich besuche die Konferenz
Ish bezooke dee konferents

I need to make a phone call (to Britain)
Ich muß (nach Großbritannien) telefonieren
ish mooss (naak grossbritannee-en) telefohneeren

I need to send a telex
Ich muß ein Telex schicken
ish moos iyn teleks shiken

I need to send this by fax
Ich muß das mit Telefax schicken
ish moos das mit telefaks shiken

I need to send this by post
Ich muß das mit der Post schicken
ish moos das mit der post shiken

I need to send this by courier
Ich muß das mit dem Kurier schicken
ish mooss das mit daym koorier shiken

I need a photocopy (of this)
Ich brauche (davon) eine Fotokopie
ish browke (daufon) iyne fotokopee

I need an interpreter
Ich brauche einen Dolmetscher
*ish **browke** iynen **dolmecher***

Can someone type a letter for me?
Kann jemand einen Brief für mich tippen?
*kan **yaymant** iynen breef fewr mish **tippen***

You may hear

Ihr Name bitte?
*eer **naame** bitte*
Your name, please?

Wie heißen Sie, bitte?
*vee **hiyssen** zee **bitte***
What is your name, please?

Wie heißt Ihre Gesellschaft?
*vee hiysst **eere gezell**shaft*
The name of your company, please?

Haben Sie einen Termin?
haaben** zee **iynen termeen
Do you have an appointment?

Haben Sie eine Geschäftskarte?
***haaben** zee **iyne gesheft**skarte*
Do you have a card?

Werden Sie erwartet?
verden** zee **ervartet
Is he/she expecting you?

(Warten Sie) einen Augenblick bitte
*(**varten** zee) **iynen owgenblick bitte***
(Wait) one moment, please

Ich sage ihm/ihr, daß Sie hier sind
*ish **zaage** eem/eer dass zee heer zint*
I'll tell him/her you're here

Er/sie kommt gleich
er/zee kommt gliysh
He/she's just coming

Bitte nehmen Sie Platz
***bitte naymen** zee platts*
Please sit down

Möchten Sie sich setzen?
mersh**ten zee zish **zettsen
Would you like to sit down?

Gehen Sie bitte hinein
gayen** zee **bitte** hin**iyn
Go in, please

Kommen Sie bitte mit
***kommen** zee **bitte** mit*
Come with me, please

Herr Kochmann ist nicht da
*herr **kok**mann ist nisht daa*
Mr Kochmann isn't in

Frau Doktor Paulick kommt um elf zurück
*frow **dok**tor **pow**lick kommt oom elf tsoo**rewk***
Dr Paulick will be back at eleven

In einer halben Stunde/in einer Stunde
*in **iy**ner **hal**ben **shtoon**de/in **iy**ner **shtoon**de*
In half an hour/an hour

Nehmen Sie den Fahrstuhl zum dritten Stock
***nay**men zee dayn **faar**shtool tsoom **dritt**en shtock*
Take the lift to the third floor

Gehen Sie den Gang entlang
gay**en zee dayn gang ent**lang
Go along the corridor

Es ist die erste/die zweite Tür
*es ist dee **erste**/dee **tsviy**te tewr*
It's the first/second door

Links/rechts
links/reshts
On the left/right

Es ist Zimmer Nummer dreihundertzwanzig
*es ist **tsimm**er **noomm**er driyhoondert**tsvan**tsig*
It's room number 320

Herein!
*her**iyn***
Come in!

SIGHTSEEING

• Opening hours vary for historic buildings, museums, galleries and so on, but most close for several hours in the afternoons and most are shut on Mondays.

• The German National Tourist Office has details of national parks and nature reserves.

• Sightseeing tours by coach with English-speaking guides are available in many cities and tourist areas.

You may see

Betreten des Rasens verboten	Keep off the grass
Bitte nicht berühren	Do not touch
Geöffnet	Open
Geschlossen (für Restaurierung)	Closed (for restoration)
Führungen	Guided tours
Öffnungszeiten	Visiting hours
Privat	Private
Zutritt verboten	No entry

You may want to say

(*See* At the tourist office, *page 76, for asking for information brochures, etc*)

Opening times

(*See* Time, *page 193*)

When is the museum open?
Wann ist das Museum geöffnet?
van is das moozayoom ge-erffnet

Is it open on Sundays?
Ist es sonntags geöffnet?
ist es zonntaags ge-erffnet

What time does the castle open?
Um wieviel Uhr öffnet das Schloß?
oom veefeel oor erffnet das shloss

What time does the palace close?
Um wieviel Uhr schließt der Palast?
oom veefeel oor shleesst der palast

Can I/we visit the monastery?
Kann man das Kloster besuchen?
kan man das klohster bezooken

Is it open to the public?
Ist es der Öffentlichkeit zugänglich?
ist es der erffentlishkiyt tsoogenglish

Can we look round?
Können wir herumsehen?
kernnen veer heroomzayen

Visiting places

One/Two, please
Eins/Zwei, bitte
iyns/tsviy bitte

Two adults and one child
Zwei Erwachsene und ein Kind
tsviy ervaksene oont iyn kint

Is there a reduction for children?
Gibt es eine Ermäßigung für Kinder?
gipt es iyne ermayssigoong fewr kinder

For pensioners?
Für Rentner?
fewr rentner

For the disabled?
Für Behinderte?
fewr behinderte

For students?
Für Studenten?
fewr shtoodenten

For groups?
Für Gruppen?
fewr grooppen

Are there guided tours (in English)?
Gibt es Führungen (auf Englisch)?
gipt es fewroongen (owf english)

Can I/we take photos?
Kann man photografieren?
kan man fotografeeren

Can you take a photo of us, please?
Können Sie uns bitte photografieren?
kernnen zee oons bitte fotografeeren

When was this built?
Wann wurde das gebaut?
*van **voorde** das **gebowt***

Who painted that picture?
Wer hat das Bild gemalt?
*ver hat das bilt **gemaalt***

In what year?
(*See* Days, Months, Dates, *page 189*)
In welchem Jahr?
*in **velshem** yaar*

What time is mass?
Um wieviel Uhr ist die Messe?
*oom **veefeel** oor ist dee **messe***

What time is the church service?
Um wieviel Uhr ist der Gottesdienst?
*oom **veefeel** oor ist der **gottesdeenst***

Is there a priest who speaks English?
Gibt es einen Geistlichen, der Englisch spricht?
*gipt es **iynen giystlishen** der **english** shprikt*

What kind of flower is that?
Was für eine Blume ist das?
*vas fewr **iyne bloome** ist das*

What is that bird called?
Was für einen Vogel ist das?
*vas fewr **iynen fohgel** ist das*

Is there a picnic area (in the park)?
Gibt es einen Rastplatz (im Park)?
*gipt es **iynen rastplatts** (im park)*

Sightseeing excursions

What excursions are there?
Was gibt es für Ausflüge?
*vas gipt es fewr **owsflewge***

Are there any excursions to Berlin?
Gibt es Ausflüge nach Berlin?
*gipt es **owsflewge** naak **berleen***

What time does it leave?
Um wieviel Uhr geht es los?
*oom **veefeel** oor gayt es lohs*

How long does it last?
Wie lange dauert es?
*vee **lange dowert** es*

What time do we get back?
Um wieviel Uhr kommen wir zurück?
*oom **veefeel** oor **kommen** veer **tsoorewk***

Where does it leave from?
Von wo fährt der Bus ab?
fon voh fayrt der boos ap

Does the guide speak English?
Kann der Führer Englisch?
*kann der **fewrer** english*

How much is it?
Was kostet das?
*vas **kostet** das*

You may hear

Das Museum ist jeden Tag außer montags geöffnet
*das moo**zayoom** ist **yay**den taag **owsser** **mohn**taags ge-**erff**net*
The museum is open every day except Mondays

Sonntags ist es geschlossen
zonn**taags ist es **geshlossen
It's closed on Sundays

Das Schloß wurde siebzehnhundertzwölf gebaut
*das shloss **voorde** zeebtsaynhoondertzwerlf **gebowt***
The castle was built in 1712

Der Maler war . . .
*der **maa**ler var*
The painter was . . .

Der Künstler war . . .
*der **koonst**ler var*
The artist was . . .

Der Architekt war . . .
*der arshee**tekt** var*
The architect was . . .

Die Ausflüge sind jeden Dienstag und Donnerstag
*dee **owsflewge** zint **yay**den **deen**ztaag oont **donner**staag*
There are excursions every Tuesday and Thursday

Der Bus fährt um zehn vom Marktplatz ab
*der boos fayrt oom tsayn fom **markt**platts ap*
The bus leaves at ten o'clock from the market square

ENTERTAINMENTS

• Films are categorised as suitable for people over 16, **ab 16**, or 18, **ab 18. Kinderfilme** are suitable for children. Many American and British films are shown in German and Austrian cinemas, most of them dubbed but sometimes with subtitles (**Untertitel**).

• The main cities for theatre in Germany are Hamburg, Berlin and Munich. Berlin and Munich in particular have a strong cabaret tradition.

• **Austria** has a famous music tradition. The Salzburg festival takes place every July and August. Vienna's musical attractions include a famous opera house and the Vienna Boys' Choir, **der Wiener Knabenchor**.

• The most popular spectator sport is football.

You may see

Abendvorstellung	Evening performance
Ausverkauft	Sold out
Diskothek	Discothèque
Durchgehende Vorstellung	Continuous performance
Einlaß ab 18	Under-18s not allowed
Eintritt für heute	Tickets for today's performances
Erster Rang	Dress circle
Erste Reihe	Orchestra stalls
Filmclub	Film club
Frühvorstellung	Matinee
Haupttribüne	Stand, grandstand
Kino	Cinema
Kein Einlaß während der Vorstellung	No entry once the performance has begun

Keine Pausen	No intervals
Konzertsaal	Concert hall
Logen	Boxes
Opernhaus	Opera house
Parkett	Stalls
Reihe	Row, tier
Rennbahn	Racecourse
Stadium	Stadium
Tanzsaal	Dance hall
Theater	Theatre
Tür	Door
Vorverkaufsstelle	Advance booking
Zirkus	Circus
Zutritt	Entry

You may want to say

What's on

(*See* Time, *page 193*)

What is there to do in the evenings?
Was kann man abends tun?
*vas kan man **aa**bents toon*

Is there a disco around here?
Gibt es eine Diskothek in der Nähe?
*gipt es **iy**ne diskot**ay**k in der **naye***

Is there any entertainment for children?
Gibt es Unterhaltung für Kinder?
*gipt es oonter**halt**oong fewr **kin**der*

What's on tonight?
Was wird heute abend gespielt?
*vas veert **hoyte** **aa**bent **geshpeelt***

What's on tomorrow?
Was wird morgen gespielt?
*vas veert **morgen** ge**shpeelt***

At the cinema
Im Kino
*im **keeno***

At the theatre
Im Theater
*im tay**aater***

Who is playing? *(music)*
Wer spielt?
ver shpeelt

Who is singing?
Wer singt?
ver zingt

Who is dancing?
Wer tanzt?
ver tantst

What time does the show start?
Um wieviel Uhr beginnt die Vorstellung?
*oom **veefeel** oor **beginnt** dee **for**shtelloong*

What time does the concert start?
Um wieviel Uhr beginnt das Konzert?
*oom **veefeel** oor **beginnt** das kon**tsert***

How long does the performance last?
Wie lange dauert die Vorstellung?
*vee **lange** **dow**ert dee **for**shtelloong*

When does it end?
Um wieviel Uhr wird es zu Ende sein?
*oom **veefeel** oor veert es tsoo **ende** ziyn*

Does the film have subtitles?
Ist der Film mit Untertiteln?
*ist der film mit **oon**terteeteln*

Is there a football match on Sunday?
Gibt es am Sonntag ein Fußballspiel?
*gipt es am **zonn**taag iyn **foos**sballshpeel*

Who's playing? *(sport)*
Wer spielt?
ver shpeelt

Where can I/we get tickets?
Wo kann man Karten kaufen?
*voh kan man **karten** **kow**fen*

Tickets

Can you get me tickets for the ballet?
Können Sie mir Karten für das Ballett besorgen?
kernnen zee meer karten fewr das ballett bezorgen

For the football match
Für das Fußballspiel
fewr das foossballshpeel

For the theatre
Für das Theater
fewr das tayaater

Two, please
Zwei, bitte
tsviy bitte

Two for tonight, please
Zwei für heute abend, bitte
tsviy fewr hoyte aabent bitte

Two for the 11 o'clock screening, please
Zwei für die Vorstellung um elf Uhr, bitte
tsviy fewr dee forshtelloong oom elf oor bitte

Are there any seats left for Saturday?
Haben Sie noch Karten für Samstag?
haaben zee nok karten fewr zamztaag

I want to book a box for four people
Ich möchte eine Loge für vier Personen buchen
ish mershte iyne loje fewr feer perzohnen booken

I want to book two seats
Ich möchte zwei Plätze buchen
ish mershte tsviy plettse booken

For Friday
Für Freitag
fewr friytaag

In the stalls
Im Parkett
im parkett

In the circle
Im ersten Rang
im ersten rang

How much are the seats?
Wieviel kosten die Plätze?
veefeel kosten dee plettse

Do you have anything cheaper?
Haben Sie etwas Billigeres?
haaben zee etvas billigeres

That's fine
Gut/In Ordnung
goot/in ortnoong

At the show/game

Where is this, please? *(showing your ticket)*
Wo ist das, bitte?
voh ist das bitte

Where is the cloakroom?
Wo ist die Garderobe?
voh ist dee garderohbe

Where is the bar?
Wo ist die Bar?
voh ist dee bar

Where are the toilets?
Wo sind die Toiletten?
voh zint dee toyletten

A programme, please
Ein Programm, bitte
iyn prohgramm bitte

Where can I/we get a programme?
Wo kann man ein Programm kaufen?
voh kan man iyn prohgramm kowfen

Is there an interval?
Gibt es eine Pause?
gipt es iyne powze

You may hear

Sie können Karten hier im Hotel vorbestellen
zee kernnen karten heer im hotel forbeshtellen
You can get tickets here in the hotel

Am Stadium
am shtaadyum
At the stadium

Es fängt um sieben Uhr an
es fengt oom zeeben oor an
It begins at seven o'clock

Es dauert zweieinviertel Stunden
es dowert tsviyiynfeertel shtoonden
It lasts two and a quarter hours

Es wird um halb zehn zu Ende sein
es veert oom halp tsayn tsoo ende ziyn
It ends at half past nine

Es gibt eine Pause von fünfzehn Minuten
es gipt iyne powze fon fewnftsayn minooten
There is a fifteen-minute interval

Für wann möchten Sie die Karten?
fewr van mershten zee dee karten
When would you like the tickets for?

Im Parkett oder im ersten Rang?
im parkett ohder im ersten rang
In the stalls or in the circle?

Es sind zwei Plätze hier im Parkett *(indicating on seating plan)*
es zint tsviy plettse heer im parkett
There are two here, in the stalls

Es tut mir leid, wir sind ausverkauft
es toot meer liyt veer zint owsferkowft
I'm sorry, we're sold out

Kann ich Ihre Karte sehen?
kan ish eere karte zayen
May I see your ticket?

SPORTS AND ACTIVITIES

• There are good facilities throughout Germany for golf, riding, tennis and other sports.

• **Fishing** There is plenty of fresh-water fishing in lakes, rivers and streams, particularly in Bavaria and the Black Forest. You need an angling permit, **Angelschein**, obtainable from the district administration or town council and a local angling permit from the owner or lessee of the waters. Local Tourist Offices will be able to supply further information. The national angling organisation is the **Verband Deutscher Sportfischer**.

• **Sailing** There are over 30 sailing schools on the North Sea, Baltic Coast and on the large inland lakes. The German National Tourist Office has a list of addresses and also further information on taking a boat on the network of inland waterways.

• **Walking and climbing** The **Verband Deutscher Gebirgs- und Wandervereine** looks after a network of well-signposted paths, mountain trails, hostels and shelters in the medium altitude ranges such as the Black Forest and the Bayrischer Wald. The **Deutscher Alpenverein (DAV)** runs huts in the Alps and runs mountaineering and ski courses.

• **Winter sports** There are resorts spread over the German Alps, the Harz, the Black Forest and the Bavarian Forest. There are Olympic skiing facilities at Garmisch-Patenkirchen. Cross-country skiing, **Langlauf**, is becoming more popular. Further information from local tourist offices.

• **Wine seminars and tastings** are held in the wine-producing areas. Tourists are welcome to join in. More information, plus details of the various wine festivals, from the German National Tourist Office.

• **Spas and health resorts** A **Kur** is a German speciality and there are registered spas in all sorts of locations from the mountains to the sea offering different treatments. More information from the German National Tourist Office.

• **Naturist holidays** The **FKK (Freikörperkultur)** offers holiday facilities at over 100 different sites.

• **Switzerland and Austria** Activities on offer are not limited to winter sports and climbing, but also include summer skiing, fishing, golf, tennis and water sports. Switzerland is a botanist's paradise, but many plants are protected. Check with local tourist offices for information on protected species.

You may see

Angeln verboten	No fishing
Drahtseilbahn	Cable car
Erste Hilfe	First Aid
Freibad	Outdoor swimming pool
Fußballplatz	Football pitch
Golfplatz	Golf course
Gefahr	Danger
Hallenbad	Indoor swimming pool
Lawinengefahr	Danger of avalanches
Piste	Ski run
Sportzentrum	Sports centre
Schwimmbad	Swimming pool
Schwimmen verboten	No swimming
Schlepplift	Drag lift
Sessellift	Chair lift
Skilift	Ski lift
Skischule	Ski school
Skiverleih	Ski hire
Strand	Beach
Tennisplatz	Tennis court
Unbefugtes Betreten verboten	Trespassers will be prosecuted

General phrases

Can I/we . . .?
Kann man . . .?
kan man

Can I/we hire bikes?
Kann man Fahrräder mieten?
*kan man **faarrayder meeten***

Can I/we go fishing?
Kann man angeln gehen?
*kan man **angeln gayen***

Can I/we go riding?
Kann man reiten gehen?
*kan man **riyten gayen***

Where can I/we . . .
Wo kann man . . .
voh kan man

Where can I/we play tennis?
Wo kann man Tennis spielen?
*voh kan man **tennis shpeelen***

Where can I/we go windsurfing?
Wo kann man windsurfen?
*voh kan man **vintsoorfen***

Are there lessons?
Gibt es Unterricht?
*gipt es **oonterrisht***

I'm a beginner
Ich bin Anfänger
*ish bin **anfenger***

I'm quite experienced
Ich bin ziemlich erfahren
*ish bin **tseemlish erfaaren***

How much does it cost per hour?
Wieviel kostet es pro Stunde?
*veefeel **kostet** es proh **shtoonde***

How much does it cost per day?
Wieviel kostet es pro Tag?
*veefeel **kostet** es proh taag*

How much does it cost per round?
Wieviel kostet die Runde?
*veefeel **kostet** dee **roonde***

Is there a reduction for children?
Gibt es eine Ermäßigung für Kinder?
*gipt es **iyne ermayssigoong** fewr **kinder***

Can we hire equipment?
Können wir die Ausrüstung mieten?
*kernnen veer dee **owsrewstoong** meeten*

Can we hire rackets?
Können wir Schläger mieten?
*kernnen veer **shlayger meeten***

Can we hire clubs?
Können wir Golfschläger mieten?
*kernnen veer **golf**shlayger **meeten***

Do we need a licence?
Brauchen wir eine Lizenz?
*browken veer **iyne leetsents***

Where can I/we get one?
Wo bekommt man das?
*voh be**kommt** man das*

Is it necessary to be a member?
Muß man Mitglied sein?
*mooss man **mit**gleet ziyn*

Beach, lake and pool

Can I/we swim here?
Kann man hier schwimmen?
*kan man heer **shvimmen***

Can I/we swim in the river?
Kann man im Fluß schwimmen?
*kan man im flooss **shvimmen***

Is it dangerous?
Ist es gefährlich?
*ist es **gefayr**lish*

Is it safe for children?
Ist es sicher für Kinder?
*ist es **zisher** fewr **kin**der*

When is high tide?
Wann ist Hochwasser?
*van ist **hohk**vasser*

Is the water clean?
Ist das Wasser sauber?
*ist das **vasser zow**ber*

Skiing

What is the snow like?
Wie ist der Schnee?
vee ist der shnay

How much is the lift pass?
Was kostet der liftpass?
*vas **kos**tet der **lift**pass*

. . . for a week
. . . für eine Woche
*fewr **iyne voke***

. . . for a day
. . . für einen Tag
*fewr **iy**nen taag*

What time is the last ascent?
Um wieviel Uhr ist der letzte Aufstieg?
oom veefeel oor ist der letste owfshteeg

Where is the nursery slope?
Wo ist der Anfängerhügel?
voh ist der anfengerhewgel

Is it steep?
Ist es steil?
ist es shtiyl

Is it icy?
Ist es eisig?
ist es iyzig

Is the run wide?
Ist die Piste breit?
ist dee peeste briyt

You may hear

Sind Sie ein Anfänger?
zint zee iyn anfenger
Are you a beginner?

Können Sie Ski fahren?
kernnen zee shee faaren
Can you ski?

Können Sie windsurfen?
kernnen zee vintsoorfen
Can you windsurf?

Es kostet zehn Mark die Stunde
es kostet tsayn mark dee shtoonde
It costs DM 10 per hour

Es gibt eine Anzahlung von fünfzig Mark
es gipt iyne antsaaloong fon fewnftsig mark
There is a deposit of DM 50

Es tut mir Leid, wir sind ausgebucht
es toot meer liyt veer zint owsgebookt
I'm sorry, we're booked up

Können Sie bitte einen Augenblick warten
kernnen zee bitte iynen owgenblik varten
Could you wait a moment, please

Kommen Sie ein bißchen später zurück
kommen zee iyn bissyen shpayter tsoorewk
Come back a bit later

Es ist sehr windig
es ist zayr vindig
It's very windy

Die Strömung ist sehr stark
*dee **shtrer**moong ist zayr shtark*
The current is very strong

Welche Größe haben Sie?
*vel**she** **grer**sse **haa**ben zee*
What size are you?

Sie brauchen ein Foto
*zee **brow**ken iyn **foh**to*
You need a photo

Der Schnee ist tief
der shnay ist teef
The snow is deep

Wir haben Pappschnee/ Pulverschnee
*veer **haa**ben **papp**shnay/ **pool**vershnay*
The snow is soft/powdery

Wir haben nicht viel Schnee
*veer **haa**ben nisht feel shnay*
There isn't much snow

HEALTH

Medical details – to show the Doctor

(Tick where appropriate, or fill in names/details

	Self **Ich**	Other members of family/party **Anderen**	
Blood group **Blutgruppe**			
Asthmatic **Asthmatisch**			
Blind **Blind**			
Deaf **Schwerhörig**			
Diabetic **Zuckerkrank**			
Epileptic **Epileptisch**			
Handicapped **Behindert**			
Heart condition **Schwaches Herz**			
High blood pressure **Hoher Blutdruck**			
Pregnant **Schwanger**			
Allergic to **Allergisch gegen**			
Antibiotics **Antibiotik**			
Penicillin **Penizillin**			
Cortisone **Kortison**			

Medicines **Medikamente**

Self **Ich** _____

Others **Anderen** _____

_____

_____

• Your local Department of Health office can provide information about medical care abroad. Within the EC you can obtain the local equivalent of NHS treatment by producing the required form – you may have to pay first and reclaim the payment when you return to Britain. Your travel insurance should also cover you for illness and accident.

• A chemist, **Apotheker**, will usually be qualified to treat minor disorders.

• In **Austria** information about the emergency medical service, **Ärztenodienst**, is available from the police.

• To indicate where the pain is you can simply point and say 'it hurts here' (**es tut hier weh**). Otherwise you'll need to look up the German for the appropriate part of the body.

You may see

Ambulanz	Surgery, Outpatients
Gift	Poison
Klinik	Clinic, hospital
Krankenhaus	Hospital
Praxis	Surgery
Sanitätswache	First aid post
Sprechstunden	Surgery hours
Unfallstation	Accident and Emergency ward

You may want to say

At the doctor's

I need a doctor
Ich brauche einen Arzt
*ish **browke** iynen artst*

Please call a doctor
Bitte, rufen Sie einen Arzt
*bitte **roofen** zee iynen artst*

My husband is ill
Mein Mann ist krank
miyn man ist krank

My wife is ill
Meine Frau ist krank
miyne frow ist krank

My friend is ill
Mein Freund *(male)*/**meine Freundin** *(female)* **ist krank**
miyn froynt/miyne froyndin ist krank

My son is ill
Mein Sohn ist krank
miyn zohn ist krank

My daughter is ill
Meine Tochter ist krank
miyne toshter ist krank

My baby is ill
Mein Baby ist krank
miyn baybee ist krank

Your symptoms

I feel unwell
Ich fühle mich nicht wohl
ish fewle mish nisht vohl

It hurts here
Es tut hier weh
es toot heer vay

My . . . hurts
Mein . . . tut weh
miyn . . . toot vay

My stomach hurts
Mein Bauch tut weh
miyn bowk toot vay

My back hurts
Mein Rücken tut weh
miyn rewken toot vay

My nose hurts
Meine Nase tut weh
miyne naaze toot vay

Someone else's symptoms

He/She feels unwell
Er/sie fühlt sich nicht wohl
er/zee fewlt zish nisht vohl

It hurts here
Es tut ihm/ihr hier weh
es toot eem/eer heer vay

His/Her . . . hurts
Sein/ihr . . . tut weh
ziyn/eer . . . toot vay

His/Her stomach hurts
Sein/ihr Bauch tut weh
ziyn/eer bowk toot vay

His/Her back hurts
Sein/ihr Rücken tut weh
ziyn/eer rewken toot vay

His/Her nose hurts
Seine/ihre Nase tut weh
ziyne/eere naaze toot vay

My . . . hurt
Meine . . . tun weh
miyne . . . toon vay

His/Her . . . hurt
Seine/ihre . . . tun weh
ziyne/eere . . . toon vay

My eyes hurt
Meine Augen tun weh
miyne owgen toon vay

His/Her eyes hurt
Seine/ihre Augen tun weh
ziyne/eere owgen toon vay

My feet hurt
Meine Füsse tun weh
miyne fewsse toon vay

His/Her feet hurt
Seine/ihre Füsse tun weh
ziyne/eere fewsse toon vay

I have a sore throat
Ich habe Halsschmerzen
ish haabe halsshmertsen

He/She has a sore throat
Er/sie hat Halsschmerzen
er/zee hat halsshmertsen

I have a temperature
Ich habe Fieber
ish haabe feeber

He/She has a temperature
Er/sie hat Fieber
er/zee hat feeber

I have diarrhoea
Ich habe Durchfall
ish haabe doorshfall

He/She has diarrhoea
Er/sie hat Durchfall
er/zee hat doorshfall

I feel dizzy
Mir ist schwindelig
meer ist shvindelig

He/She feels dizzy
Ihm/ihr ist es schwindelig
eem/eer ist es shvindelig

I have been sick
Ich habe mich übergeben
ish haabe mish ewbergayben

He/She has been sick
Er/sie hat sich übergeben
er/zee hat zish ewbergayben

I can't sleep
Ich kann nicht schlafen
ish kan nisht shlaafen

He/She can't sleep
Er/sie kann nicht schlafen
er/zee kan nisht shlaafen

I can't breathe
Ich kann nicht atmen
ish kan nisht aatmen

He/She can't breathe
Er/sie kann nicht atmen
er/zee kan nisht aatmen

My . . . is bleeding
Mein(e) . . . blutet
miyn/miyne . . . blootet

His/Her . . . is bleeding
Sein(e)/Ihr(e) . . . blutet
ziyn(e)/eer(e) . . . blootet

I think that . . .
Ich glaube, . . .
*ish **glowbe***

He/she thinks that . . .
Er/sie glaubt, . . .
er/zee glowbt

It's my . . .
Es ist mein(e) . . .
*es ist miyn/**miyne***

It's his/her . . .
Es ist sein(e)/ihr(e) . . .
es ist ziyn(e)/eer(e)

It's my arm
Es ist mein Arm
es ist miyn arm

It's his/her leg
Es ist sein/ihr Bein
es ist ziyn/eer biyn

It's my leg
Es ist mein Bein
es ist miyn biyn

It's his/her ankle
Es ist sein/ihr Knöchel
*es ist ziyn/eer **knerkel***

It's broken
Es ist gebrochen
*es ist **gebroken***

It's broken
Es ist gebrochen
*es ist **gebroken***

It's sprained
Es ist verstaucht
*es ist **fershtowkt***

It's sprained
Es ist verstaucht
*es ist **fershtowkt***

I have cut myself
Ich habe mich geschnitten
*ish **haabe** mish **geshnitten***

He/she has cut him/herself
Er/sie hat sich geschitten
er/zee hat zish ge***shnitten***

I have burnt myself
Ich habe mich verbrannt
*ish **haabe** mish **ferbrannt***

He/she has burnt him/herself
Er/sie hat sich verbrannt
*er/zee hat zish **ferbrannt***

I have been stung by an insect
Ein Insekt hat mich gestochen
*iyn in**zekt** hat mish **geshtoken***

He/she has been stung by an ins
Ein Insekt hat ihn/sie gestochen
*iyn in**zekt** hat een/zee **geshtoken***

I have been bitten by a dog
Ein Hund hat mich gebissen
*iyn hoont hat mish **gebissen***

He/she has been bitten by a dog
Ein Hund hat ihn/sie gebissen
*iyn hoont hat een/zee **gebissen***

You may hear

Wo tut es weh?
voh toot es vay
Where does it hurt?

Tut es hier weh?
toot es heer vay
Does it hurt here?

Sehr? Nur ein bißchen?
*zayr, noor iyn **bissyen***
A lot? A little?

Seit wann fühlen Sie sich so?
*ziyt van **fewlen** zee zish zoh*
How long have you been feeling like this?

Wie alt sind Sie?
vee alt zint zee
How old are you?

Wie alt ist er/sie
vee alt ist er/zee
How is he/she?

Machen Sie bitte den Mund auf
***maaken** zee **bitte** dayn moont owf*
Open your mouth, please

Ziehen Sie sich bitte aus
***tsee**-en zee zish **bitte** ows*
Get undressed, please

Machen Sie sich oben frei
***maaken** zee zish **ohben** friy*
Take your top off

Legen Sie sich bitte da drüben hin
***laygen** zee zish **bitte** daa **drewben** hin*
Lie down over there, please

Nehmen Sie irgendwelche Medikamente?
naymen zee eergentvelshe maydikamente
Are you taking any medicines?

Sind Sie gegen irgendein Medikament allergisch?
zint zee gaygen eergentiyn maydikament allergish
Are you allergic to any medicine?

Sind Sie gegen Wundstarrkrampf geimpft?
zint zee gaygen voontshtarrkrampf geimpft
Have you been vaccinated against tetanus?

Was haben Sie (heute) gegessen?
vas haaben zee (hoyte) gegessen
What have you eaten (today)?

Ich gebe Ihnen ein Rezept
ish gaybe eenen iyn raytsept
I am going to give you a prescription

Nehmen Sie dreimal täglich eine Tablette
naymen zee driymal tayglish iyne tablette
Take a tablet three times a day

Nach dem Essen
naak daym essen
After meals

Abends
aabents
At night

Sie haben eine Entzündung
zee haaben iyne enttsewndoong
You've got an infection

Es ist infiziert
es ist infitseert
It's infected

Ich werde Ihren Blutdruck messen
ish verde eeren blootdrook messen
I'm going to take your blood pressure

Ich muß Ihnen eine Spritze geben
ish mooss eenen iyne shprittse gayben
I have to give you an injection

Das muß genäht werden
das mooss genayt verden
That needs some stitches

Ich muß eine Röntgenaufnahme machen
ish mooss iyne rerntgenowfnaame maaken
I have to take an X-ray

Ich brauche eine Blutprobe
ish browke iyne blootprohbe
I need a blood sample

Ich brauche eine Urinprobe
ish browke iyne ooreen prohbe
I need a urine sample

Sie haben Lebensmittelvergiftung
zee haaben laybenzmittelfergiftoong
You have food poisoning

Es ist ein Infarkt
es ist iyn infarkt
It's a heart attack

Sie müssen sich ausruhen
zee mewssen zish owsroo-en
You must rest

Sie müssen drei Tage im Bett bleiben
zee mewssen driy taage im bett bliyben
You must stay in bed for three days

Sie müssen in fünf Tagen wiederkommen
*zee **mew**ssen in fewnf **taa**gen **vee**derkommen*
You must come back in five days' time

Ich muß Sie ins Krankenhaus einweisen
*ish mooss zee ins **kran**kenhows **iyn**viyzen*
I'll have to send you to hospital

Es ist nichts Ernstes
*es ist nishts **ern**stes*
It is nothing serious

Sie sind gesund
*zee zint **gezoont***
There is nothing wrong with you

Sie können sich anziehen
*zee **kern**nen zish **ant**see-en*
You can get dressed again

At the dentist's

I need a dentist
Ich brauche einen Zahnarzt
*ish **brow**ke **iy**nen **tsaan**artst*

I have toothache
Ich habe Zahnschmerzen
*ish **haa**be **tsaan**shmertsen*

This tooth hurts
Dieser Zahn tut weh
*dee**ze**r tsaan toot vay*

I have broken a tooth
Ich habe mir ein Stück vom Zahn abgebrochen
*ish **haa**be meer iyn shtewk fom tsaan **ap**gebroken*

I have lost a filling
Ich habe eine Plombe verloren
*ish **haa**be **iy**ne **plom**be **fer**loren*

I have lost a crown/cap
Ich habe eine Krone verloren
*ish **haa**be **iy**ne **kroh**ne **fer**loren*

He/She has toothache
Er/sie hat Zahnschmerzen
*er/zee hat **tsaan**shmertsen*

He/She has broken a tooth
Er/sie hat sich ein Stück vom Zahn abgebrochen
*er/zee hat zish iyn shtewk vom tsaan **ap**gebroken*

He/She has lost a filling
Er/sie hat eine Plombe verloren
*er/zee hat **iyne plom**be ferloren*

He/She has lost a crown/cap
Er/sie hat eine Krone verloren
*er/zee hat **iyne krohn**e ferloren*

Can you fix it temporarily?
Können Sie es provisorisch behandeln?
kernnen zee es provizorish behandeln

How much will it cost?
Was wird es kosten?
vas virt es kosten

Can you give me an injection?
Können Sie mir eine Spritze geben?
kernnen zee meer iyne shprittse gayben

Can you give him/her an injection?
Können Sie ihm/ihr eine Spritze geben?
kernnen zee eem/eer iyne shprittse gayben

This denture is broken
Das Gebiß ist gebrochen
das gebiss ist gebroken

Can you repair it temporarily?
Können Sie es provisorisch reparieren
kernnen zee es provizorish repareeren

You may hear

Machen Sie den Mund auf
maaken zee dayn moont owf
Open your mouth

Sie brauchen eine Plombe
zee browken iyne plombe
You need a filling

Ich muß es rausnehmen
ish moos es rowsnaymen
I'll have to extract it

Ich gebe Ihnen eine Spritze
ish gaybe eenen iyne shprittse
I'm going to give you an injection

Ankle	**der Knöchel**	***kner**shel*
Appendix	**der Blinddarm**	***blint**darm*
Arm	**der Arm**	*arm*
Artery	**die Schlagader**	***shlaag**aader*
Back	**der Rücken**	***rew**ken*
Bladder	**die Blase**	***blaa**ze*
Blood	**das Blut**	*bloot*
Body	**der Körper**	***ker**per*
Bone	**der Knochen**	***knok**en*
Bottom	**der Hintern**	***hin**tern*
Bowels	**der Darm**	*darm*
Breast	**die Brust**	*broost*
Buttock	**der Po**	*poh*
Cartilage	**der Knorpel**	***knor**pel*
Chest	**der Brustkorb**	***broost**korp*
Chin	**das Kinn**	*kin*
Ear	**das Ohr**	*ohr*
Elbow	**der Ellenbogen**	***ell**enbohgen*
Eye	**das Auge**	***ow**ge*
Face	**das Gesicht**	*gezi**sht***
Finger	**der Finger**	***fin**ger*
Foot	**der Fuß**	*fooss*
Genitals	**die Genitalien**	*geni**taa**lee-en*
Gland	**die Drüse**	***drew**ze*
Hair	**das Haar**	*haar*
Hand	**die Hand**	*hant*
Head	**der Kopf**	*kopf*
Heart	**das Herz**	*herts*
Heel	**die Ferse**	***fayr**ze*
Hip	**die Hüfte**	***hew**fte*
Jaw	**der Kiefer**	***kee**fer*
Joint	**das Gelenk**	*ge**lenk***
Kidney	**die Niere**	***nee**re*
Knee	**das Knie**	*k-nee*

Leg	**das Bein**	*biyn*
Ligament	**das Ligament**	*ligament*
Lip	**die Lippe**	*lippe*
Liver	**die Leber**	*layber*
Lung	**die Lunge**	*loonge*
Mouth	**der Mund**	*moont*
Muscle	**der Muskel**	*mooskel*
Nail	**der Nagel**	*naagel*
Neck	**der Hals**	*hals*
Nerve	**der Nerv**	*nerf*
Nose	**die Nase**	*naaze*
Penis	**der Penis**	*peenis*
Private parts	**die Geschlechtsteile**	*geshleshtstiyle*
Rib	**die Rippe**	*rippe*
Shoulder	**die Schulter**	*shoolter*
Skin	**die Haut**	*howt*
Spine	**das Rückgrat**	*rewkgraat*
Stomach	**der Magen**	*maagen*
Tendon	**die Sehne**	*zayne*
Testicle	**der Testikel**	*testikel*
Thigh	**der Oberschenkel**	*ohbershenkel*
Throat	**die Kehle**	*kayle*
Thumb	**der Daumen**	*dowmen*
Toe	**der Zeh**	*tsay*
Tongue	**die Zunge**	*tsoonge*
Tonsils	**die Mandeln**	*mandeln*
Tooth	**der Zahn**	*tsaan*
Vagina	**die Vagina**	*vageena*
Vein	**die Ader**	*aader*
Wrist	**das Handgelenk**	*hantgelenk*

PROBLEMS AND COMPLAINTS

• If you lose anything or have anything stolen, you must report it to the police within 24 hours so that you can make a valid insurance claim.

You may see

Außer Betrieb	Out of order

You may want to say

General phrases

Can you mend this (immediately)?
Können Sie das (gleich) reparieren?
kernnen zee das (gliysh) repareeren

When can you mend this?
Wann können Sie das reparieren?
van kernnen zee das repareeren

Can you help me?
Können Sie mir helfen?
kernnen zee meer helfen

Can I speak to the manager?
Kann ich den Geschäftsführer sprechen?
kan ish dayn gesheftsfewrer shpreken

There's a problem with . . .
Es gibt ein Problem mit . . .
es gipt iyn problaym mit

There isn't any . . .
Es gibt kein/keine/keinen . . .
es gipt kiyn/kiyne/kiynen

I need . . .
Ich brauche . . .
ish browke

The . . . doesn't work
Der/die/das . . . funktioniert nicht
der/dee/das . . . foonktsyoneert nisht

The . . . is broken
Der/die/das . . . ist kaputt
der/dee/das . . . ist kapoot

I can't
Ich kann nicht
ish kan nisht

It's not my fault
Ich bin nicht schuldig daran
*ish bin nisht **shooldig daran***

I have forgotten . . .
Ich habe . . . vergessen
*ish **haabe** . . . **fergessen***

I have lost . . .
Ich habe . . . verloren
*ish **haabe** . . . **ferloren***

Someone has stolen . . .
Man hat . . . gestohlen
*man hat . . . **geshtohlen***

My . . . has disappeared
Meine/meine . . . ist verschwunden
*miyn/**miyne** . . . ist **fershvoonden***

My money isn't there
Mein Geld ist nicht da
miyn gelt ist nisht daa

My travellers' cheques aren't there
Meine Reiseschecks sind nicht da
***miyne riyzeshecks** zint nisht daa*

Something is missing
Etwas ist weg
etvas ist vek

The . . . is missing
Der/die/das . . . ist weg
der/dee/das . . . ist vek

This isn't mine
Das gehört mir nicht
*das **gehert** meer nisht*

Where you're staying

There isn't any hot water
Es gibt kein heißes Wasser
*es gipt kiyn **hiysses vasser***

There isn't any toilet paper
Es gibt kein Toilettenpapier
*es gipt kiyn toy**lettenpapeer***

There isn't any electricity
Es gibt keinen Strom
*es gipt **kiynen** shtrohm*

There aren't any towels
Es gibt keine Handtücher
*es gipt **kiyne** hant**tewsher***

The light doesn't work
Das Licht funktioniert nicht
*das lisht foonktsyo**neert** nisht*

The shower doesn't work
Die Dusche funktioniert nicht
*dee **dooshe** foonktsyo**neert** nisht*

I need another pillow
Ich brauche noch ein Kopfkissen
*ish **browke** nok iyn **kopf**kissen*

I need another blanket
Ich brauche noch eine Bettdecke
*ish **browke** nok **iyne** **bett**deke*

The lock/the key is broken
Das Schloß/der Schlüssel ist kaputt
*das shloss/der **shlew**ssel ist ka**poot***

The bed is broken
Das Bett ist kaputt
*das bett ist ka**poot***

I can't open the window
Ich kann das Fenster nicht öffnen
*ish kan das **fen**ster nisht **erf**nen*

I can't turn the tap off
Ich kann den Hahn nicht zudrehen
*ish kan dayn haan nisht **tsoo**drayen*

The drain is blocked
Der Abfluß ist verstopft
*der **apf**looss ist fer**shtopft***

The toilet doesn't flush
Die Toilette spült nicht
*dee toy**lette** shpewlt nisht*

The wash basin is dirty
Das Waschbecken ist schmutzig
*das **vash**beken ist **shmoottsig***

The room is . . .
Das Zimmer ist . . .
*das **tsimmer** ist*

The room is too hot/cold
Das Zimmer ist zu heiß/kalt
*das **tsimmer** ist tsoo hiyss/kalt*

The room is too dark
Das Zimmer ist zu dunkel
*das **tsimmer** ist tsoo **doon**kel*

The room is too small
Das Zimmer ist zu klein
*das **tsimmer** ist tsoo kliyn*

The bed is uncomfortable
Das Bett ist unbequem
*das bett ist **un**bekvaym*

There's a lot of noise
Es ist zu laut
es ist tsoo lowt

There's a smell of gas
Es riecht nach Gas
es reesht naak gas

In restaurants and bars

This isn't cooked
Das ist nicht gar
das ist nisht gar

This is burnt
Das ist angebrannt
*das ist **an**gebrannt*

This is cold
Das ist kalt
das ist kalt

I didn't order this
Ich habe das nicht bestellt
*ish **haa**be das nisht be**shtellt***

This glass is cracked
Dieses Glas hat einen Sprung
***dee**zes glas hat **iy**nen shproong*

This is dirty
Dies ist schmutzig
*dees ist **shmoottsig***

This smells bad
Das riecht shlecht
das reesht shlesht

This tastes strange
Das schmeckt komisch
*das shmeckt **koh**mish*

There's a mistake here
Da stimmt etwas nicht
*daa shtimmt **et**vas nisht*

My bill is too much
Meine Rechnung ist zu viel
***miy**ne **resh**noong ist tsoo feel*

In shops

I bought this here (yesterday)
Ich habe das (gestern) hier gekauft
*ish **haa**be das (**ge**stern) heer **ge**kowft*

Can I change it?
Kann ich es umtauschen?
*kan ish es **oom**towshen*

I want to return this
Ich möchte das zurückbringen
*ish **mersh**te das tsoo**rewk**bringen*

Can you give me my money back?
Können Sie mein Geld zurückerstatten?
***kern**nen zee miyn gelt tsoo**rewk**ershtatten*

Here is the receipt
Hier ist die Quittung
*heer ist dee **kvit**toong*

It's no good
Es funktioniert nicht
*es foonktsyo**neert** nisht*

It has a flaw
Es hat einen Fehler
*es hat **iy**nen **fay**ler*

It has a hole
Es hat ein Loch
es hat iyn lok

There is a stain/mark
Es gibt einen Fleck
*es gipt **iy**nen flek*

This is off
Das ist schlecht
das ist shlesht

This isn't fresh
Dies ist nicht frisch
dees ist nisht frish

The lid is missing
Der Deckel fehlt
*der **dekel** faylt*

Forgetting and losing things and theft

I have forgotten my ticket
Ich habe meine Fahrkarte vergessen
*ish **haabe miyne faarkarte fergessen***

I have forgotten my key
Ich habe meinen Schlüssel vergessen
*ish **haabe miynen shlewssel fergessen***

I have lost my driving licence
Ich habe meinen Führerschein verloren
*ish **haabe miynen fewrershiyn ferloren***

I have lost my passport
Ich habe meinen Paß verloren
*ish **haabe miynen pass ferloren***

We've lost our rucksacks
Wir haben unsere Rucksäcke verloren
*veer **haaben oonzere rookzeke ferloren***

Where is the lost property office?
Wo ist das Fundbüro?
*voh ist das **foontbewroh***

Where is the police station?
Wo ist die Polizeiwache?
*voh ist dee **politsiyvake***

Someone has stolen my bag
Man hat meine Handtasche gestohlen
*man hat **miyne hanttashe geshtohlen***

Someone has stolen our car
Man hat unser Auto gestohlen
*man hat **oonzer owto geshtohlen***

Someone has stolen my money
Man hat mein Geld gestohlen
*man hat miyn gelt **geshtohlen***

If someone is bothering you

Leave me alone please
Lassen Sie mich bitte allein
*lassen zee mish **bitte alliyn***

Go away or I'll call the police
Gehen Sie weg sonst rufe ich die Polizei
*gayen zee vek zonst **roofe** ish dee politsiy*

There's someone annoying me
Jemand belästigt mich
*yaymant **belestigt** mish*

You may hear

Helpful and unhelpful replies

Einen Augenblick, bitte
*iynen owgenblick **bitte***
Just a moment, please

Natürlich/Selbstverständlich
natewrlish/zelbstfershtentlish
Of course

Ich werde Ihnen noch einen/eine/ein . . . bringen
*ish **verde eenen** nok **iynen/iyne/iyns bringen***
I'll bring you another one

Ich werde Ihnen eines sofort bringen
*ish **verde** **eenen** **iynes** zoh**fort** **bringen***
I'll bring you one immediately

Sofort/gleich
*zoh**fort**/gliysh*
Immediately

Ich werde es für Sie morgen reparieren
*ish **verde** es fewr zee **morgen** repa**reeren***
I'll fix it for you tomorrow

Es tut mir leid, es ist unmöglich
*es toot meer liyt es ist **oon**merglish*
I'm sorry, it's not possible

Es tut mir leid, ich kann nichts machen
*es toot meer liyt ish kan nishts **maa**ken*
I'm sorry, there's nothing I can do

Ich bin nicht dafür zuständig
*ish bin nisht daa**fewr** **tsoo**shtendig*
I'm not responsible for that

Wir sind nicht dafür verantwortlich
*veer zint nisht daa**fewr** fe**rant**vortlish*
We aren't responsible

Questions you may be asked

Wann haben Sie's gekauft?
*van **haaben** zeez **gekowft***
When did you buy it?

Haben Sie die Quittung?
haaben** zee dee **kvittoong
Have you got the receipt?

Wann ist es passiert?
*van ist es **passeert***
When did it happen?

Wie sieht Ihr Auto aus?
*vee zeeht eer **owto** ows*
What does your car look like?

Was haben Sie für ein Auto?
*vas **haaben** zee fewr iyn **owto***
What make of car is it?

Was ist das Kraftfahrzeugkennzeichen?
*vas ist das **kraftfaartsoyg-kenntsiyken***
What is the registration number of your car?

Wie heißen Sie?
*vee **hiyssen** zee*
What's your name?

Wo wohnen Sie?
*voh **vohnen** zee*
Where are you staying?

Was ist Ihre Adresse?
*vas ist **eere adresse***
What's your address?

Wo haben Sie's verloren?
*voh **haaben** zeez **ferloren***
Where did you lose it?

Wo ist es gestohlen worden?
*voh ist es **geshtohlen vorden***
Where was it stolen?

Wie sieht Ihre Tasche aus?
*vee zeet **eere tashe** ows*
What does your bag look like?

Was ist Ihre Zimmernummer?
*vas ist **eere tsimmernoommer***
What's your room number?

Welche Nummer hat Ihre Ferienwohnung?
velshe noommer** hat **eere fayrienvohnoong
What's the number of your apartment?

Ihre Paßnummer, bitte?
Eere passnoommer bitte
What's your passport number?

Sind Sie versichert?
*zint zee **ferzishert***
Are you insured?

Bitte füllen Sie das Formular aus
***bitte fewllen** zee das **formoolar** ows*
Please fill in this form

BASIC GRAMMAR

Nouns

Nouns in German have one of three genders, masculine, feminine or neuter. There are certain endings which show what gender a noun is. For example **-heit**, **-keit**, **-ung** are always feminine endings and the suffix **-chen** always makes a word neuter, **das Mädchen** – the girl. On the whole though genders have to be learnt from hearing and reading the language.

Nouns in German are always written with a capital letter.

Plurals

Plurals are formed by adding an ending and/or an umlaut on to the noun. Endings vary and although feminine words ending in **-keit**, **-heit** and **-ung** usually add **-en** to make the plural, most plural endings have to be learnt. Dictionaries give the plural endings of words in the German–English section. Some words don't change in the plural, e.g. **der Knochen** – bone.

Definite article – 'the'

The definite article changes according to whether the noun is masculine, feminine, neuter or plural:
der – masculine
die – feminine
das – neuter
die – plural, all genders

e.g.	**der Mann** – the man	**die Männer** – the men
	die Frau – the woman	**die Frauen** – the women
	das Haus – the house	**die Häuser** – the houses

The indefinite article – 'a', 'an'

The indefinite articles are:

ein – masculine **eine** – feminine **ein** – neuter

The word **kein**, which has the same endings, means 'no', 'not any' and can also be used in the plural.

kein Mann – no man **keine Männer** – no men
keine Frau – no woman **keine Frauen** – no women
kein Haus – no house **keine Häuser** – no houses

Cases

German has four cases: nominative, accusative, genitive and dative. The nominative case is used for the subject of a sentence, the accusative for the direct object, the genitive is the possessive case and the dative goes with the indirect object. There are also certain prepositions (see page 182) which either take the accusative or the dative and verbs which take the dative.

The definite and indefinite articles may change according to what case the noun is in:

Definite article

	Masculine	*Feminine*	*Neuter*	*Plural*
Nom.	**der** Mann	**die** Frau	**das** Haus	**die** Männer
Acc.	**den** Mann	**die** Frau	**das** Haus	**die** Männer
Gen.	**des** Mannes	**der** Frau	**des** Hauses	**der** Männer
Dat.	**dem** Mann	**der** Frau	**dem** Haus	**den** Männern

Indefinite article

	Masculine	*Feminine*	*Neuter*	*Plural*
Nom.	**ein** Mann	**eine** Frau	**ein** Haus	**keine** Männer
Acc.	**einen** Mann	**eine** Frau	**ein** Haus	**keine** Männer
Gen.	**eines** Mannes	**einer** Frau	**eines** Hauses	**keiner** Männer
Dat.	**einem** Mann	**einer** Frau	**einem** Haus	**keinen** Männern

Possessive adjectives

The possessive adjectives add the same endings as the indefinite article:

mein my	**mein Vater** my father	**meine Mutter** my mother
dein your*	**deine Schwester** your sister	**deine Kinder** your children
sein – his, its **ihr** – her	**unser** – our **euer** – your*	**Ihr** – your* **ihr** – their

* See **'You'** on page 183

Adjectives

Adjectives come before the noun and the ending changes according to the gender of the noun, whether the noun is singular or plural, and whether the noun is with a definite or indefinite article or with no article at all.

Definite article

	Masculine	*Feminine*	*Neuter*
Nom.	**der** arme Mann	**die** arme Frau	**das** arme Mädche
Acc.	**den** arm**en** Mann	**die** arme Frau	**das** arme Mädche
Gen.	**des** arm**en** Mannes	**der** arm**en** Frau	**des** arm**en** Mädch
Dat.	**dem** arm**en** Mann	**der** arm**en** Frau	**dem** arm**en** Mädc

	Plural
Nom.	**die** arm**en** Männer
Acc.	**die** arm**en** Männer
Gen.	**der** arm**en** Männer
Dat.	**den** arm**en** Männern

Indefinite article

	Masculine	*Feminine*	*Neuter*
Nom.	**ein** arm**er** Mann	**eine** arme Frau	**ein** arm**es** Mädchen
Acc.	**einen** arm**en** Mann	**eine** arme Frau	**ein** arm**es** Mädchen
Gen.	**eines** arm**en** Mannes	**einer** arm**en** Frau	**eines** arm**en** Mädchens
Dat.	**einem** arm**en** Mann	**einer** arm**en** Frau	**einem** arm**en** Mädchen

	Plural
Nom.	**keine** arm**en** Männer
Acc.	**keine** arm**en** Männer
Gen.	**keiner** arm**en** Männer
Dat.	**keinen** arm**en** Männer**n**

No article

	Masculine	*Feminine*	*Neuter*
Nom.	gut**er** Wein	gut**e** Milch	gut**es** Bier
Acc.	gut**en** Wein	gut**e** Milch	gut**es** Bier
Gen.	gut**en** Weins	gut**er** Milch	gut**en** Bier
Dat.	gut**em** Wein	gut**er** Milch	gut**em** Bier

	Plural
Nom.	gut**e** Leute
Acc.	gut**e** Leute
Gen.	gut**er** Leute
Dat.	gut**en** Leute**n**

Comparatives and superlatives

To make an adjective comparative, add **-er** on to the stem and then add the endings as above.

e.g. **der reiche Mann** – the rich man
der reichere Mann – the richer man
ein schnelles Auto – a fast car
ein schnelleres Auto – a faster car

To make an adjective superlative, add **-st** on to the stem and then the endings.

e.g. **der reichste Mann** – the richest man
das schnellste Auto – the fastest car

Some common adjectives e.g. **groß** (big), **lang** (long), **alt** (old), add an umlaut as well to make the comparative and superlative.

e.g. **meine ältere Schwester** – my older sister
das größte Land – the biggest country
der längste Fluß – the longest river

Prepositions

Aus, **bei**, **mit**, **seit**, **nach**, **von** and **zu** always take the dative. **Bis**, **entlang**, **durch**, **ohne**, **gegen**, **wider**, **um** and **für** always take the accusative.

Other prepositions can take either the accusative or the dative. The accusative usually indicates movement, e.g. **in den Garten**, into the garden, while the dative indicates position, e.g. **im (in + dem) Garten**, in the garden.

Subject pronouns ('I', 'you', 'he', 'she', etc.)

I	**ich**
you (informal)	**du**
he	**er**
she	**sie**
it	**es**
we	**wir**
you (informal)	**ihr**
you (formal)	**Sie**
they	**sie**

'You'

There are three words for 'you' in German:

Du is informal and is used when you are talking either to someone you know well, or to a child or someone much younger than yourself. Young people tend to address each other as **du** as well.

Ihr is informal and is used in the same situations as **du** when you are addressing more than one person.

Sie is always written with a capital letter and is the formal word for 'you'. It can be used to address one person or a group of people. Always use it when you don't know the person you are talking to, or if they are much older than you.

If in doubt about which word for 'you' to use, stick to **Sie**.

The possessive adjective 'your' (**dein**, **euer** or **Ihr** in German), follows the same guidelines.

Word order

Normally the main verb of a sentence comes second; however, there are certain words which send the verb to the end of the sentence or clause. The most common of these are:

daß	that
weil	because
wenn	when, if

e.g. **Sie kommt nicht, weil sie krank ist**
She's not coming because she's ill

The present perfect tense (I have been, we have seen etc.) is made up of two parts in German: the auxiliary verb (**haben** or **sein**) and the past participle which always goes to the end of the sentence or clause.

e.g. **Ich habe ihn im Theater gesehen**	I've seen him in the theatre
Wir haben sie für nächsten Dienstag eingeladen	We've invited them/her for next Tuesday

Verbs

Endings change on verbs according to (i) the subject of the verb and (ii) the tense of the verb. Regular verbs are known as 'weak' verbs and the endings in the present tense are as follows:

sagen to say

Ich	sage
du	sagst
er, sie, es	sagt
wir	sagen
ihr	sagt
Sie	sagen
sie	sagen

The endings are added to the stem of the verb. To find the stem, knock **-en** off the infinitive (which is the form of the verb given in a dictionary).

Irregular verbs are known as 'strong' verbs.
Sein to be and **haben** to have, are both strong verbs.

sein		**haben**	
ich	**bin**	**ich**	**habe**
du	**bist**	**du**	**hast**
er, sie, es	**ist**	**er, sie, es**	**hat**
wir	**sind**	**wir**	**haben**
ihr	**seid**	**ihr**	**habt**
Sie	**sind**	**Sie**	**haben**
sie	**sind**	**sie**	**haben**

Some strong verbs change the vowel in the second person singular (**du**) and the third person singular (**er**, **sie**, **es**)
e.g.

fahren to drive, to go

ich	**fahre**
du	**fährst**
er, sie, es	**fährt**
wir	**fahren**
ihr	**fahrt**
Sie	**fahren**
sie	**fahren**

geben to give

ich	**gebe**
du	**gibst**
er, sie, es	**gibt**
wir	**geben**
ihr	**gebt**
Sie	**geben**
sie	**geben**

Another useful irregular verb is **wissen** to know

ich	**weiß**
du	**weißt**
er, sie, es	**weiß**
wir	**wissen**
ihr	**wißt**
Sie	**wissen**
sie	**wissen**

Negatives

To make a verb negative, add **nicht**

e.g. **Ich kann nicht**	I can't
Wir verstehen nicht	We don't understand

Separable verbs

A lot of verbs change or add to their meaning simply by adding a prefix.

e.g. **fahren**	to go, to drive
abfahren	to leave
kommen	to come
ankommen	to arrive

In a sentence the prefix splits from the rest of the verb and goes to the end of the sentence.

e.g. **Er kommt um neun Uhr an** He's arriving at nine o'clock

Some prefixes are inseparable and don't go to the end of the sentence.

Modal verbs

Modals are a group of verbs which are very useful if you want to express attitudes or intentions. Modal verbs include:

dürfen: ich darf – I may, I am allowed to
darf ich? – may I?
Sie dürfen – you may, you are allowed to

können: ich kann – I can
Sie können – you can

mögen: ich mag – I like
Sie mögen – you like

müssen: ich muß – I must, have to
Sie müssen – you must, have to

sollen: ich soll – I am supposed to
Sie sollen – you are supposed to

wollen: ich will – I want
Sie wollen – you want

They are often used in the 'conditional' form or in the simple past rather than in the present:
e.g.
ich könnte – I could
wir/Sie könnten – we/you could

ich möchte – I'd like
wir/Sie möchten – we'd/you'd like
Was möchten Sie? – what would you like?

ich sollte – I should, I ought to
wir/Sie sollten – we/you should, ought to

Ich mußte – I had to

Ich wollte – I wanted to

Verbs in other tenses you may find useful:

sein	**ich war**	I was, I used to be
	wir waren	we were, we used to be
	ich bin gewesen	I have been
	wir sind gewesen	we have been
haben	**ich hatte**	I had, I used to have
	wir hatten	we had, we used to have
gehen	**ich ging**	I went, I used to go
	wir gingen	we went, we used to go

The future tense is used relatively little in German and the verb tends to stay in the present tense, especially when time is mentioned.
e.g. You'll pick me up tomorrow morning then
Du holst mich also morgen früh ab
We're going there tomorrow
Wir gehen morgen dahin

Questions

To ask a question, use a question word and invert the subject and verb:

e.g. **Was machst du?**	What are you doing?
Was wollen Sie?	What do you want?
Wer bist du?	Who are you?

If there is no question word simply invert the subject and verb:

e.g. **Kommen Sie?**	Are you coming?
Verstehst du?	Do you understand?

DAYS, MONTHS, DATES

Days

Monday	**Montag**	*mohntaag*
Tuesday	**Dienstag**	*deenztaag*
Wednesday	**Mittwoch**	*mittvok*
Thursday	**Donnerstag**	*donnerztaag*
Friday	**Freitag**	*friytaag*
Saturday	**Samstag/Sonnabend**	*zamstaag/zonnaabent*
Sunday	**Sonntag**	*zonntaag*

Months

January	**Januar**	*yanoo-ar*
February	**Februar**	*faybroo-ar*
March	**März**	*merts*
April	**April**	*april*
May	**Mai**	*miy*
June	**Juni**	*yoonee*
July	**Juli**	*yoolee*
August	**August**	*owgoost*
September	**September**	*zeptember*
October	**Oktober**	*oktohber*
November	**November**	*november*
December	**Dezember**	*detsember*

Seasons

Spring	**der Frühling**	*frewling*
Summer	**der Sommer**	*zommer*
Autumn	**der Herbst**	*herpst*
Winter	**der Winter**	*vinter*

General phrases

Day	**der Tag**	*taag*
Week	**die Woche**	*voke*
Fortnight	**vierzehn Tage**	*feertsayn taage*
Month	**der Monat**	*mohnaat*
Year	**das Jahr**	*yaar*
Six months	**ein halbes Jahr**	*iyn halbez yaar*
on Monday	**(am) Montag**	*am mohntaag*
on Tuesdays	**dienstags**	*deenztaagz*
every Wednesday	**jeden Mittwoch**	*yayden mittvok*
in August	**im August**	*im owgoost*
at the beginning of March	**Anfang März**	*anfang merts*
in the middle of June	**Mitte Juni**	*mitte yoonee*
at the end of September	**Ende September**	*ende zeptember*
in six months' time	**in einem halben Jahr**	*in iynem halben yaar*
during the summer	**während des Sommers**	*vayrent des zommerz*
two years ago	**vor zwei Jahren**	*for tsviy yaaren*
(in) the nineties	**in den neunziger Jahren**	*in dayn noyntsiger yaaren*
last ...	**letzten/letzte/letztes**	*lettsten/lettste/lettstes*
last Monday	**letzten Montag**	*lettsten mohntaag*
last week	**letzte Woche**	*lettste voke*
last month	**letzten Monat**	*letsten mohnaat*
last year	**letztes Jahr**	*lettstes yaar*
next ...	**nächsten/nächste/nächstes**	*neksten/nekste/nekstes*
next Tuesday	**nächsten Dienstag**	*neksten deenztaag*
next week	**nächste Woche**	*nekste voke*

next month	**nächsten Monat**	*neksten mohnaat*
next year	**nächstes Jahr**	*nekstes yaar*

What day is it today? **Welchen Tag haben wir heute?**
velshen taag haaben veer hoyte

What is the date today? **Was ist das heutige Datum?**
vas ist das hoytige daatoom

When is your birthday? **Wann hast du Geburstag?**
van hast doo geboortstaag

Today	**heute**	*hoyte*
This morning	**heute morgen**	*hoyte morgen*
This afternoon	**heute nachmittag**	*hoyte naakmittaag*
(In the) morning	**am Morgen**	*am morgen*
(In the) afternoon	**am Nachmittag**	*am naakmittaag*
(In the) evening	**am Abend**	*am aabent*
(At) night	**in der Nacht**	*in der naakt*
Yesterday	**gestern**	*gestern*
The day before yesterday	**vorgestern**	*forgestern*
Yesterday morning	**gestern morgen**	*gestern morgen*
Yesterday evening	**gestern abend**	*gestern aabent*
Tomorrow	**morgen**	*morgen*
The day after tomorrow	**übermorgen**	*ewbermorgen*
Tomorrow afternoon	**morgen nachmittag**	*morgen naakmittaag*
Tomorrow morning	**morgen früh**	*morgen frew*
Before Saturday	**vor Samstag**	*for zamztaag*
After Thursday	**nach Donnerstag**	*naak donnerstaag*
Until/by Friday	**bis Freitag**	*bis friytaag*
Two days ago	**vor zwei Tagen**	*for tsviy taagen*

On the first of January	**am ersten Januar** *am **ersten** **yanoo**-ar*
On Tuesday 10 May	**am Dienstag den zehnten Mai** *am **deenz**taag dayn **tsaynten** miy*
1990	**neunzehnhundertneunzig** *noyntsaynhoondert**noyntsig***
In the 15th century	**im fünfzehnten Jahrhundert** *im **fewnf**tsaynten yaar**hoondert***

TIME

• To say that it's 'half past . . .' in German you have to say that it's half way round to the next hour, e.g. half past five is **halb sechs**, because it's half way round to six; half past two is **halb drei**, because it's half way to three o'clock.

One o'clock
Ein Uhr
iyn oor

Two o'clock
Zwei Uhr
tsviy oor

Three o'clock etc.
Drei Uhr
driy oor

Quarter past . . .
Viertel nach . . .
feertel naak

Half past . . .
Halb . . .
halp

Five past . . .
Fünf nach . . .
fewnf naak

Twenty-five past . . .
Fünfundzwanzig nach . . .
fewnfoonttsvantsig naak
Fünf vor halb . . .
fewnf for halp

Just after . . .
Kurz nach . . .
koorts naak

Quarter to . . .
Viertel vor . . .
feertel for

Ten to . . .
Zehn vor . . .
tsayn for

Twenty to . . .
Zwanzig vor . . .
tsvantsig for

Quarter past one
Viertel nach eins
feertel naak iyns

Half past three
Halb vier
halp feer

Half past seven
Halb acht
halp aakt

Five past nine
Fünf nach neun
fewnf naak noyn

Just after four o'clock
Kurz nach vier
koorts naak feer

Quarter to five
Viertel vor fünf
feertel for fewnf

Ten to eleven
Zehn vor elf
tsayn for elf

Noon/midday
Zwölf Uhr mittags/Mittag
zwerlf oor mittaags/mittaag

Midnight
Mitternacht
mitternaakt

In the morning (am)
Morgens
morgenz

In the afternoon (pm)
Nachmittags
naakmittaags

In the evening
Abends
aabents

A quarter of an hour
Eine Viertelstunde
iyne feertelshtoonde

Three quarters of an hour
Eine Dreiviertelstunde
iyne driyfeertelshtoonde

Half an hour
Eine halbe Stunde
iyne halbe shtoonde

24-hour clock

0045
null Uhr fünfundvierzig
nooll oor fewnfoontfeertsig

0900
neun Uhr
noyn oor

1300
dreizehn Uhr
driytsayn oor

1430
vierzehn Uhr dreißig
feertsayn oor driyssig

2149
einundzwanzig Uhr neunundvierzig
iynoonttsvantsig oor noynoontfeertsig

General phrases

What time is it?
Wieviel Uhr ist es?
veefeel oor ist es

It's . . .
Es ist . . .
es ist

It's one o'clock
Es ist ein Uhr
es ist iyn oor

It's six o'clock
Es ist sechs Uhr
es ist zeks oor

It's quarter past eight
Es ist viertel nach acht
es ist veertel naak aakt

What time . . .?
Um wieviel Uhr . . .?
oom veefeel oor

At . . .
Um . . .
oom

At half past one
Um halb zwei
oom halp tsviy

At quarter to seven
Um viertel vor sieben
oom feertel for zeeben

At 2155
Um einundzwanzig Uhr fünfundfünfzig
oom iynoonttsvantsig oor fewnfoontfewnftsig

At exactly/precisely two o'clock
Punkt um zwei Uhr
poonkt oom tsviy oor

Exactly two o'clock
Punkt zwei Uhr
poonkt tsviy oor

About half past six
Ungefähr halb sieben
oongefayr halp zeeben

Nearly quarter to five
Fast viertel vor fünf
fast feertel for fewnf

Soon
Bald
balt

Early
Früh
frew

Late
Spät
shpayt

On time
Pünktlich
pewnktlish

Earlier
Früher
frewer

Later
Später
shpayter

Half an hour ago
Vor einer halben Stunde
for iyner halben shtoonde

In ten minutes' time
In zehn Minuten
in tsayn minooten

In quarter of an hour
In einer Viertelstunde
in iyner feertelshtoonde

COUNTRIES AND NATIONALITIES

• It's usual in German to refer to someone's nationality by saying 'he is a Dane', **Er ist Däner**, or 'She is a Frenchwoman', **Sie ist Französin**, rather than saying 'he is Danish', 'she is French' etc.

• Languages, where appropriate, are the same as the adjective, but written with a capital letter.

Country	Nationality *masculine/feminine*	Adjective
Africa **Afrika**	**Afrikaner(in)**	**afrikanisch**
Asia **Asien**	**Asiat(in)**	**asiatisch**
Austria **Österreich**	**Österreicher(in)**	**österreichisch**
Australia **Australien**	**Australier(in)**	**aus Australien**
Belgium **Belgien**	**Belgier(in)**	**belgisch**
Bulgaria **Bulgarien**	**Bulgare/Bulgarin**	**bulgarisch**
Canada **Kanada**	**Kanadier(in)**	**kanadisch**
Central America **Mittelamerika**	**Mittelamerikaner(in)**	**aus Mittelamerika**
China **China**	**Chinese/Chinesin**	**chinesisch**
Cuba **Kuba**	**Kubaner(in)**	**kubanisch**
Czechoslovakia **die Tschechoslowakei**	**Tscheche/Tschechin**	**tschechisch**

Denmark		
Dänemark	**Däne/Dänin**	**dänisch**
Egypt		
Ägypten	**Ägypter(in)**	**ägyptisch**
Eire		
Eire	**Ire/Irin**	**irisch**
England		
England	**Engländer(in)**	**englisch**
Europe		
Europa	**Europäer**	**europäisch**
Finland		
Finnland	**Finne/Finnin**	**finnisch**
France		
Frankreich	**Franzose/Französin**	**französisch**
Germany		
Deutschland	**Deutscher/Deutsche**	**deutsch**
Great Britain		
Großbritannien	**Brite/Britin**	**britisch**
Greece		
Griechenland	**Grieche/Griechin**	**griechisch**
Hungary		
Ungarn	**Ungar(in)**	**ungarisch**
India		
Indien	**Inder(in)**	**indisch**
Ireland		
Irland	**Ire/Irin**	**irisch**
Israel		
Israel	**Israeli**	**israelisch**
Italy		
Italien	**Italiener(in)**	**italienisch**
Japan		
Japan	**Japaner(in)**	**japanisch**
Luxembourg		
Luxemburg	**Luxemburger(in)**	**aus Luxemburg**
Malta		
Malta	**Malteser(in)**	**aus Malta**

Mexico **Mexiko**	**Mexikaner(in)**	**mexikanisch**
Netherlands **Holland**	**Holländer(in)**	**holländisch**
New Zealand **Neuseeland**	**Neuseeländer(in)**	**neuseeländisch**
Northern Ireland **Nordirland**	**Ire/Irin**	**irisch**
Norway **Norwegen**	**Norweger(in)**	**norwegisch**
Poland **Polen**	**Pole/Polin**	**polnisch**
Portugal **Portugal**	**Portugiese/ Portugiesin**	**portugiesisch**
Rumania **Rumänien**	**Rumäne/Rumänin**	**rumänisch**
Russia **Rußland**	**Russe/Russin**	**russisch**
Scotland **Schottland**	**Schotte/Schottin**	**schottisch**
South America **Südamerika**	**Südamerikaner(in)**	**südamerikanisch**
Soviet Union **die Sowjetunion**	**Sowjetbürger(in)**	**sowjetisch**
Spain **Spanien**	**Spanier(in)**	**spanisch**
Sweden **Schweden**	**Schwede/Schwedin**	**schwedisch**
Switzerland **die Schweiz**	**Schweizer(in)**	**schweizerisch**
Turkey **die Türkei**	**Türke/Türkin**	**türkisch**
United Kingdom **Vereinigtes Königreich**		

United States		
die Vereinigten Staaten/Amerika/ USA	**Amerikaner(in)**	**amerikanisch**
Wales		
Wales	**Waliser(in)**	**walisisch**
West Indies		
Westindische Inseln	**Westinder(in)**	**westindisch**
Yugoslavia		
Jugoslawien	**Jugoslawe/ Jugoslawin**	**jugoslawisch**

GENERAL SIGNS AND NOTICES

Achtung	Caution
Aufzug	Lift
. . . Auf eigene Gefahr	At your own risk
Ausgang	Exit
Auskunft	Information
Ausverkauf	Sale
Außer Betrieb	Out of order
Baustelle	Building site
Belegt	Full, no vacancies
Besetzt	Engaged
Betreten verboten	No trespassing
Betriebsferien	Closed for holidays
Bitte klingeln	Please ring
Bitte klopfen	Please knock
Bitte nicht stören	Do not disturb
Damen	Ladies, Women
Drücken	Push
Eingang	Entrance
Eintreten ohne zu klopfen	Enter without knocking
Eintritt frei	Admission free
Entwerter	Ticket stamping machine
Erdgeschoß	Ground floor
Erste Hilfe	First Aid
Fahrstuhl	Lift
Feiertags geschlossen	Closed on public holidays
Feuermelder	Fire alarm
Frei	Free, vacant
Frisch gestrichen	Wet paint
Für Unbefugte verboten	Trespassers will be prosecuted
Gefahr	Danger
Geldeinwurf	Insert money

Geöffnet	Open
Geschlossen	Closed
Heiß	Hot
Herren	Men, Gentlemen
Kalt	Cold
Kasse	Cashier
Kein Durchgang für Fußgänger	No thoroughfare for pedestrians
Kein Trinkwasser	Not drinking water
Kein Zutritt	No entrance
Kundendienst	Customer service
Lebensgefahr	Danger of death
Mehrwertsteuer	VAT
Münzrückgabe	Coin return button
Nicht berühren	Do not touch
Notausgang	Emergency exit
Polizei	Police
Privatweg	Private road
Radweg	Cycle path
Rauchen verboten	No smoking
Reserviert	Reserved
Rolltreppe	Escalator
Ruhetag	Closed all day
Schlussverkauf	Sale
Sonderangebot	Special offer
Spätvorstellung	Late performance
Stehplätze	Standing room
Trinkwasser	Drinking water
Verboten	Forbidden, prohibited
Vorsicht	Caution
Vorsicht, bissiger Hund	Beware of the dog
Werktags geöffnet	Open on workdays
Ziehen	Pull
Zimmer frei	Rooms to let
Zu verkaufen	For sale
Zu vermieten	To let, for hire

CONVERSION TABLES (approximate equivalents)

Linear measurements

centimetres	**Zentimeter (cm)**
metres	**Meter (m)**
kilometres	**Kilometer (km)**

10 cm = 4 inches	1 inch = 2.45 cm
50 cm = 19.6 inches	1 foot = 30 cm
1 metre = 39.37 inches (just over 1 yard)	1 yard = 0.91 m
110 metres = 100 yards	
1 km = 0.62 miles	1 mile = 1.61 km

To convert
km to miles: divide by 8 and multiply by 5
miles to km: divide by 5 and multiply by 8

Miles		Kilometres
0.6	1	1.6
1.2	2	3.2
1.9	3	4.8
2.5	4	6.4
3	5	8
6	10	16
12	20	32
19	30	48
25	40	64
31	50	80
62	100	161
68	110	177
75	120	193
81	130	209

Liquid measures

litre	**Liter (l)**
1 litre = 1.8 pints	1 pint = 0.57 litre
5 litres = 1.1 gallons	1 gallon = 4.55 litres

'A litre of water's a pint and three quarters'

Gallons		Litres
0.2	1	4.5
0.4	2	9
0.7	3	13.6
0.9	4	18
1.1	5	23
2.2	10	45.5

Weights

gram	**Gramm (g)**
100 grams	**Hundert Gramm**
200 grams	**Zweihundert Gramm**
pound	**Pfund (pfd)**
kilo	**Kilo (kg)**
100 g = 3.5 oz	1 oz = 28 g
200 g = 7 oz	¼ lb = 113 g
½ kilo = 1.1 lb	½ lb = 225 g
1 kilo = 2.2 lb	1 lb = 450 g

Pounds		Kilos (Grams)
2.2	1	0.45 (450)
4.4	2	0.9 (900)
6.6	3	1.4 (1400)
8.8	4	1.8 (1800)
11	5	2.3 (2300)
22	10	4.5 (4500)

Area

hectare
1 hectare = 2.5 acres

Hektar
1 acre = 0.4 hectares

To convert
hectares to acres: divide by 2 and multiply by 5
acres to hectares: divide by 5 and multiply by 2

Hectares		Acres
0.4	1	2.5
2.0	5	12
4	10	25
10	50	124
40.5	100	247

Clothing and shoe sizes

Women's dresses and suits

UK	10	12	14	16	18	20
Continent	36	38	40	42	44	46

Men's suits and coats

UK	36	38	40	42	44	46
Continent	46	48	50	52	54	56

Men's shirts

UK	14	14½	15	15½	16	16½	17
Continent	36	37	38	39	41	42	43

Shoes

UK	2	3	4	5	6	7	8	9	10	11
Continent	35	36	37	38	39	41	42	43	44	45

Waist and chest measurements

inches	28	30	32	34	36	38	40	42	44	46	48	50
centimetres	71	76	80	87	91	97	102	107	112	117	122	127

Tyre pressures

lb/sq in	15	18	20	22	24	26	28	30	33	35
kg/sq cm	1.1	1.3	1.4	1.5	1.7	1.8	2.0	2.1	2.3	2.5

NATIONAL HOLIDAYS

G = Germany, S = Switzerland, A = Austria

Neujahrstag	New Year's Day	1 January *(GSA)* 2 January *(S)*
Dreikönigsfest	Epiphany	6 January *(A)*
Faschingsdienstag	Shrove Tuesday *(afternoon)*	*(GSA)*
Karfreitag	Good Friday	*(GS)*
Ostermontag	Easter Monday	*(GSA)*
Tag der Arbeit	Labour Day	1 May *(GA)*
Himmelfahrt	Ascension	*(GSA)*
Pfingstmontag	Whit Monday	*(GSA)*
Fronleichnam	Corpus Christi	*(A, and parts G)*
Siebzehnter Juni	Day of Unity	17 June *(G)*
Maria Himmelfahrt	Assumption	15 August *(A)*
Nationalfeiertag	National Day	26 October *(A)*
Allerheiligen	All Saints Day	1 November *(A, and parts G)*
Buß- und Bettag	Day of Prayer and Repentance	*(G)*
Die unbefleckte Empfängnis	Immaculate Conception	8 November *(A)*
Heiligabend	Christmas Eve	24 December *(Half day)* *(GSA)*
Erster Weihnachtstag	Christmas Day	25 December *(GSA)*
Zweiter Weihnachtstag	Boxing Day	26 December *(G)*
Stephanstag	St Stephen's Day	26 December *(SA)*

USEFUL ADDRESSES

Tourist offices in the UK

German National Tourist Office
Nightingale House
65 Curzon Street
London W1Y 7PE
Tel: 071-495 3990/91

Austrian National Tourist Office
30 St George Street
London W1R 0AL
Tel: 071-629 0461

Swiss National Tourist Office
Swiss Centre
New Coventry Street
London W1V 8EE
Tel: 071-734 1921

Embassies in UK

Embassy of the Federal Republic of Germany
23 Belgrave Square
Chesham Place
London SW1X 8PZ
Tel: 071-235 5033

Austrian Embassy
18 Belgrave Mews West
London SW1X 8HU
Tel: 071-235 3731

Embassy of Switzerland
16/18 Montagu Place
London W1H 2BQ
Tel: 071-723 0701

Embassies in Ireland

Embassy of the Federal Republic of Germany
31 Trimleston Avenue
Booterstown
Blackrock
County Dublin
Tel: Dublin 69 30 11

Austrian Embassy
15 Ailesbury Court
93 Ailesbury Road
Dublin 4
Tel: Dublin 69 45 77

Embassy of Switzerland
6 Ailesbury Road
Ballsbridge
Dublin 4
Tel: Dublin 69 25 15

Other organisations

Goethe Institute
(for information about cultural events and language courses)
50/51 Prince's Gate
Exhibition Road
London SW77 2PH
Tel: 071-581 3344/7

Goethe Institute
37 Merrion Square
Dublin 2
Tel: Dublin 76 64 51

German Chamber of Industry and Commerce
12–13 Suffolk Street
London SW1Y 4HG
Tel: 071-930 7251

DER Travel Service
(Deutsches Reisebüro GmbH)
18 Conduit Street
London W1
Tel: 071-408 0111

British embassies abroad

Germany
Friedrich-Ebert Allee 77
5300 Bonn 1
Tel: 23 40 61
There are also consulates in:
Berlin, Bremen, Düsseldorf, Frankfurt, Freiburg, Hamburg, Hanover, Kiel, Munich, Nuremberg and Stuttgart

Austria
Jauresgaße 12
1030 Wien
Tel: 713 15 75/9
There are also consulates in:
Bregenz, Graz, Innsbruck and Salzburg

Switzerland
Thunstraße 50
3005 Berne
Tel: 44 50 21/6
There are also consulates in:
Geneva, Lugano, Montreux and Zurich

Irish embassies abroad

Germany
Godesberger Allee 119
5300 Bonn 2
Tel: 37 69 37

Austria
Hilton Centre
1030 Wien
Tel: 75 42 46

Switzerland
Eigerstraße 71
3007 Berne
Tel: 46 23 53

NUMBERS

0	**null**	*nooll*
1	**eins**	*iyns*
2	**zwei**	*tsviy*
3	**drei**	*driy*
4	**vier**	*feer*
5	**fünf**	*fewnf*
6	**sechs**	*zeks*
7	**sieben**	*zeeben*
8	**acht**	*aakt*
9	**neun**	*noyn*
10	**zehn**	*tsayn*
11	**elf**	*elf*
12	**zwölf**	*zwerlf*
13	**dreizehn**	*driytsayn*
14	**vierzehn**	*feertsayn*
15	**fünfzehn**	*fewnftsayn*
16	**sechzehn**	*zektsayn*
17	**siebzehn**	*zeebtsayn*
18	**achtzehn**	*aakttsayn*
19	**neunzehn**	*noyntsayn*
20	**zwanzig**	*tsvantsig*
21	**einundzwanzig**	*iynoonttsvantsig*
22	**zweiundzwanzig**	*tsviyoonttsvantsig*
23	**dreiundzwanzig**	*driyoonttsvantsig*
24	**vierundzwanzig**	*feeroonttsvantsig*
25	**fünfundzwanzig**	*fewnfoonttsvantsig*
26	**sechsundzwanzig**	*zeksoonttsvantsig*
27	**siebenundzwanzig**	*zeebenoonttsvantsig*
28	**achtundzwanzig**	*aaktoonttsvantsig*
29	**neunundzwanzig**	*noynoonttsvantsig*
30	**dreißig**	*driyssig*
31	**einunddreißig**	*iynoontdriyssig*

32 etc.	**zweiunddreißig**	*tsviyoontdriyssig*
40	**vierzig**	*feertsig*
50	**fünfzig**	*fewnftsig*
60	**sechzig**	*zektsig*
70	**siebzig**	*zeebtsig*
80	**achtzig**	*aakttsig*
90	**neunzig**	*noyntsig*
100	**hundert**	*hoondert*
101	**hunderteins**	*hoondertiyns*
102 etc.	**hundertzwei**	*hoondertsviy*
150	**hundertfünfzig**	*hoondertfewnftsig*
200	**zweihundert**	*tsviyhoondert*
300	**dreihundert**	*driyhoondert*
400	**vierhundert**	*feerhoondert*
500	**fünfhundert**	*fewnfhoondert*
600	**sechshundert**	*zekshoondert*
700	**siebenhundert**	*zeebenhoondert*
800	**achthundert**	*aakthoondert*
900	**neunhundert**	*noynhoondert*
1000	**tausend**	*towzent*
1100 etc.	**tausendeinhundert**	*towzentiynhoondert*
2000 etc.	**zweitausend**	*tsviytowzent*
100000	**hunderttausend**	*hoonderttowzent*
1000000	**eine Million**	*iyne millyohn*
2000000 etc.	**zwei Millionen**	*tsviy millyohnen*

• One: use **ein** or **eine** with a noun to mean 'one' or 'a', e.g. **ein Bier** (one/a beer), **eine heiße Schokolade** (a/one hot chocolate).

• The word for a hundred, **hundert**, doesn't change in the plural – **zweihundert**, **dreihundert** etc. The same applies to **tausend**, a thousand.

• Years:

1990	**neunzehnhundertneunzig**
1815	**achtzehnhundertfünfzehn**

DICTIONARY

Words for food and drink are given in the Menu reader, page 113.

See also General signs and notices, page 201, and the lists of Signs you may see in the individual sections.

German nouns are given with the definite article ('the') to show their gender: **der** for masculine, **die** for feminine, **das** for neuter (**die** in the plural).

Adjective endings change according to the case, gender and number of the noun the adjective is describing. A full table of adjective endings is given in the Basic grammar section, page 178.

Other abbreviations: acc. – accusative case; dat. – dative case (see page 179); adj. – adjective.

German-English

A

abbiegen to turn off
der **Abend** evening
das **Abendbrot** supper
das **Abendessen** dinner (*evening meal*)
aber but
abfahren to depart (*bus, car*)
die **Abfahrt** departure (*bus, car*)
der **Abfahrtslauf** downhill skiing
der **Abfall** rubbish, litter
der **Abfertigungsschalter** check-in desk
abfliegen to depart (*plane*)
der **Abflug** departure (*plane*)
das **Abflußrohr** drain
das **Abführmittel** laxative
die **Abholung** collection (*post, rubbish*)
der **Absatz** heel (*shoe*)
abschicken to post, send off
abschleppen to tow
das **Abschleppseil** tow rope
der **Abschleppwagen** breakdown truck
abschließen to lock
das **Abteil** compartment
die **Abteilung** department
die **Agentur** agency
ähnlich similar
der **Alkohol** alcohol
alkoholfrei non-alcoholic
der **Alkoholiker** alcoholic (*person*)
alkoholisch alcoholic (*content*)

alle all
die **Allee** avenue
allein alone
alles everything
allgemein general
im allgemeinen in general
als as, when (*with past tense*); than
also so, well, therefore
alt old
altmodisch old fashioned
das **Amtzeichen** dialling tone
an at, on
andere other
die **anderen** the others
anders different(ly)
der **Anfang** beginning
anfangen to begin
der **Anfänger** beginner, learner
das **Angebot** offer
angebrannt burnt (*food*)
angeln to fish, go fishing
die **Angelrute** fishing rod
angenehm pleasant
der **Anhänger** fan (*supporter*); trailer (*car*)
ankommen to arrive
die **Anlegestelle** jetty, pier
anprobieren to try on
der **Anruf** call (*phone*)
anrufen to telephone
ansehen to look at
sich ansehen to look at each other
ansteckend infectious
das **Antibiotikum** antibiotic
die **Antiquität** antique
antiseptisch antiseptic
die **Antwort** answer
antworten to answer
die **Anzahlung** deposit

anziehen to put on
sich anziehen to dress, get dressed
der **Anzug** suit
anzünden to light (*fire*)
die **Arbeit** job, work
arbeiten to work
arbeitslos unemployed
arm poor
der **Arm** arm
die **Armbanduhr** watch
die **Art** kind (*sort of*)
der **Artikel** article
der **Arzt, die Ärztin** doctor
der **Assistent, die Assistentin** assistant
atmen to breathe
die **Atmosphäre** atmosphere
auch also
auf on, on top of, up
aufgeregt excited
auf jeden Fall in any case
auflegen to hang up (*telephone*)
aufstehen to stand up, get u
Auf Wiedersehen goodbye
Auf Wiederschauen goodby (*Austria*)
das **Auge** eye
der **Augenblick** moment
aus out, from, off (*light etc.*
die **Auseinandersetzung** argument
der **Ausflug** trip, excursion
ausgeben to spend (*money*)
ausgebucht full up (*booked up*)
ausgehen to go out
ausgezeichnet excellent
die **Auskunft** information

das **Ausland** abroad
im Ausland sein to be abroad
ins Ausland fahren to go abroad
der **Ausländer, die Ausländerin** foreigner
ausländisch foreign
auspacken to unpack
sich ausruhen to rest, relax
ausschalten to turn out, switch off
außer except
außerdem besides
die **Aussicht** view
aussprechen to pronounce
die **Ausstattung** equipment
aussteigen to get off (*bus*)
die **Ausstellung** exhibition
der **Ausverkauf** sale (*bargains*)
ausziehen to move out (*house*)
sich ausziehen to get undressed
das **Auto** car
mit dem Auto by car
die **Autobahn** motorway
automatisch automatic
die **Autovermietung** car hire

B

das **Baby** baby
die **Babynahrung** baby food
die **Babywischtücher** baby wipes
das **Bad** bath
ein Bad nehmen to have a bath
der **Badeanzug** bathing costume
die **Badehose** swimming trunks
der **Bademeister** attendant (*bathing*), lifeguard
baden to bathe
das **Badezimmer** bathroom
die **Bahn** track, way
der **Bahnhof** station
der **Bahnhofsvorsteher** stationmaster
der **Bahnsteig** platform
bald soon
so bald wie möglich as soon as possible
der **Ball** ball (*tennis, football etc.*)
das **Ballet** ballet
die **Banane** banana
der **Bankier** banker
das **Bargeld** cash
bar bezahlen to pay cash
die **Batterie** battery
der **Bauarbeiter** builder
bauen to build
der **Bauer** farmer
der **Bauernhof** farm
der **Baum** tree
die **Baumwolle** cotton
die **Baustelle** building site
der **Becher** mug
bedeuten to mean, signify
was bedeutet das? what does this mean?
bedienen to serve
begeistert enthusiastic
beginnen to begin
behalten to keep
die **Behandlung** treatment
behindert disabled, handicapped
die **Beilage** side dish, side salad
das **Bein** leg
das **Beispiel** example
zum Beispiel for example

bekannt famous
bekommen to get
beleidigt insulted
beliebt popular
benutzen to use
das **Benzin** petrol
bequem comfortable
der **Berg** mountain
bergauf up the hill
berichten to report
der **Beruf** career, profession
was sind Sie vom Beruf? what do you do?
das **Beruhigungsmittel** sedative
berühren to touch
beschäftigt busy
beschränkt limited
beschreiben to describe
besetzt taken, engaged, occupied
besichtigen to visit (*tourist sites*)
der **Besitzer, die Besitzerin** owner
besondere special, particular
besonders especially
besorgt worried
besser better
das **Beste** the best
bestehen to insist
bestellen to order
bestimmt definitely
besuchen to go round, visit
der **Besucher, die Besucherin** visitor
der **Betrag** amount (*money*)
betrunken drunk
das **Bett** bed, berth
die **Bettdecke** blanket
das **Bettuch** sheet
bevor before

bewegen to move
bezahlen to pay
beziehungsweise (bzw) respectively
die **Bibel** the Bible
die **Bibliothek** library
das **Bier vom Faß** draught beer
das **Bild** picture
der **Bildschirm** screen
billig cheap
bis until
ein bißchen a little
bitte please; not at all
blaß pale
blau blue
das **Blei** lead
bleiben to remain
das **Bleichmittel** bleach
bleifrei lead free
der **Bleistift** pencil
blind blind
der **Blitz** lightning
die **Blume** flower
das **Blut** blood
bluten to bleed
blutig rare (*steak*)
der **Boden** ground, floor
der **Bogen** arch
die **Bordkarte** boarding card
die **Börse** stock exchange
die **Botschaft** embassy
brauchen to need
die **Braut** bride
der **Bräutigam** bridegroom
brechen to break
breit broad, wide
brennen to burn
der **Brennstoff** fuel
der **Brief** letter
der **Brieffreund, die Brieffreund** penfriend
der **Briefkasten** letterbox

die Briefmarke stamp (*postage*)
das Briefpapier writing paper
die Brieftasche wallet
der Briefträger, die Briefträgerin postman, postwoman
der Briefumschlag envelope
die Brille glasses
bringen to bring
das Brot bread
das Brötchen bread roll
die Brücke bridge
der Bruder brother
der Brunnen fountain, well
das Buch book
buchen to book, reserve
die Bucht bay
das Bügeleisen iron (*for clothes*)
die Burg castle, fortress
das Büro office
die Bürste brush
der Bus bus
mit dem Bus by bus
der Busbahnhof bus station
der Busfahrer bus driver
das Butangas butane gas

C

der Chef head (*boss*)
die Chips potato crisps
der Cousin cousin (*male*)
die Creme lotion, cream

D

da there
das Dach roof
Damen Ladies (*toilets*)
die Damenbinden sanitary towels
der Dampf steam
der Dampfer steamer
dankbar grateful
danke thank you
dann then
das the, this, that, which (*neuter*)
das Datum date (*date*)
dauern to last, take time
der Daumen thumb
dein/e your (*adj.*) (*familiar*)
dein/e/r yours (*familiar*)
denken to think
das Denkmal monument
denn for, as
der the, who, which (*masculine*)
der-/die-/dasselbe the same
deshalb therefore, for that reason
das destillierte Wasser distilled water
das Detail detail
deutsch German
die deutsche Frage the German question
Deutschland (das) Germany
dich you (*familiar*)
dick thick, fat
die the, who, which (*feminine*)
der Dieb thief
dies this
diese these
dir (to) you
der Direktor, die Direktorin director
das Dokument document
der Dom cathedral
der Donner thunder
das Doppelbett double bed
doppelt double
das Dorf village
dort there

die Dose can, tin
die Dosenmilch tinned milk
der Dosenöffner can opener
der Dozent, die Dozentin lecturer
die Drahtseilbahn cable car
draußen outside
drehen to turn
dringend urgent
drinnen indoors
dritte/r/s third
die Droge drug
drucken to print
drücken to press, push
du you (*familiar*)
dumm stupid
dunkel dark
dünn thin
durch through; cooked, well done (*steak*)
der Durchfall diarrhoea
durchgehend direct (*train*)
durchkommen to get through
durstig thirsty
die Dusche shower

E

echt genuine, real
die Ecke corner
egal: es ist mir egal I don't mind
ehrlich honest
ehrlich gesagt frankly
das Ei, die Eier egg(s)
das gekochte Ei boiled egg
eigentlich in fact
in Eile sein hurry; to be in a hurry
der Eimer bucket
ein one, a
eindrucksvoll impressive
eine one, a (*feminine*)
einfach simple, plain
einige some
einkaufen gehen to go shopping
das Einkaufszentrum shopping centre
das Einkommen income
einladen to invite
die Einladung invitation
einmal once
auf einmal all of a sudden
eins one (*number*)
einsam lonely
einschalten to switch on
einschiffen to embark (*boat*)
einsteigen to enter, get on (*bus, train*)
der Eintritt admission
das Eintrittsgeld admission charge
die Eintrittskarte ticket (*theatre etc.*)
einzel single
das Einzelbett single bed
das Eis ice
das Eisen iron (*metal*)
die Eisenbahn railway
der Elektriker electrician
die Elektrizität electricity
der Empfang reception
empfehlen to recommend
das Ende end
die Endstation last stop, terminus
die Energie energy
eng narrow, tight
englisch English
der Enkel grandson

die Enkelin granddaughter
die Enkelkinder grandchildren
die Ente duck
entlang along
sich entschließen to decide
entschuldigen Sie mich excuse me
enttäuscht disappointed
entweder either
entweder . . . oder either . . . or
entwickeln to develop
die Entzündung inflammation
er he
das Erdbeben earthquake
die Erde earth
das Erdgeschoß ground floor
die Erdnuß peanut
die Erfahrung experience
der Erfolg success
sich erholen to recover
sich erinnern an to remember
erkennen to recognise
erklären to declare, explain
erlauben to let (*allow*)
die Ermäßigung reduction, discount
ernst serious
erreichen to reach
der Ersatzreifen spare tyre
erste/r/s first
die Erste Hilfe first aid
der/die Erwachsene adult
erwarten expect
erzählen to tell
es it
es sei denn unless
es tut mir leid I'm sorry
der Esel donkey
essen to eat
das Essen food, meal
der Essig vinegar
das Eßzimmer dining-room
das Etikett label
etwas something
etwas gern tun to like doing something
euch (to) you (*familiar*)
euer/e your (*adj.*) (*familiar*)
eure/r/s yours (*familiar*)
eventuell perhaps
das Examen examination
der Export export
expreß express

F

die Fabrik factory
die Fähre ferry
fahren to drive
der Fahrer driver
das Fahrgeld fare
die Fahrkarte ticket (*travel*)
der Fahrkartenschalter ticket office
der Fahrplan timetable (*travel*)
das Fahrrad bicycle
die Fahrt trip, journey, tour
das Fahrzeug vehicle
falls in case
falsch false, wrong
die Familie family
fantastisch fantastic
die Farbe colour
farbecht colour fast
fast nearly
faul lazy; rotten
das Federbett duvet
der Fehler fault, flaw, mistake
einen Fehler machen to make a mistake
fehlerhaft faulty

das Feld field
das Fenster window
die Ferien holidays (*school*)
das Ferienhaus holiday house
die Ferienwohnung holiday flat
Fern- long-distance
das Ferngespräch long-distance call
das Fernsehen television
fernsehen to watch television
die Ferse heel (*foot*)
fertig ready
das Fest festival, party
fest firm, solid
das Fett fat
fettarm low-fat
fettig greasy
feucht damp
das Feuer fire
das Feuerwerk firework
das Feuerzeug lighter (*cigarette*)
das Fieber fever, temperature
finden to find
der Finger finger
die Firma firm (*company*)
der Fisch fish
flach level (*flat*)
die Flasche bottle
der Flaschenöffner bottle opener
das Fleisch meat
die Fliege fly
fliegen to fly
fließend fluent (*languages*)
die Flitterwochen honeymoon
der Flohmarkt flea market
der Flügel wing
der Flug flight
die Fluggesellschaft airline
der Flughafen airport
das Flugzeug aeroplane, aircraft
der Fluß river
die Flüssigkeit liquid
folgen to follow
der Fön hairdrier
fönen to blow-dry (*hair*)
formell formal
nicht formell informal
fortgeschritten advanced
der Fortschritt progress
die Frage question
fragen to ask
Frau Mrs
die Frau woman
Fräulein Miss
frech cheeky
frei free (*available, unoccupied*)
die Freiheit freedom
der/die Fremde stranger
der Freund friend, boyfriend
die Freundin friend, girlfriend
der Frieden peace
der Friedhof cemetery
frieren to freeze
frisch fresh
der Frostschutz antifreeze
die Frucht fruit
früh early
früher earlier
der Frühling spring
das Frühstück breakfast
sich fühlen to feel
sich unwohl/wohl fühlen to feel ill/well
der Führerschein driving licence
die Führung guided tour
füllen to fill
funktionieren to work (*function*)
für for

furchtbar dreadful
der Fuß foot
zu Fuß on foot
der Fußball football
der Fußweg footpath
füttern to feed (*inc. baby*)

G

die Gabel fork
die Galerie gallery
der Gang corridor, gangway
ganz bestimmt yes, absolutely
die Garantie guarantee
der Garten garden
die Gartenbohnen kidney beans, haricot beans
die Gaskartusche gas refill
der Gast guest
der Gastgeber, die Gastgeberin host, hostess
das Gebäude building
geben to give
das Gebiet district, region
das Gebiß denture
die Gebühr charge, fee
der Geburtstag birthday
die Gefahr danger
gefährlich dangerous
das Gefängnis prison
gefroren frozen
der Gegenstand object (*thing*)
gegenüber opposite
das Geheimnis secret
gehen to go
das Gehirn brain
das Gehör hearing
gehören to belong (to)
der Gehsteig pavement
der Geistliche priest
gelähmt paralysed
gelb yellow
das Geld money
der Geldbeutel purse
das Gelee jelly
das Gemälde painting
gemeinsam common (*shared*)
genau exact(ly)
genießen to enjoy
genug enough
das Gepäck luggage
gerade straight, even (*not odd*)
der Geruch smell
das Geschäft shop, business
geschäftlich on business
der Geschäftsführer, die Geschäftsführerin managing director
die Geschäftsreise business trip
das Geschenk gift, present
die Geschichte history
geschieden divorced
das Geschirrtuch drying-up cloth
geschlossen closed
der Geschmack flavour, taste
geschnitten cut, sliced
die Geschwindigkeit speed
die Geschwindigkeitsbegrenzung speed limit
die Geschwister brothers and sisters
die Gesellschaft society, company (*business*)
das Gesicht face
die Gesichtscreme face cream
der Gesichtspuder face powder

gesperrt closed (*road*)
gestern yesterday
gestohlen stolen
gestreift striped
gesund fit (*healthy*)
die **Gesundheit** health
das **Getränk** drink
getrennt separated
die **Gewerkschaft** trade union
das **Gewicht** weight
gewöhnlich usual, common
das **Gewürz** spice
gibt es . . . ? is there . . . ?
gießen to pour
das **Gift** poison
giftig poisonous
der **Gipfel** summit, top
das **Glas** glass
glatt smooth
glauben to believe, think
gleich equal
der/die/das **Gleiche** the same
der **Gleisanschluß** junction (*rail*)
die **Glocke** bell
das **Glück** luck
Glück haben to be lucky
glücklich happy
die **Glühbirne** light bulb
gnädige Frau madam
der **Golfplatz** golf course
die **Golfschläger** golf clubs
Gott God
der **Gottesdienst** church service
grau grey
die **Grenze** frontier, border
der **Griff** handle
die **Grippe** flu
groß big, tall
die **Größe** size
die **Großeltern** grandparents
größer bigger
die **Großmutter** grandmother
der **Großvater** grandfather
großzügig generous
grün green
der **Grund** reason
die **Gruppe** group
gültig valid
der **Gummi** rubber
günstig convenient
die **Gurke** cucumber
der **Gürtel** belt
gut good, well
guten Abend good evening
gute Nacht good night
guten Morgen good morning
guten Tag good day

H

das **Haar, die Haare** hair
die **Haarschnellkur** conditioner
der **Haarschnitt** haircut
haben to have
er/sie hat he/she has
das **Hackfleisch** mince (*meat*)
der **Hafen** harbour
die Hafenrundfahrt harbour trip
der **Hahn** tap
halb half (*adj.*)
eine halbe Stunde half-hour, half an hour
die **Hälfte** half
die **Halspastillen** throat lozenge
halt! stop!
halten to hold, stop
die **Hand** hand
die **Handelsmesse** trade fair
handgearbeitet hand made
das **Handgepäck** hand luggage

der **Händler** dealer
der **Handschuh, die Handschuhe** glove, gloves
die **Handtasche** handbag
das **Handtuch** towel
hart hard
häßlich ugly
häufig frequent
haupt main
die **Hauptstadt** capital city
die **Hauptstraße** high (main) street
das **Haus** house
nach Hause gehen to go home
zu Hause at home
die **Hausarbeit** housework
die **Hausfrau** housewife
die **Haut** skin
das **Heftpflaster** sticking plaster
heilig holy
Heiligabend Christmas Eve
die **Heimat** home
Heimweh haben to be homesick
heiß hot
heißen to be called
ich heiße . . . my name is . . .
wie heißen Sie? what's your name?
was heißt das? what does this mean?
helfen to help
hell light (*coloured*)
das helle Bier lager
das **Hemd** shirt
herausnehmen to take out, remove
der **Herbst** autumn
der **Herd** stove, cooker
herein! come in!
hereinkommen to come in
Herr Mr
der **Herr** man, gentleman
herum around
das **Herz** heart
der Herzanfall heart attack
heute today
heute abend this evening, tonight
hier here
hier ist . . . here is . . .
die **Hilfe** help
Hilfe! help!
der **Himmel** sky, heaven
hinauslehnen to lean out
hineingehen to enter
sich hinlegen to lie down
hinstellen to put down
hinten at the back
hinter behind
hin und wieder occasionally
hin und zurück return (*ticket*)
hinunter down (*movement*)
die **Hitze** heat
hoch high
das **Hochwasser** high tide
die **Hochzeit** wedding
hoffen to hope
höflich polite
die **Höhle** cave
holen to fetch
das **Holz** wood
homeopatisch homeopathic
homosexuell homosexual
hören to hear
der **Hörer** receiver (*telephone*)
die **Hose** trousers
hübsch pretty
der **Hubschrauber** helicopter

der **Hügel** hill
der **Hund** dog
Hunger haben to be hungry
hungrig hungry
husten to cough
der **Hut** hat

I

ich I
die **Idee** idea
ihm (to) him
ihn him
ihnen (to) them
Ihnen (to) you (*polite*)
ihr (to) her
ihr/e her, their (*adj.*)
ihre/r/s hers, theirs
Ihr/e your (*adj.*) (*polite*)
Ihre/r/s yours (*polite*)
immer always
immer geradeaus straight on
immer wieder again and again
in in
inbegriffen included
die **Infektion** infection
der **Ingenieur, die Ingenieurin** engineer
innere inner
innerhalb within
das **Insekt** insect
das Insektenbekämpfungsmittel insect repellent
die **Insel** island
insgesamt altogether
das **Institut** college, institute
interessant interesting
irgendwie somehow
irgendwo somewhere

sich irren to make a mistak
Sie haben sich geirrt you've made a mistake

J

die **Jacke** jacket
das **Jahr** year
die **Jahreszeit** season
der **Jahrmarkt** fair
der **Jeansstoff** denim
jede/r/s each, every
jemand someone
jene those
jenseits beyond
jetzt now
das **Jod** iodine
jüdisch Jewish
die **Jugend** youth
die **Jugendherberge** youth host
jung young
der **Junge** boy
Jura law (*study subject*)

K

die **Kabine** cabin
der **Kaffee** coffee
kalt cold
der **Kamm** comb
kämpfen to fight
das **Kaninchen** rabbit
der **Kanister** petrol can
die **Kanne** jug
die **Kapelle** chapel
kaputt broken
Karfreitag (der) Good Fric
die **Karte** map
der **Käse** cheese
der **Kater** cat; hangover
die **Katze** cat

kaufen to buy
keine/r/s no, none
der **Keks** biscuit
der **Keller** cellar
der **Kellner** waiter
die **Kellnerin** waitress
kennen to know (*someone*)
die **Kernkraft** nuclear power
die **Kerze** candle
die **Kette** chain
der **Kiefer** jaw
das **Kind** child
die **Kinder** children
das **Kinderbett** cot
der **Kinderwagen** pram
das **Kino** cinema
die **Kirche** church
das **Kissen** cushion, pillow
klar clear
die **Klasse** class
das **Klavier** piano
klebrig sticky
das **Kleid** dress
die **Kleider** clothes
klein little
der **Kleinbus** minibus
das **Kleingeld** change
klemmt: es klemmt it's stuck
der **Klempner** plumber
das **Klima** climate
die **Klimaanlage** air conditioning
klopfen to knock
das **Kloster** monastery
klug clever
das **Knäckebrot** crispbread
der **Kochtopf** saucepan
der **koffeinfreie Kaffee** decaffeinated coffee
der **Koffer** suitcase
die **Kohlensäure** carbon dioxide
mit Kohlensäure fizzy
ohne Kohlensäure still
komisch funny (*peculiar*)
kommen to come
kommerziell commercial
kompliziert complicated
die **Konferenz** conference
die **Konfitüre** jam
der **König** king
die **Königin** queen
können to be able (*see grammar, p. 186–7*)
könnte could (*see grammar, p.* 186–7)
das **Konto** bank account
die **Kontaktlinsen** contact lenses
der **Kontrolleur, die Kontrolleurin** inspector
das **Konzert** concert, concerto
der **Kopf** head
die Kopfschmerzen headache
der **Kopfsalat** lettuce
der **Korb** basket
der **Korken** cork
der **Korkenzieher** corkscrew
der **Körper** body
kosten to cost
was kostet das? how much does it cost?
was kosten sie? how much do they cost?
das **Kostüm** suit (*lady's*)
das **Kraftfahrzeugkennzeichen** registration number
krank ill
das **Krankenhaus** hospital
der **Krankenpfleger, die Krankenschwester** nurse
der **Krankenwagen** ambulance
die **Krankheit** illness
das **Kraut** herb
der **Krebs** cancer
der **Kreis** circle

der Kreisverkehr roundabout
das Kreuz cross
die Kreuzfahrt cruise
der Krieg war
der Kuchen cake
die Kuh cow
die Küche kitchen
kühl cool
der Kühlschrank fridge
die Kunst art
die schönen Künste the fine arts
der Künstler artist
künstlich artificial
die Kurve curve, bend
der Kurs course
die Kusine cousin (*female*)
die Küste coast
der Kuß kiss

L

lachen to laugh
lächeln to smile
der Laden shop
die Lampe lamp
das Land country, land
die Landschaft countryside, scenery
lang long (*inc. hair*)
der Langlauf cross-country skiing
langsam slow(ly)
langweilig boring
der Lärm noise
lassen to leave
laut loud, noisy
die Lawine avalanche
leben to live
das Leben life
die Lebensmittelvergiftung food poisoning
lecker delicious
das Leder leather
ledig single (*unmarried*)
leer empty
legal legal
der Lehrer, die Lehrerin instructor, teacher
leicht easy, light (*weight*)
leider unfortunately
die Leiter ladder
lernen to learn
lesen to read
letzte/r/s last
die Leukämie leukaemia
die Leute people
das Licht light
lieben to love
Lieblings- favourite
das Lied song
die Lieferung delivery
der Lieferwagen delivery van
der Liegestuhl deckchair
der Liegewagen couchette
die Linie line
links left
die Linse lens (*camera*)
die Lippe lip
die Liste list
der Liter litre
die Lizenz licence (*fishing etc.*)
der LKW (Lastkraftwagen) lor
der Löffel spoon
der Lohn wage
lohnen: es lohnt sich nicht i not worth it
los:was ist los? what's the matter?
der Löwe lion
die Lotion lotion

die Lungenentzündung pneumonia
lustig funny (*amusing*)

M

machen to do, make
es macht nichts it doesn't matter
macht das Ihnen etwas aus, wenn . . . ? do you mind if . . . ?
das Mädchen girl
der Magen stomach
die Magenschmerzen stomach ache
die Magenverstimmung indigestion
die Magermilch skimmed milk
der Maler, die Malerin painter
man one (*pronoun*)
manchmal sometimes
der Mann man, husband
männlich male, masculine
der Mantel coat
die Marine navy
der Markt market
die Maschine machine
die Masern measles
die Maske mask (*diving*)
das Maß measurement
der Matrose sailor
die Mauer wall
das Medikament medicine (*drug*)
medizinisch medical
das Meer sea
das Mehl flour
mehr more
nicht mehr no more
mehrere several
der Mehrfachstecker adaptor (*electrical*)
die Mehrwertsteuer VAT
mein/e my (*adj.*)
mein/e/s mine (*of me*)
die Meinung opinion
meiner Meinung nach in my opinion
die meisten (von) most (of)
der Mensch human being
merkwürdig odd
die Messe mass (*church*); trade fair
messen to measure
das Messer knife
das Metall metal
mich me
mieten to hire, rent
die Milch milk
mild mild
mindestens at least
der Minister minister
der Ministerpräsident, die Ministerpräsidentin prime minister
die Minute minute (*time*)
mir (to) me
mit with
das Mitglied member
der Mittag midday
das Mittagessen lunch
die Mitte middle
mittel: das kontrazeptive Mittel contraceptive
mittelalterlich medieval
das Mittelmeer mediterranean
die Mitternacht midnight
die Mode fashion
möchte (he, she) would like (*see grammar, p. 186–7*)
mögen to like

möglich possible
möglicherweise possibly
die **Möglichkeiten** facilities
der **Monat** month
monatlich monthly
der **Mond** moon
morgen tomorrow
morgen früh tomorrow morning
der **Morgen** morning
der **Motor** engine
das **Motorboot** motorboat
das **Motorrad** motorbike
der **Mülleimer** dustbin
müde tired
der **Mund** mouth
die **Münze** coin
das **Museum** museum
die **Musik** music
der **Musiker, die Musikerin** musician
Sie müssen . . . must; you must . . .
das **Muster** pattern, sample
mutig brave
die **Mutter** mother

N

nach to, towards, after
der **Nachbar, die Nachbarin** neighbour
nachfüllen to refill
der **Nachmittag** afternoon
der **Nachname** surname
die **Nachrichten** news
nächste/r/s next
die **Nacht** night
das **Nachthemd** nightdress
der **Nachtklub** nightclub
die **Nadel** needle
der **Nagel** nail
nah near
nähe: in der Nähe nearby
der **Name** name
die **Nase** nose
die Nase voll haben to be fed up
das **Nasenbluten** nosebleed
naß wet
die **Nässe** wet(ness)
national national
die **Nationalität** nationality
natürlich natural(ly)
der **Naturschutz** conservation
der **Nebel** fog
nebelig foggy
neben next to
der **Neffe** nephew
das **Negativ** negative
nehmen to take, catch (*train etc.*)
ich nehm' es wohl an I suppose so
nein no
nervös nervous
nett kind (*generous*), nice
das **Netz** net
die **Netzkarte** all zone travel card
neu new
der Neujahrstag New Year's Day
nicht not
die **Nichte** niece
nichts nothing
nie never
niedrig low
das **Niedrigwasser** low tide
niemand nobody
die **Niere** kidney
niesen to sneeze
nirgendwo nowhere

das **Niveau** level
noch still, yet
der **Norden** north
der **Notfall** emergency
nötig necessary
die **Notrufsäule** emergency telephone (*on motorway*)
nüchtern sober
die **Nummer** number
nur just, only
die **Nuß** nut
nützlich useful
nutzlos useless

O

ob whether, if
oben on top of, above, upstairs
der **Ober** waiter
das **Obst** fruit
obwohl although
offensichtlich obviously
öffentlich public (*adj.*)
die **Öffentlichkeit** public
öffnen to open
oft often
ohne without
das **Ohr** ear
der **Ohrring** earring
das **Öl** oil
die **Oma** granny
der **Onkel** uncle
der **Opa** grandpa
die **Oper** opera
ordentlich tidy
Ordnung: in Ordnung all right, OK, fine
der **Ort** place
örtlich local
der **Osten** east

P

das **Paar** pair, couple
ein **paar** (a) few
das **Paket** packet, parcel
das **Papier** paper
die **Papiertaschentücher** tissues
der **Paprika** pepper (*vegetable*)
der **Papst** pope
die **Parkscheibe** parking disc
die **Partei** party (*political*)
der **Paß** passport
passen to fit
das paßt dir gut it fits you well, it suits you
passieren to happen
die **Pastille** lozenge
die **Pauschalreise** package tour
die **Pause** interval (*theatre etc.*)
peinlich embarrassing
pensioniert retired
persönlich personal(ly)
der **Pfeffer** pepper (*spice*)
die **Pfeife** pipe
das **Pferd** horse
die **Pflanze** plant
das **Pflaster** (sticking) plaster
der **Photoapparat** camera
der **Pier** jetty
die **Plastiktüte** plastic bag
die **Platte** puncture
der **Plattenspieler** record-player
der **Platz** place, seat (*in theatre etc.*), space, square (*in town*)
die **Plombe** filling (*dental*)
plötzlich suddenly
die **Polizei** police
die **Polizeiwache** police station
die **Pommes frites** chips
die **Post** mail
die **Postkarte** post card
die **Postleitzahl** post code

prima! great!
pro per
der **Produzent, die Produzentin** producer (*radio, television*)
der **Prospekt** brochure, leaflet
Prost! cheers!
provisorisch temporarily
prüfen to check
das **Pulver** powder
purpur purple
die **Putzfrau** cleaning lady

Q

die **Qualität** quality
die **Qualle** jellyfish
die **Quittung** receipt

R

der **Rabbiner** rabbi
das **Rad** wheel
das **Radfahren** cycling
der **Rasierer** razor
das **Rathaus** town hall
rauchen to smoke
rauh rough
der **Raum** room, space
die **Rechnung** bill
rechts right
der **Rechtsanwalt, die Rechtsanwältin** lawyer
die **Reformkost** health foods
die **Regelschmerzen** period pains
der **Regen** rain
es regnet it's raining
der **Regenschirm** umbrella
die **Regierung** government
reich rich
reif mature
rein clean, pure
die **Reise** journey
das **Reisebüro** travel agent
der **Reiseführer** guidebook
reisekrank travel sick
das **Reiseziel** destination
reiten to ride
rennen to run
der **Rentner, die Rentnerin** pensioner
reparieren fix (*mend*)
retten to save, rescue
das **Rettungsboot** lifeboat
der **Rettungsgürtel** lifebelt
das **Rezept** recipe, prescription
der **Richter** judge
richtig right, correct
die **Richtung** direction
riechen to smell
der **Rock** skirt
roh raw
das **Rohr** pipe
der **Rollstuhl** wheel chair
die **Rolltreppe** escalator
rosa pink
rot red
die **Röteln** German measles
der **Rowdy** yob
die **Rückerstattung** refund
die **Rückseite** the back (*reverse side*)
rückwärts backwards
rufen to call
ruhig calm, quiet
rund round
die **Rundfunkstation** radio station
rutschig slippery

S

die Sache thing
die Sahne cream
das Salz salt
sammeln to collect
sauber clean
saubermachen to clean
sauer acid, sour
der Sauerregen acid rain
das Schaf sheep
schaffen to manage (*cope*)
die Schallplatte record (*disc*)
der Schalter counter (*post office, ticket office etc.*)
die Schaltiere shellfish
scharf sharp, hot (*spicy*)
der Schatten shade, shadow
das Schaufenster shop window
der Scheck cheque
die Scheibe slice, disc (*parking*)
der Schein note (*bank*)
scheinen to seem, appear
die Schere scissors
scheußlich horrible
schicken to send
das Schiff ship, boat
das Schild sign
der Schinken ham
schlafen to sleep
der Schlafsack sleeping bag
das Schlafzimmer bedroom
schlagen to hit
die Schlange queue, snake
schlecht bad
schließen to close, shut
das Schließfach locker
schlimm bad, serious
schlimmer worse
das Schlimmste the worst
der Schlips tie
der Schlitten toboggan
die Schlittschuhbahn ice rink
die Schlittschuhe skates (*ice*)
das Schloß castle, palace; lock
der Schlüssel key
der Schlüsselring key ring
der Schluß finish
schmecken to taste
schmeckt es Ihnen? does it taste all right?
der Schmerz pain
schmerzhaft painful
das Schmerzmittel pain killer
der Schminkstoff make-up
schmutzig dirty
der Schnee snow
schneiden to cut
schneien to snow
schnell fast
der Schnurrbart moustache
die Schokolade chocolate
schon already
schön pretty, nice, fine (*weather*)
der Schrank cupboard
schrecklich awful, dreadful
schreiben to write
die Schreibmaschine typewriter
der Schriftsteller writer
der Schritt (foot)step
die Schublade drawer
die Schuld debt
schuldig guilty
die Schule school
die Schüssel bowl, dish
der Schuster shoe mender
der Schutz shelter, protection
die Schutzbrille goggles
der Schwager brother-in-law
die Schwägerin sister-in-law
der Schwamm sponge
schwanger pregnant

schwarz black
schwarzweiß black and white
schwarzfahren to travel without a ticket
das **Schwein** pig
schwer difficult, hard, heavy
schwerhörig deaf
die **Schwester** sister
die **Schwiegermutter** mother-in-law
der **Schwiegersohn** son-in-law
die **Schwiegertochter** daughter-in-law
der **Schwiegervater** father-in-law
das **Schwimmbad** swimming bath
das **Schwimmbecken** swimming pool
schwimmen to swim
die **Schwimmflossen** flippers
die **Schwimmweste** lifejacket
schwindelig dizzy
schwitzen to sweat
der **See** lake
die **See** sea
seekrank seasick
segeln to sail
sehen to see
die **Sehenswürdigkeit** tourist site
sehr very
die **Seife** soap
das **Seil** rope
sein to be (*see grammar, p. 184*)
sein/e his (*adj. and pronoun*)
seit since
die **Seite** side, page
der **Sekt** German equivalent of Champagne
die **Selbstbedienung** self-service
Selbstversorger: für Selbstversorger self catering
selten seldom, rare
seltsam strange
die **Semmel** bread roll (*Austria*)
der **Senf** mustard
sicher certain, sure, positive, safe
der **Sicherheitsgurt** seat belt
sicherlich certainly
die **Sicherung** fuse
der **Sicherungskasten** fusebox
sie she, her, they, them (*pronoun*)
Sie you (*polite*)
das **Silvester** New Year's Eve
sind are (*see grammar, p.184*)
der **Sitz** seat
Ski laufen to ski
die **Skischuhe** ski boots
der **Slip** knickers
sofort immediately
sogar even (*including*)
der **Sohn** son
solche/r/s such
der **Sommer** summer
die **Sonne** sun
der **Sonnenbrand** sunburn
die **Sonnenbrille** sunglasses
der **Sonnenschirm** sunshade
der **Sonnenstich** sunstroke
sonst otherwise
sowieso anyway
der **Sozialarbeiter, die Sozialarbeiterin** social worker
sparen to save (*money*)
Spaß machen to be fun
das hat Spaß gemacht that was fun
spät late

später later
der **Spaziergang** walk
die **Speisekarte** menu (*à la carte*)
der **Speisewagen** dining car
sperren to block
der **Spiegel** mirror
das **Spiel** game
das **Spielen** gambling
spielen to play
das **Spielzeug** toy
der **Sportwagen** push-chair
die **Sprache** language
der **Sprachführer** phrase book
sprechen to speak
springen to jump
das **Spülbecken** sink
der **Staat** state
das **Stadion** stadium
die **Stadt** town, city
der **Stadtplan** town plan
das **Stadtzentrum** town centre
die **Starthilfekabel** jump leads
statt instead of
der **Staub** dust
stechen to sting (*insect*)
die **Stechmücke** mosquito
die **Steckdose** socket
der **Stecker** plug (*electrical*)
stehen to stand
steil steep
der **Stein** stone
sterben to die
der **Stern** star
die **Steuer** tax, duty
Stief- step-
die Stiefmutter stepmother
die **Stiefel** boots
der **Stift** pen
der **Stil** style
still quiet, silent
die **Stimme** voice
stimmen: das stimmt that's true
der **Stock** stick
das **Stockwerk** floor, storey
im ersten Stock on the first floor
der **Stoff** fabric, material
die **Stoßzeit** rush hour
der **Strand** beach
die **Straße** street
die Straße hoch up the road
die **Straßenbahn** tram
die **Straßenbauarbeiten** roadworks
der **Streifen** stripe
streuen to scatter
der **Strom** current (*electricity*)
der **Stromanschluß** electricity (*wiring etc.*)
die **Stromsperre** power cut
die **Strümpfe** stockings
das **Stück** piece, bit
das **Stückchen** little bit
der **Stuhl** chair
die **Stunde** hour
eine halbe Stunde half-hour
suchen to look for
das **Surfbrett** surfboard
süß sweet
die **Süßigkeiten** sweets
synchronisiert dubbed
die **Szene** scene

T

der **Tabak** tobacco
der **Tag** day
die **Tage** days, period
täglich daily

das Tal valley
tanken to fill up with petrol
die Tankstelle garage (*for petrol*)
die Tante aunt
der Tanz dance
die Tasche bag, pocket
das Taschenmesser penknife
das Taschentuch handkerchief
die Tasse cup
die Tatsache fact
tatsächlich really, actually, indeed
tauchen to dive
der Tee tea
der Teebeutel tea bag
der Teelöffel teaspoon
der Teil part, piece
zum Teil partly
teilweise partly
die Telefonkarte telephone card
die Telefonzelle telephone box
der Teller plate
der Teppich carpet
der Termin date, appointment
teuer dear (*expensive*)
das Theater theatre
das Theaterstück play (*theatre*)
tief deep
das Tier animal
der Tierarzt, die Tierärztin vet
der Tiergarten zoo
tippen to type
der Tisch table
die Tochter daughter
toll lovely, wonderful
das Tonbandgerät tape recorder
der Topf pot
das Tor gate; goal (*football*)
tot dead
tragbar portable
tragen to carry
das Tragflächenboot hydrofoil
trampen to hitchhike
traurig sad
die Treppe stairs
trinken to drink
das Trinkgeld tip
trocken dry
tropfen to drip
Tschüß goodbye (*casual*)
das Tuch cloth
tun to do, make
die Tür door
der Turm tower
die Turnschuhe plimsolls, trainers
die Tüte bag

U

über over, above, via
überall everywhere
die Überfahrt crossing (*sea*)
überfallen to attack, mug
das Übergewicht excess luggage
überholen to overtake
übermorgen day after tomorrow
überrascht surprised
übersetzen to translate
das Überzelt fly sheet
die Übung exercise
die Uhr clock, time
wieviel Uhr ist es? what time is it?
die Umleitung diversion
umsonst free
umsteigen to change (*trains*)
die Umwelt environment
umweltfreundlich environmentally friendly

umziehen to change (*clothes*); to move house
unabhängig independent
unangenehm unpleasant
unbeleuchtet unlit
unbequem uncomfortable
und and
der **Unfall** accident
ungeduldig impatient
ungefähr roughly, about
ungerade odd (*number*)
ungewöhnlich unusual
unglücklich unhappy, unlucky
unhöflich rude
unmöglich impossible
uns us, to us
unschuldig innocent
unser our
unsere/r/s ours
unten downstairs, below
unter under, underneath
die **Unterführung** underpass
das **Untergeschoß** basement
die **Unterhaltung** entertainment
das **Unterhemd** vest
die **Unterhose** underpants
die **Unterkunft** accommodation
der **Unterricht** lesson (*instruction*)
unterrichten to teach, instruct
unterschreiben to sign
die **Unterschrift** signature
die **Untertasse** saucer
die **Untertitel** subtitles
die **Unterwäsche** underclothes
unvorsichtig careless
unwohl unwell
der **Urlaub** holiday (*period of time*)
im Urlaub on holiday
ursprünglich original(ly)

V

der **Vater**
verantwortlich responsible
verärgert annoyed
der **Verbandskasten** first aid kit
die **Verbindung** connection (*travel*)
verboten forbidden, prohibited
verderben to spoil, ruin
verdienen to earn
vereinbaren to agree
die **Vergangenheit** past
vergessen to forget
vergewaltigen to rape
vergleichen to compare
der **Vergnügungspark** amusement park
verhaftet: Sie sind verhaftet you're under arrest
sich verheiraten to get married
verheiratet married
verkaufen to sell
der **Verkäufer, die Verkäuferin** shop assistant
der **Verkehr** traffic
die **Verkehrsampel** traffic light
der **Verkehrsstau** traffic jam
verleihen to lend
verletzen to injure
verletzt injured
verlieren to lose
verlobt engaged (*to be married*)
der/die Verlobte fiancé(e)
vermeiden to avoid
vermieten to let (*rent*)
vermissen to miss (*nostalgia*)
vernünftig sensible, reasonable

verpacken to wrap (up)
verpassen to miss (*bus etc.*)
verrenkt twisted
verrückt mad, crazy
verschieden different
die **Verschmutzung** pollution
versichert insured
die **Versicherung** insurance
die **Versicherungskarte** insurance document
die **Verspätung** delay
versprechen to promise
verstauchen to sprain
verstehen to understand
verstopft blocked
die **Verstopfung** constipation
der/die **Verwandte** relation
das **Verzeichnis** directory (*index*)
viel (von) a lot (of), much
nicht viel not much
viele many
nicht viele not many
vielen Dank thank you very much
vielleicht perhaps
ein Viertel quarter
vierzehn Tage fortnight
das **Visum** visa
der **Vogel** bird
das **Volk** people, nation
voll full
das **Vollkornbrot** wholemeal bread
von from, by
vor before, in front of
vor allem above all, especially
vorbereiten to prepare
vorgestern day before yesterday
der **Vorname** first name
vorne in front (of)
der **Vorort** suburb
die **Vorsicht** caution
vorsichtig careful
vorstellen to introduce
sich vorstellen to imagine
die **Vorstellung** performance
die **Vorverkaufsstelle** booking office (*theatre*)
die **Vorwahl** dialling code
vorwärts forward
vorziehen to prefer

W

der **Wagen** carriage (*on train*)
die **Wahl** election
wählen to choose, vote; d (*telephone*)
wahr true
während during, while
wahrscheinlich probably, likely
der **Wald** forest
die **Wand** wall (*inside*)
wann? when?
das **Warenhaus** department s
warten (auf) to wait (for)
der **Warteraum** waiting roon
waschbar washable
das **Waschbecken** sink, wash basin
die **Wäsche** laundry
waschen to wash
das **Wasser** water
wasserdicht waterproof
wechseln to change, exchange (*money*)
der **Wecker** alarm clock
weder . . . noch . . . neith . . . nor . . .

weg away
der **Weg** path
wegen because of
weggehen to go away
wegnehmen to take away
wegwerfbar disposable
weh tun to hurt
es tut mir weh it hurts
weiblich female, feminine
weich soft
Weihnachten (das) Christmas
der Weihnachtsabend Christmas Eve
der erste Weihnachtstag Christmas Day
weil because
der **Weinberg** vineyard
weinen to cry
die **Weintraube** grape
weiß white
weit far (*away*)
wie weit . . . ? how far . . . ?
ist es weit? is it far?
weiter further
welche/r/s which
die **Welle** wave
die **Welt** world
der erste/zweite Weltkrieg the First/Second World War
weniger less
wenigstens at least
wenn if, when, whenever
wer? who?
werfen to throw
der **Werktag** weekday
die **Wertsachen** valuables
wertvoll valuable
wesentlich essential
das **Wetter** weather
die **Wettervorhersage** weather forecast
wichtig important, serious
wie like, as, how
wie bitte? pardon?
wie immer as usual
wie ist . . . ? what is . . . like?
wie lange? how long?
wie sind . . . ? what are . . . like?
wieviel? how much?
wie viele? how many?
wie weit? how far?
wieder again
wiederholen to repeat
wiederkommen to return
der **Winter** winter
wir we
wirklich really
der **Wirt, die Wirtin** landlord, landlady
die **Wirtschaft** economy
das Wirtschaftswunder the economic miracle
wissen to know (*something*)
die **Wissenschaft** science
die **Witwe** widow
der **Witwer** widower
der **Witz** joke
wo where
die **Woche** week
wochentlich weekly
wohnen to live (*dwell*)
die **Wohnung** flat (*apartment*)
der **Wohnwagen** caravan
das **Wohnzimmer** living-room, lounge
die **Wolke** cloud
die **Wolle** wool
wollen to want (to)

das **Wort** word
das **Wörterbuch** dictionary
wünschen to wish
würzig spicy

Z

zäh tough (*meat*)
zählen to count
der **Zähler** meter
der **Zahn** tooth
der **Zahnarzt, die Zahnärztin** dentist
die **Zahnbürste** toothbrush
die **Zahnpasta** toothpaste
die **Zahnschmerzen** toothache
der **Zahnstocher** toothpick
zart tender
das **Zeichen** signal
zeichnen to draw
die **Zeichnung** drawing
zeigen to show
die **Zeit** time
die **Zeitkarte** season ticket
die **Zeitschrift** magazine
die **Zeitung** newspaper
das **Zelt** tent
der **Zeltboden** groundsheet
zelten to camp
die **Zeltschnur** guy rope
zentral central
die **Zentralheizung** central heating
das **Zentrum** centre
ziehen to pull
das **Ziel** goal
ziemlich fairly
die **Zigarette** cigarette
der **Zirkus** circus
die **Zitrone** lemon
zu to, too
der **Zucker** sugar
der **Zug** train
mit dem Zug by train
zum Beispiel for example
zum Wohl! cheers!
die **Zunge** tongue
zurück back
zurückerstatten to refund
zurückgeben to give back
zurücklegen to put by
zusätzlich extra
der **Zuschlag** supplement
die **Zweigstelle** branch (*of ban*
etc.)
zweimal twice
zweite/r/s second
die **Zwillinge** twins
zwischen between

There is a list of car and bicycle parts on page 43, and parts of the body on page 168. See also the menu reader on page 113, numbers on page 211 and pages 189–202.

A

a, an **ein, eine**
abbey **die Klosterkirche**
about (*relating to*) **über + acc.** (*see grammar, p. 182*)
(*approximately*) **ungefähr**
above **über + acc./dat.** (*see grammar, p. 182*)
abroad **im Ausland**
abscess **der Abszeß**
accept (*take*) **nehmen**
accident **der Unfall**
accommodation **die Unterkunft**
account (*bank*) **das Konto**
accountant **der Buchhalter**
ache **der Schmerz**
acid (*adj.*) **sauer**
across **über + acc.**
(*opposite*) **gegenüber + dat.** (*see grammar, p. 182*)
acrylic (*noun/adj.*) **das Akryl, aus Akryl**
act **spielen**
actor **der Schauspieler**
actress **die Schauspielerin**
adaptor (*electrical*) **der Mehrfachstecker**
add **hinzufügen**
addicted **süchtig**
address **die Adresse**
adhesive tape **der Klebstreifen**
admission **der Eintritt**
admission charge **das Eintrittsgeld**
adopted **adoptiert**
adult **der/die Erwachsene**
advance: in advance **im voraus**
advanced (*level*) **fortgeschritten**
advertisement, advertising **die Werbung**
aerial **die Antenne**
aeroplane **das Flugzeug**
afford: I can't afford it **das kann ich mir nicht leisten**
afraid: I'm afraid **Ich habe Angst**
after **nach + dat.** (*see grammar, p. 182*)
afterwards **nachher**
afternoon **der Nachmittag**
aftershave **das After-Shave**
again **wieder**
against **gegen + acc.** (*see grammar, p. 182*)
age **das Alter**
agency **die Agentur**
ago **vor + dat.** (*see grammar, p. 182*)
to agree **vereinbaren**
AIDS **AIDS**
air **die Luft**
by air **per Flugzeug**
(by) air mail **per Luftpost**

air conditioning **die Klimaanlage**
air force **die Luftwaffe**
airline **die Fluggesellschaft**
airport **der Flughafen**
aisle **der Gang**
alarm **der Alarm**
alarm clock **der Wecker**
alcohol **der Alkohol**
alcoholic (*content*) **alkoholisch**
(*person*) **der Alkoholiker**
alive **lebendig**
all **alle**
allergic to **allergisch gegen + acc.** (*see grammar, p.182*)
alley **die Gasse**
to allow **erlauben**
allowed **erlaubt**
all right (*OK*) **in Ordnung**
almond **die Mandel**
alone **allein**
along **entlang + acc.** (*see grammar, p.182*)
already **schon**
also **auch**
although **obwohl**
always **immer**
am (*see 'to be'*) **bin**
ambassador **der Botschafter**
ambition **die Ambition**
ambitious **ehrgeizig**
ambulance **der Krankenwagen, die Ambulanz**
among **unter + acc./dat.** (*see grammar, p. 182*)
amount (*money*) **der Betrag**
amusement park **der Vergnügungspark**
anaesthetic (*local*) **die örtliche Betäubung**
(*general*) **die volle Narkose**

and **und**
angry **zornig**
animal **das Tier**
anniversary **der Jahrestag**
annoyed **verärgert**
anorak **der Anorak**
another (one) **noch ein/eine**
answer **die Antwort**
to answer **antworten**
antibiotic **das Antibiotikum**
antifreeze **der Frostschutz**
antique **die Antiquität**
antiseptic **antiseptisch**
anxious **ängstlich**
any **irgendein(e)**
anyone **jemand**
anything **(irgend)etwas**
anything else **noch etwas**
anyway **auf jeden Fall**
anywhere **irgendwo**
apart (from) **außer + dat.** (*see grammar, p. 182*)
apartment **das Appartement**
appendicitis **die Blinddarmentzündung**
apple **der Apfel**
appointment **der Termin**
approximate(ly) **ungefähr**
apricot **die Aprikose /die Marille** (*Austria*)
arch **der Bogen**
archaeology **die Archäologie**
architect **der Architekt**
are (*see 'to be'*) **sind**
area **die Gegend**
argument **die Auseinandersetzung**
arm **der Arm**
armbands (*swimming*) **die Schwimmflügel**

army **die Armee**
around **herum**
to arrange (*fix*) **vereinbaren**
arrest: under arrest **verhaftet**
arrival **die Ankunft**
to arrive **ankommen**
he's arriving at 5.00 pm **er kommt um fünf an**
art **die Kunst**
art gallery **die Kunsthalle**
fine arts **die schönen Künste**
arthritis **die Arthritis**
artichoke **die Artischocke**
article **der Artikel**
artificial **künstlich**
artist **der Künstler**
as (*like*) **wie**
as far as **soviel**
as far as I know **soviel ich weiß**
ash **die Asche**
ashtray **der Aschenbecher**
to ask **fragen**
asparagus **der Spargel**
aspirin **das Aspirin**
assistant **der Assistent/die Assistentin**
asthma **das Asthma**
at **an + dat. or acc.** (*see grammar, p. 182*)
athletics **die Leichtathletik**
atmosphere **die Atmosphäre**
to attack **angreifen** (*mug*) **überfallen**
attendant (*bathing*) **der Bademeister**
attractive **attraktiv**
aubergine **die Aubergine**
auction **die Auktion**
aunt **die Tante**
author **der Schriftsteller**
automatic **automatisch**
autumn **der Herbst**
avalanche **die Lawine**
avenue **die Allee**
avocado **die Avocatobirne**
to avoid **vermeiden**
away **entfernt**
awful **schrecklich**

B

baby **das Baby**
baby food **die Babynahrung**
baby wipes **die Babywischtücher**
baby's bottle **die (Knockel)flasche**
babysitter **der Babysitter/die Babysitterin**
back (*reverse side*) **die Rückseite**
back: at the back **hinten**
backwards **rückwärts**
bacon **der Speck**
bad **schlecht**
bag **die Tüte, die Tasche**
baggage **das Gepäck**
baker **der Bäcker/die Bäckerin**
baker's **die Bäckerei**
balcony (*theatre etc.*) **der Balkon**
bald **kahl**
ball (*tennis, football etc.*) **der Ball**
ballet **das Ballett**
ballpoint pen **der Kugelschreiber**
banana **die Banane**
band (*music*) **die Band**
bandage **die Binde**
bank (*money*) **die Bank**
banker **der Bankier**
bar **die Bar**
barber's **der (Herren)friseur**
bargain **das Sonderangebot**

baseball **der Baseball**
basement **das Untergeschoß**
basin (*bowl*) **die Schüssel**
(*sink*) **das Waschbecken**
basket **der Korb**
basketball **der Basketball**
bath **das Bad**
to have a bath **ein Bad nehmen**
to bathe **baden**
bathing costume **der Badeanzug**
bathroom **das Badezimmer**
battery **die Batterie**
bay **die Bucht**
to be **sein** (*see grammar, p. 184*)
beach **der Strand**
beans **die Bohnen**
French/green **grüne Bohnen**
kidney/haricot **die Gartenbohnen**
red/white/black **rote/weiße/schwarze Bohnen**
beard **der Bart**
beautiful **schön**
because **weil**
bed **das Bett**
bedroom **das Schlafzimmer**
bee **die Biene**
beef **das Rindfleisch**
beer **das Bier**
beetroot **die rote Bete**
before **bevor, vor + dat.** (*see grammar, p. 182*)
to begin **beginnen, anfangen**
it begins at 8.00 pm **es fängt um acht Uhr abends an**
beginner **der Anfänger**
beginning **der Anfang**
behind **hinter + dat. or acc.** (*see grammar, p. 182*)

beige **beige**
to believe **glauben**
bell **die Glocke**
to belong to **gehören + dat.** (*see grammar, p. 179*)
below **unten**
belt **der Gürtel**
bend **die Kurve**
bent **gebogen**
berry **die Beere**
berth **das Bett**
(*on ship*) **die Koje**
besides **außerdem**
best **beste/r/s**
better **besser**
between **zwischen + dat.** (*see grammar, p. 182*)
beyond **jenseits + gen.** (*see grammar, p. 182*)
bib **das Lätzchen**
Bible **die Bibel**
bicycle **das Fahrrad**
big **groß**
bigger **größer**
bill **die Rechnung**
bin (*rubbish*) **der Mülleimer**
bin liners **die Abfallbeutel**
binding (*ski*) **die Bindung**
binoculars **das Fernglas**
biochemistry **die Biochemie**
biology **die Biologie**
bird **der Vogel**
birthday **der Geburtstag**
biscuit **der Keks**
bishop **der Bischof**
a bit **ein bißchen**
to bite **beißen**
bitter **bitter**
black **schwarz**
black and white (*film*) **schwarzweiß**

black coffee **schwarzer Kaffee**
blackberry **die Brombeere**
blackcurrant **die Johannisbeere**
blanket **die Bettdecke**
bleach **das Bleichmittel**
to bleed **bluten**
blind **blind**
blister **die Blase**
to block (*road*) **sperren**
blocked **verstopft**
(*road*) **gesperrt**
blond(e) **blond**
blood **das Blut**
blouse **die Bluse**
to blow **blasen**
to blow-dry **fönen**
blue **blau**
blusher **das Rouge**
to board **an Bord gehen**
boarding card **die Bordkarte**
boat **das Schiff**
boat trip **die Schiffahrt**
body **der Körper**
to boil **kochen**
boiled egg **das gekochte Ei**
boiler **der Boiler**
bomb **die Bombe**
bone **der Knochen**
book **das Buch**
to book **buchen**
booking **die Buchung**
booking office (*rail*) **der Fahrkartenschalter**
(*theatre*) **die Vorverkaufsstelle**
booklet (*bus tickets*) **das Fahrscheinheft**
bookshop **die Buchhandlung**
boot (*shoe*) **der Stiefel**
border (*edge*) **der Rand**
(*frontier*) **die Grenze**
boring **langweilig**
both **beide**
bottle **die Flasche**
bottle opener **der Flaschenöffner**
bottom **der Boden**
bow (*ship*) **der Bug**
bow (*knot*) **die Schleife**
bowl **die Schüssel**
box **die Kiste**
(*theatre*) **die Loge**
box office **die Kasse**
boy **der Junge**
boyfriend **der Freund**
bra **der Büstenhalter (BH)**
bracelet **das Armband**
braces **die Hosenträger**
brain **das Gehirn**
branch (*bank etc.*) **die Zweigstelle**
brand **die Marke**
brandy **der Weinbrand**
brass **das Messing**
brave **mutig**
bread **das Brot**
bread roll **das Brötchen, die Semmel** (*Austria*)
wholemeal bread **das Vollkornbrot**
to break (*inc. limb*) **brechen**
to break down **eine Panne haben**
breakdown truck **der Abschleppwagen**
breakfast **das Frühstück**
breast **die Brust**
to breathe **atmen**
bricklayer **der Maurer**

bride **die Braut**
bridegroom **der Bräutigam**
bridge **die Brücke**
briefcase **die Aktentasche**
bright (*colour*) **leuchtend**
(*light*) **strahlend**
to bring **bringen**
British **britisch**
broad **breit**
brochure **der Prospekt**
broken **kaputt**
bronchitis **die Bronchitis**
bronze **die Bronze**
brooch **die Brosche**
broom **der Besen**
brother **der Bruder**
brother-in-law **der Schwager**
brown **braun**
brown sugar **der braune Zucker**
bruise **der blaue Fleck**
brush **die Bürste**
bucket **der Eimer**
budgerigar **der Wellensittich**
buffet **das Büffet**
to build **bauen**
builder **der Bauarbeiter**
building **das Gebäude**
building site **die Baustelle**
bulb (*light*) **die Glühbirne**
bull **der Stier**
bumper (*car*) **die Stoßstange**
burn (*on skin*) **die Brandwunde**
to burn **brennen**
burnt (*food*) **angebrannt**
bus **der Bus**
by bus **mit dem Bus**
bus-driver **der Busfahrer**
bush **der Busch**

business **das Geschäft**
business trip **die Geschäftsreise**
on business **geschäftlich**
businessman/woman **der Geschäftsmann/die Geschäftsfrau**
business studies **die Wirtschaftslehre**
bus station **der Busbahnhof**
bus stop **die Bushaltestelle**
busy **beschäftigt**
but **aber**
butane gas **das Butangas**
butcher's **die Metzgerei/die Fleischerei**
butter **die Butter**
butterfly **der Schmetterling**
button **der Knopf**
to buy **kaufen**
by (*author etc.*) **von + dat.** (*see grammar, p. 182*)

C

cabbage **der Kohl**
cabin **die Kabine**
cable car **die Drahtseilbahn**
café **das Café**
cake **der Kuchen**
cake shop **die Konditorei**
calculator **der Taschenrechner**
call (*phone*) **der Anruf**
to call **rufen**
to be called **heißen**
calm **ruhig**
camera **der Photoapparat**
camomile tea **der Kamillentee**
to camp **zelten**
campbed **die Campingliege**

camping **das Camping**
camping gas **das Campinggas**
campsite **der Campingplatz**
can (*to be able*) **können**
could **könnte**
can (*tin*) **die Dose**
(*petrol*) **der Kanister**
can opener **der Dosenöffner**
to cancel **stornieren**
an appointment **absagen**
cancer **der Krebs**
candle **die Kerze**
canoe **das Kanu**
capital (*city*) **die Hauptstadt**
captain (*boat*) **der Kapitän**
car **das Auto**
by car **mit dem Auto**
car hire **die Autovermietung**
car park **der Parkplatz**
carafe **die Karaffe**
caravan **der Wohnwagen**
caravan site **der Campingplatz für Wohnwagen**
cardigan **die Strickjacke**
care: I don't care **das macht mir nichts aus**
careful **vorsichtig**
careless (*driver*) **unvorsichtig**
carpenter **der Tischler**
carpet **der Teppich**
carriage (*rail*) **der Wagen**
carrier bag **die Tragetasche**
carrot **die Mohrrübe, die Karotte, die Möhre**
to carry **tragen**
to carry on (*walking/driving*) **weitergehen**
car wash **die Autowäsche**
case: in case **falls**
cash **das Bargeld**
to pay cash **bar bezahlen**
to cash **einlösen**
cash desk, cashier **die Kasse**
cassette **die Kassette**
castle (*palace*) **das Schloß**
(*fortress*) **die Burg**
cat **die Katze**
catalogue **der Katalog**
to catch (*train/bus*) **nehmen**
cathedral **die Kathedrale, der Dom**
Catholic **katholisch**
cauliflower **der Blumenkohl, der Karfiol** (*Austria*)
to cause **verursachen**
caution **die Vorsicht**
cave **die Höhle**
ceiling **die Decke**
celery **die Stangensellerie**
cellar **der Keller**
cemetery **der Friedhof**
centimetre **der Zentimeter**
central **zentral**
central heating **die Zentralheizung**
centre **das Zentrum**
century **das Jahrhundert**
cereal (*food*) **die Getreideflocken**
certain **sicher**
certainly **sicherlich**
certificate **die Bescheinigung**
CFCs **FKWs**
chain **die Kette**
chair **der Stuhl**
chair lift **der Sessellift**
chalet **das Chalet**
champagne **der Sekt**
change (*small coins*) **das Kleingeld**

to change (*clothes*) **umziehen**
(*money*) **wechseln**
(*trains*) **umsteigen**
changing room **die Umkleidekabine**
chapel **die Kapelle**
charcoal **die Holzkohle**
charge (*money*) **die Gebühr**
charter flight **der Charterflug**
cheap **billig**
to check **prüfen**
checked (*pattern*) **kariert**
check-in (*desk*) **der Abfertigungsschalter**
to check in **einchecken**
cheek **die Backe**
cheeky **frech**
cheers! **Prost!/zum Wohl!**
cheese **der Käse**
cheesecake **der Käsekuchen, die Käsesahne**
chef **der Chefkoch**
chemist **der Chemiker**
chemistry **die Chemie**
cheque **der Scheck**
cherry **die Kirsche**
chess **das Schachspiel**
chestnut **die Kastanie**
chewing gum **das Kaugummi**
chicken **das Hähnchen**
chickenpox **die Windpocken**
child **das Kind**
children **die Kinder**
chimney (*exterior*) **der Schornstein**
(*hearth*) **der Kamin**
chin **das Kinn**
china **das Porzellan**
chips **die Pommes frites**
chocolate **die Schokolade**
chocolates **die Pralinen**
to choose **wählen**

chop (*lamb/pork*) **das Kotelett**
Christian **christlich**
Christian name **der Vorname**
Christmas **das Weihnachten**
Christmas Day **der erste Weihnachstag**
Christmas Eve **der Heiligabend**
church **die Kirche**
cigar **die Zigarre**
cigarette **die Zigarette**
cigarette paper **das Zigarettenpapier**
cinema **das Kino**
circle **der Kreis**
(*theatre*) **der erste Rang**
city **die Stadt**
civil servant **der Staatsbeamte, die Staatsbeamtin**
class **die Klasse**
classical music **die klassische Musik**
claustrophobia **die Klaustrophobie**
to clean **saubermachen**
clean **sauber**
cleaner **die Putzfrau/der Putzmann**
cleansing lotion **die Reinigungsmilch**
clear **klar**
clerk **der/die Büroangestellte**
clever **klug**
cliff **der Felsen**
climate **das Klima**
to climb **klettern**
climber **der Bergsteiger/die Bergsteigerin**
clinic **die Klinik**
cloakroom **die Garderobe**

clock **die Uhr**
close (*by*) **in der Nähe**
to close **schließen**
closed **geschlossen**
cloth **das Tuch**
clothes **die Kleider**
clothes pegs **die Wäscheklammern**
cloud **die Wolke**
cloudy **bewölkt**
club **der Klub**
coach **der Bus**
(*railway*) **der Wagen**
coal **die Kohle**
coarse **grob**
(*food*) **einfach**
coast **die Küste**
coat **der Mantel**
coat-hanger **der Kleiderbügel**
cocktail **der Cocktail**
coffee **der Kaffee**
coin **die Münze**
cold: to have a cold **erkältet sein**
collar **der Kragen**
colleague **der Kollege/die Kollegin**
collect **sammeln**
collection (*e.g. stamps*) **die Sammlung**
(*postal/rubbish*) **die Abholung**
college **das Institut**
colour **die Farbe**
colour-blind **farbenblind**
colour-fast **farbecht**
comb **der Kamm**
come **kommen**
to come back **zurückkommen**
to come in **hereinkommen**
come in! **herein!**
to come off (*e.g. button*) **herunterfallen**
comedy **die Komödie**
comfortable **bequem**
comic (*magazine*) **das Comic-Heft**
commercial **kommerziell**
common (*usual*) **gewöhnlich**
(*shared*) **gemeinsam**
communion **das Abendmahl**
communism **der Kommunismus**
compact disc **die CD**
company **die Gesellschaft**
compared with **verglichen mit + dat.** (*see grammar, p. 182*)
compartment **das Abteil**
compass **der Kompaß**
to complain **klagen**
complaint **die Klage**
complete (*finished*) **fertig**
(*whole*) **komplett**
complicated **kompliziert**
compulsory **obligatorisch**
composer **der Komponist**
computer **der Computer**
operator **der EDV Arbeiter/die EDV Arbeiterin**
programmer **der Programmierer/die Programmiererin**
science **die Informatik**
concert **das Konzert**
concert hall **die Konzerthalle**
concussion **die Gehirnerschütterung**
condition (*state*) **der Zustand**
conditioner **die Pflegespülung**
condom **der Kondom**
conference **die Konferenz**
confirm **bestätigen**
conjunctivitis **die Konjunktivitis**
connection (*travel*) **die Verbindung**

conscious **bei Bewußtsein**
conservation **der Naturschutz**
conservative **konservativ**
constipation **die Verstopfung**
consulate **das Konsulat**
consultant **der Berater/die Beraterin**
contact lens **die Kontaktlinse**
contact lens cleaner **der Kontaktlinsenreiniger**
continent **der Kontinent**
contraceptive **das kontrazeptive Mittel**
contract **der Vertrag**
control (*passport*) **die Kontrolle**
convent **das Frauenkloster**
convenient **günstig**
cook **der Koch**
to cook **kochen**
cooked **gekocht**
cooker **der Herd**
cool **kühl**
cool box **die Kühlbox**
copper **das Kupfer**
copy **die Kopie**
cork **der Korken**
corkscrew **der Korkenzieher**
corner (*outside*) **die Ecke**
correct **richtig**
corridor **der Gang**
cosmetics **das Kosmetikum**
to cost **kosten**
cot **das Kinderbett**
cottage **das Häuschen**
cotton (*material*) **die Baumwolle**
(*thread*) **das Nähgarn**
cotton wool **die Watte**
couchette **der Liegewagen**
cough **der Husten**
to cough **husten**
(I, he, she, it) could (*see 'can'*) **könnte**

to count **zählen**
counter (*post office*) **der Schalter**
country (*nation*) **das Land**
country(side) **die Landschaft**
in the country **auf dem Lande**
couple (*pair*) **das Paar**
courgettes **die Zucchini**
course (*lessons*) **der Kurs**
court (*law*) **der Gerichtshof**
(*tennis*) **der Platz**
cousin **der Cousin/die Kusine**
cover (*lid*) **der Deckel**
cow **die Kuh**
crab **der Krebs**
cramp **der Muskelkater**
crayon **der Buntstift**
crazy **verrückt**
cream **die Sahne**
(*lotion*) **die Creme**
(*colour*) **creme**
credit card **die Kreditkarte**
cricket **das Kricket**
crispbread **das Knäckebrot**
crisps **die Chips**
cross **das Kreuz**
Red Cross **das rote Kreuz**
to cross (*border*) **hinüberfahren**
cross-country (*skiing*) **der Langlauf**
crossing (*sea*) **die Überfahrt**
crossroads **die Kreuzung**
crowd **die Menschenmenge**
crowded **überfüllt, voll**
crown **die Krone**
cruise **die Kreuzfahrt**
crutch **die Krücke**
to cry **weinen**
crystal **kristall**
cucumber **die Gurke**
cuff **die Manschette**

cup **die Tasse**
cupboard **der Schrank**
cure (*remedy*) **das Heilmittel**
o cure **heilen**
curler (*hair*) **der Lockenwickler**
curly **lockig**
curry **der Curry**
current (*electricity*) **der Strom**
curtain **die Gardine**
curve **die Kurve**
cushion **das Kissen**
custard **die Vanillesoße**
customs **der Zoll**
cut **der Schnitt**
o cut **schneiden**
to cut oneself **sich schneiden**
cutlery **das Besteck**
cycling **das Radfahren**
cylinder (*car*) **der Zylinder**
cyclist **der Radfahrer**
cystitis **die Blasenentzündung**

D

daily **täglich**
damage **der Schaden**
• damage **schaden + dat.** (*see grammar, p. 179*)
damp **feucht**
dance **der Tanz**
• dance **tanzen**
danger **die Gefahr**
dangerous **gefährlich**
dark **dunkel**
darling **der Liebling**
darts **das Dartspiel**
data (*information*) **die Daten**
date (*day*) **das Datum**
(*fruit*) **die Dattel**
daughter **die Tochter**
daughter-in-law **die Schwiegertochter**
day **der Tag**
day after tomorrow **übermorgen**
day before yesterday **vorgestern**
day after/before **der Tag danach/davor**
dead **tot**
deaf **schwerhörig**
dealer **der Händler**
dear (*loved*) **liebe**
(*expensive*) **teuer**
death **der Tod**
debt **die Schuld**
decaffeinated coffee **der koffeinfreie Kaffee**
deck **das Deck**
deckchair **der Liegestuhl**
to decide **sich entschließen**
to declare **erklären**
deep **tief**
deer **der Hirsch**
defect **der Fehler**
defective **fehlerhaft**
definitely **bestimmt**
defrost (*food*) **auftauen**
degree (*temperature*) **der Grad**
(*university*) **der Universitätsabschluß**
delay **die Verspätung**
delicate **fein**
delicious **lecker**
to deliver **liefern**
delivery **die Lieferung**
demonstration **die Demonstration**
denim **der Jeansstoff**
dentist **der Zahnarzt**
denture **das Gebiß**
deodorant **das Deo(dorant)**

to depart (*bus, car*) **abfahren**
(*plane*) **abfliegen**
department **die Abteilung**
department store **das Kaufhaus**
departure (*bus, car*) **die Abfahrt**
(*plane*) **der Abflug**
departure lounge **die Abflughalle**
deposit **die Anzahlung**
desert **die Wüste**
to describe **beschreiben**
description **die Beschreibung**
design **der Entwurf**
(*dress*) **das Design**
to design **entwerfen**
designer **der Designer**
dessert **die Nachspeise**
destination **das Reiseziel**
detail **das Detail**
detergent **das Reinigungsmittel**
to develop **entwickeln**
diabetes **der Diabetes**
diabetic (*adj.*) **diabetisch**
to dial **wählen**
dialling code **die Vorwahl**
dialling tone **das Amtzeichen**
diamond **der Diamant**
diarrhoea **der Durchfall**
diary **das Tagebuch**
dice **der Würfel**
dictator **der Diktator**
dictionary **das Wörterbuch**
to die **sterben**
. . . died **gestorben**
diesel **das Dieselöl**
diet **die Diät**
different(ly) **verschieden, anders**
difficult **schwer**

dining room **das Eßzimmer**
dinner **das Abendessen**
dinner jacket **der Smoking**
diplomat **der Diplomat**
direct (*train*) **durchgehend**
direction **die Richtung**
director **der Direktor/die Direktorin**
directory (index) **das Verzeichnis**
dirty **schmutzig**
disabled **behindert**
disappointed **enttäuscht**
disc **die Scheibe**
(*computer*) **die Platte**
(*record*) **die Schallplatte**
disc film **der Discfilm**
disc jockey **der Discjockey**
disco(thèque) **die Diskothek**
discount **der Rabatt**
dish **die Schüssel**
dishwasher **die Geschirrspülmaschine**
disinfectant **das Desinfektionsmittel**
dislocated **verrenkt**
disposable **wegwerfbar**
disposable nappies **die Papierwindeln**
distance **die Entfernung**
distilled water **das destilliert Wasser**
district **das Gebiet**
to dive **tauchen**
diversion **die Umleitung**
diving **das Tauchen**
diving-board **das Springbret**
divorced **geschieden**
dizzy **schwindelig**
to do **machen, tun**
dock **das Dock**

doctor **der Arzt/die Ärztin**
document **das Dokument**
dog **der Hund**
doll **die Puppe**
dollar **der Dollar**
dome **die Kuppel**
dominoes **das Dominospiel**
donkey **der Esel**
door **die Tür**
double **doppelt**
double bed **das Doppelbett**
dough **der Teig**
down (*movement*) **hinunter**
downstairs **unten**
drain **das Abflußrohr**
drama **das Drama**
draught (*air*) **der Luftzug**
draught beer **das Bier vom Faß**
to draw **zeichnen**
drawer **die Schublade**
drawing **die Zeichnung**
drawing-pin **die Reißzwecke**
dreadful **furchtbar**
dress **das Kleid**
to dress, get dressed **sich anziehen**
dressing (*medical*) **der Verband**
(*salad*) **die Soße, die Beilage**
drink **das Getränk**
to drink **trinken**
to drip **tropfen**
to drive **fahren**
driver **der Fahrer**
(*bus/train*) **der Busfahrer/der Zugfahrer**
driving licence **der Führerschein**
to drown **ertrinken**
drug **die Droge**
drug addict **der/die Drogensüchtige**
drum **die Trommel**
drunk **betrunken**
dry **trocken**
(*wine*) **herb/trocken**
dry-cleaner's **die chemische Reinigung**
dubbed **synchronisiert**
duck **die Ente**
dull (*weather*) **trüb**
dumb **taub**
dummy (*baby's*) **der Schnuller**
during **während + gen.** (*see grammar, p. 182*)
dust **der Staub**
dustbin **der Mülleimer**
dusty **staubig**
duty (*tax*) **die Steuer**
duty-free **anmeldefrei**
duvet **das Federbett**

E

each **jede/r/s**
ear **das Ohr**
earache **die Ohrenschmerzen**
eardrops **die Ohrentropfen**
earlier **früher**
early **früh**
to earn **verdienen**
earring **der Ohrring**
earth **die Erde**
earthquake **das Erdbeben**
east **der Osten**
eastern **östlich**
Easter **das Ostern**
easy **leicht**
to eat **essen**
economical **ökonomisch**
economics **die Volkswirtschaft**
economy **die Wirtschaft**
the economic miracle **das Wirtschaftswunder**

edible **eßbar**
egg **Ei**
either **entweder**
either . . . or **entweder . . . oder**
elastic band **das Gummiband**
election **die Wahl**
electric **elektrisch**
electrician **der Elektriker**
electricity **die Elektrizität**
(*wiring etc.*) **der Stromanschluß**
electronic **elektronisch**
to embark (*boat*) **einschiffen**
embarrassing **peinlich**
embassy **die Botschaft**
emergency **der Notfall**
emergency telephone (*on motorway*) **die Notrufsäule**
empty **leer**
to empty **leeren**
enamel **das Email**
end **das Ende**
to end **enden**
energy **die Energie**
engaged (*to be married*) **verlobt**
(*occupied*) **besetzt**
engine **der Motor**
engineer **der Ingenieur/die Ingenieurin**
England **England (das)**
English **englisch**
to enjoy **genießen**
enough **genug**
to enter **hineingehen**
(*bus, train*) **einsteigen**
entertainment **die Unterhaltung**
enthusiastic **begeistert**
entrance **der Eingang**
envelope **der Briefumschlag**
environment **die Umwelt**
environmentally friendly **umweltfreundlich**
equal **gleich**
equipment **die Ausstattung**
escalator **die Rolltreppe**
especially **besonders**
essential **wesentlich**
estate agent **der Hausmakler**
evaporated milk **die Dosenmilch**
even (*including*) **sogar**
(*not odd*) **gerade**
evening **der Abend**
every **jede/r/s**
everyone **alle**
everything **alles**
everywhere **überall**
exact(ly) **genau**
examination **das Examen**
example **das Beispiel**
for example **zum Beispiel**
excellent **ausgezeichnet**
except **außer + dat.** (*see grammar, p. 182*)
excess luggage **das Übergewicht**
to exchange **tauschen**
(*money*) **wechseln**
exchange rate **der Wechselkurs**
excited **aufgeregt**
exciting **aufregend**
excursion **der Ausflug**
excuse me **Entschuldigen Sie**
executive (*adj.*) **exekutiv**
exercise **die Übung**
exhibition **die Ausstellung**
exit **der Ausgang**
to expect **erwarten**
expensive **teuer**
experience **die Erfahrung**

experiment **der Versuch**
expert **der Experte/die Expertin**
to explain **erklären**
explosion **die Explosion**
export **der Export**
to export **exportieren**
express **expreß**
extension cable **das Verlängerungskabel**
external **äußere**
extra **zusätzlich**
eye **das Auge**
eyebrow **die Augenbraue**
eyebrow pencil **der Augenbrauenstift**
eyelash **die Augenwimper**
eyeliner **der Eyeliner**
eyeshadow **der Lidschatten**

F

fabric **der Stoff**
face **das Gesicht**
face cream **die Gesichtscreme**
face powder **der Gesichtspuder**
facilities **die Möglichkeiten**
fact **die Tatsache**
in fact **eigentlich**
factory **die Fabrik**
to fail (*exam/test*) **durchfallen**
failure **der Mißerfolg**
to faint **ohnmächtig werden**
fair (*haired*) **blond**
fair **der Jahrmarkt**
trade fair **die Handelsmesse**
fairly **ziemlich**
faith **der Glaube**
fake **die Imitation**
to fall (*down/over*) **hinfallen**
false **falsch**
familiar **vertraut**
family **die Familie**
famous **bekannt**
fan (*air*) **der Ventilator**
(*supporter*) **der Anhänger**
fantastic **fantastisch**
far (*away*) **weit weg**
how far . . . ? **wie weit . . . ?**
is it far? **ist es weit?**
fare **das Fahrgeld**
farm **der Bauernhof**
farmer **der Bauer**
fashion **die Mode**
fashionable/in fashion **modisch**
fast **schnell**
fat (*adj./noun*) **dick/das Fett**
fatal **tödlich**
father **der Vater**
father-in-law **der Schwiegervater**
fault **der Fehler**
faulty **fehlerhaft**
favourite **Lieblings-**
(*e.g. favourite film*) **der Lieblingsfilm**
fax **der Telefax**
feather **die Feder**
to be fed up **die Nase voll haben**
fee **die Gebühr**
to feed (*inc. baby*) **füttern**
to feel **sich fühlen**
(*ill/well*) **sich unwohl/wohl fühlen**
felt-tip pen **der Filzstift**
female, feminine **weiblich**
feminist **der Feminist/die Feministin**

fence **der Zaun**
ferry **die Fähre**
festival **das Fest**
to fetch **holen**
fever **das Fieber**
(a) few **ein paar**
fiancé(e) **der/die Verlobte**
fibre **die Faser**
field **das Feld**
fig **die Feige**
to fight **kämpfen**
file (*documents*) **der Aktenordner**
(*nail/DIY*) **die Feile**
to fill **füllen**
filling (*dental*) **die Plombe**
film (*cinema/for camera*) **der Film**
film star **der/die Filmstar**
filter **der Filter**
finance **die Finanzen**
to find **finden**
fine (*OK*) **in Ordnung**
(*penalty*) **die Geldstrafe**
(*weather*) **schön**
finger **der Finger**
finish **der Schluß**
fire **das Feuer**
fire brigade **die Feuerwehr**
fire extinguisher **der Feuerlöscher**
firewood **das Brennholz**
firework **das Feuerwerk**
firm **fest**
firm (*company*) **die Firma**
first **erste/r/s**
first aid **die Erste Hilfe**
first aid kit **der Verbandskasten**
fish **der Fisch**
to fish/go fishing **angeln**
fishing **das Angeln**
fishing rod **die Angelrute**
fishmonger's **das Fischgeschäft**
fit (*healthy*) **gesund**
to fit **passen**
that fits you well **das paßt dir gut**
fitting room **die Umkleidekabine**
to fix (*mend*) **reparieren**
fizzy **mit Kohlensäure**
flag **die Fahne**
flash (*camera*) **das Blitzlicht**
flat (*apartment*) **die Wohnung**
flat (*level*) **platt**
(*battery*) **leer**
flavour **der Geschmack**
flaw **der Fehler**
flea market **der Flohmarkt**
flight **der Flug**
flight bag **die Schultertasche**
flippers **die Schwimmflossen**
flood **die Flut**
floor **der Boden**
(*storey*) on the first floor **im ersten Stock**
ground floor **das Erdgeschoß**
flour **das Mehl**
flower **die Blume**
flu **die Grippe**
fluent (*language*) **fließend**
fluid **flüssig**
fly **die Fliege**
fly sheet **das Überzelt**
fly spray **der Fliegenspray**
to fly **fliegen**
fog **der Nebel**
foggy **nebelig**
foil **die Folie**

folding (*e.g. chair*) **Klapp- (der Klappstuhl)**
folk music **die Volksmusik**
to follow **folgen**
following (*next*) **folgend**
food **das Essen**
food poisoning **die Lebensmittelvergiftung**
foot **der Fuß**
on foot **zu Fuß**
football **der Fußball**
footpath **Fußweg**
for **für**
forbidden **verboten**
foreign **ausländisch**
foreigner **der Ausländer/die Ausländerin**
forest **der Wald**
to forget **vergessen**
to forgive **vergeben**
fork **die Gabel**
form **die Form**
fortnight **vierzehn Tage**
forward **vorwärts**
forwarding address **die Nachsendeadresse**
foundation (*make-up*) **die Grundierungscreme**
fountain **der Brunnen**
fox **der Fuchs**
foyer **das Foyer**
fracture **der Bruch**
fragile **zerbrechlich**
frankly **ehrlich gesagt**
freckles **die Sommersprossen**
free **frei/umsonst**
(*available, unoccupied*) **frei**
freedom **die Freiheit**
to freeze **frieren**
freezer **die Tiefkühltruhe**
frequent **häufig**
fresh **frisch**
fridge **der Kühlschrank**
fried **Brat-**
friend **der Freund/die Freundin**
friends **die Freunde**
frightened **erschrocken**
fringe **die Fransen**
frog **der Frosch**
from **von + dat.** (*see grammar, p. 182*)
front **die Vorderseite**
in front of **vorne, vor**
front door **die Haupttür**
frontier **die Grenze**
frost **der Frost**
frozen **gefroren**
fruit **das Obst, die Frucht**
fruit shop **die Obst- und Gemüsehandlung**
to fry **braten**
frying pan **die Bratpfanne**
fuel **der Brennstoff**
full **voll**
full board **die Vollpension**
full up (*booked up*) **ausgebucht**
to have fun **Spaß haben**
it was fun **es hat Spaß gemacht**
funeral **die Beerdigung**
funfair **der Jahrmarkt**
funny (*amusing*) **lustig**
(*peculiar*) **komisch**
fur **der Pelz**
furniture **die Möbel**
further on **weiter**
fuse **die Sicherung**
fusebox **der Sicherungskasten**

G

gallery **die Galerie**
gambling **das Spielen**
game (*match*) **das Spiel**
(*hunting*) **das Wild**
gangway **der Gang**
garage (*for parking*) **die Garage**
(*for petrol*) **die Tankstelle**
garden **der Garten**
gardener **der Gärtner/die Gärtnerin**
garlic **der Knoblauch**
gas **das Gas**
gas bottle/cylinder **die Gasflasche**
gas refill **die Gaskartusche**
gastritis **die Gastritis**
gate **das Tor**
(*airport*) **der Flugsteig**
gel (*hair*) **das Haargel**
general **allgemein**
in general **im allgemeinen**
generous **großzügig**
gentle **sanft**
gentleman/men **der Herr, die Herren**
(*gents*) **Herren**
genuine **echt**
geography **die Geographie**
Germany **Deutschland (das)**
to get **bekommen**
to get off (*bus*) **aussteigen**
to get on (*bus*) **einsteigen**
to get through (*phone*) **durchkommen**
gift **das Geschenk**
gin **der Gin**
and tonic **der Gin-Tonic**
girl **das Mädchen**
girlfriend **die Freundin**
to give **geben**
to give back **zurückgeben**
glass **das Glas**
glasses **die Brille**
gloves **die Handschuhe**
glue **der Klebstoff**
to go **gehen**
to go away **weggehen**
to go down **hinuntergehen**
to go in **eingehen**
to go out **ausgehen**
to go round (*visit*) **besuchen**
let's go! **gehen wir!**
goal **das Ziel**
(*football*) **das Tor**
goat **die Ziege**
God **Gott**
goggles **die Schutzbrille**
gold **das Gold**
golf **das Golf**
golf clubs **die Golfschläger**
golf course **der Golfplatz**
good **gut**
good day **guten Tag**
good evening **guten Abend**
good morning **guten Morgen**
goodnight **gute Nacht**
goodbye **Auf Wiedersehen/ Auf Wiederschauen** (*Austria*) (*casual*) **Tschüß**
goods **die Waren**
Good Friday **Karfreitag (der)**
government **die Regierung**
gram **das Gramm**
grammar **die Grammatik**
grandchildren **die Enkelkinde**
granddaughter **die Enkelin**
grandfather **der Großvater**
grandmother **die Großmutter**
grandparents **die Großeltern**

grandson **der Enkel**
grandstand **die Haupttribüne**
grape **die Weintraube**
grapefruit **die Pampelmuse**
grass **das Gras**
grateful **dankbar**
greasy **fettig**
great! **prima!**
green **grün**
green card **die grüne Karte**
(*environmentally aware*) **grün**
greengrocer's **die Obst- und Gemüsehandlung**
to greet **grüßen**
grey **grau**
grilled **gegrillt**
grocer's **der Lebensmittelhändler**
ground **der Boden**
groundsheet **der Zeltboden**
ground floor **das Erdgeschoß**
group **die Gruppe**
guarantee **die Garantie**
guest **der Gast**
guest house **die Pension**
guide **der Führer**
guided tour **die Führung**
guidebook **der Reiseführer**
guilty **schuldig**
guitar **die Gitarre**
gun **das Gewehr**
guy rope **die Zeltschnur**
gymnastics **die Gymnastik**

H

habit **die Gewohnheit**
hail **der Hagel**
hair **das Haar, die Haare**
hairbrush **die Haarbürste**
haircut **der Haarschnitt**
hairdresser **der Friseur**
hairdrier **der Fön**
hairgrip **die Haarklemme**
hairspray **der Haarspray**
half **die Hälfte**
half (*adj.*) **halb**
half board **die Halbpension**
half price/fare **zum halben Preis**
half-hour/half an hour **eine halbe Stunde**
half past . . . (*see Time p. 193*) **halb . . .**
hall (*in house*) **die Diele**
ham **der Schinken**
cured ham **geräucherter Schinken**
hamburger **der Hamburger**
hammer **der Hammer**
hand **die Hand**
hand cream **die Handcreme**
hand luggage **das Handgepäck**
hand made **handgearbeitet**
handbag **die Handtasche**
handicapped **behindert**
handkerchief **das Taschentuch**
handle **der Griff**
hangover **der Kater**
to hang up **auflegen**
to happen **passieren**
happy **glücklich**
harbour **der Hafen**
harbour trip **die Hafenrundfahrt**
hard **hart**
(*difficult*) **schwer**
hard shoulder **der Seitenstreifen**
hat **der Hut**
to hate **hassen**
to have **haben**

hay **das Heu**
hay fever **der Heuschnupfen**
hazelnut **die Haselnuß**
he **er**
head **der Kopf**
(*boss*) **der Chef**
headache **die Kopfschmerzen**
headphones **die Kopfhörer**
to heal **heilen**
health **die Gesundheit**
healthy **gesund**
health foods **die Reformkost**
to hear **hören**
hearing **das Gehör**
hearing aid **das Hörgerät**
heart **das Herz**
heart attack **der Herzanfall**
heat **die Hitze**
heater **das Heizgerät**
heating **die Heizung**
heaven **der Himmel**
heavy **schwer**
hedge **die Hecke**
heel **die Ferse**
(*shoe*) **der Absatz**
height **die Höhe**
helicopter **der Hubschrauber**
hell **die Hölle**
hello **Hallo**
helmet (*motorbike*) **der Helm**
help **die Hilfe**
help! **Hilfe!**
to help **helfen**
her (*adj. and pronoun*) **ihr/sie**
(to) her **ihr**
herb **das Kraut**
herbal tea **der Kräutertee**
here **hier**
here is . . . **hier ist . . .**
hers **ihre/r/s**
hiccups: to have hiccups **(den) Schluckauf haben**

high **hoch**
high chair **der Hochstuhl**
to hijack **entführen**
hill **der Hügel**
him **ihn**
(to) him **ihm**
to hire **mieten**
his (*adj. and pronoun*) **sein**
history **die Geschichte**
to hit **schlagen**
to hitchhike **trampen**
hobby **das Hobby**
to hold **halten**
hole **das Loch**
holiday (*period of time*) **der Urlaub**
holidays (*school*) **die Ferien**
on holiday **im Urlaub**
holy **heilig**
Holy Week **die Passionswoche**
home **die Heimat**
at home **zu Hause**
to go home **nach Hause gehen**
homeopathic **homeopathisch**
to be homesick **Heimweh haben**
homosexual **homosexuell**
honest **ehrlich**
honeymoon **die Flitterwochen**
to hope **hoffen**
I hope so **ich hoffe schon**
horrible **scheußlich**
horse **das Pferd**
hose **der Schlauch**
hospital **das Krankenhaus**
host **der Gastgeber/die Gastgeberin**
hot **heiß**
(*spicy*) **scharf**
hotel **das Hotel**
hour **die Stunde**

half-hour **eine halbe Stunde**
house **das Haus**
housewife **die Hausfrau**
housework **die Hausarbeit**
hovercraft **das Hovercraft**
how **wie**
how far? **wie weit?**
how long? **wie lange?**
how many? **wie viele?**
how much? **wieviel?**
how much does it cost? **was kostet das?**
how much do they cost? **was kosten sie?**
human **menschlich**
human being **der Mensch**
hungry **hungrig**
to be hungry **Hunger haben**
to hunt **jagen**
hunting **die Jagd**
hurry: to be in a hurry **in Eile sein**
to hurt **weh tun**
it hurts **es tut weh**
husband **der Mann**
hut **die Hütte**
hydrofoil **das Tragflächenboot**

I

I **ich**
ice **das Eis**
(*on roads*) **das Glatteis**
ice cream **das Eis**
ice rink **die Schlittschuhbahn**
icy **eisig**
idea **die Idee**
if **wenn**
ill **krank**
illness **die Krankheit**
imagine **sich vorstellen**
imagination **die Phantasie**
immediately **sofort**
immersion heater **der Boiler**
impatient **ungeduldig**
important **wichtig**
impossible **unmöglich**
impressive **eindrucksvoll**
in **in + acc. or dat** (*see grammar, p. 182*)
included **inbegriffen**
income **das Einkommen**
indeed **tatsächlich**
independent **unabhängig**
indigestion **die Magenverstimmung**
indoors **drinnen**
industry **die Industrie**
infected **infiziert**
infection **die Infektion**
infectious **ansteckend**
inflamed **entzündet**
inflammation **die Entzündung**
influenza **die Grippe**
informal **nicht formell**
information **die Auskunft**
information desk/office **das Auskunftsbüro**
injection **die Spritze**
to injure **verletzen**
injured **verletzt**
injury **die Verletzung**
ink **die Tinte**
inner **innere**
innocent **unschuldig**
insect **das Insekt**
insect bite **der Insektenstich**
insect repellent **das Insektenbekämpfungsmittel**
inside **das Innere**
to insist **bestehen**
inspector **der Kontrolleur/die Kontrolleurin**

instant coffee **der Pulverkaffee**
instead of **statt + dat.** (*see grammar, p. 182*)
instructor **der Lehrer/die Lehrerin**
insulin **das Insulin**
insult **die Beleidigung**
insurance **die Versicherung**
insurance document **die Versicherungskarte**
to insure **versichern**
insured **versichert**
intelligent **intelligent**
interested **interessiert**
interesting **interessant**
international **international**
to interpret **dolmetschen**
interpreter **der Dolmetscher/die Dolmetscherin**
interval (*theatre etc.*) **die Pause**
interview **das Interview**
into **in + acc.** (*see grammar p. 182*)
to introduce **vorstellen**
invitation **die Einladung**
invite **einladen**
iodine **das Jod**
Ireland **Irland (das)**
Irish **irisch**
iron (*metal*) **das Eisen**
(*for clothes*) **das Bügeleisen**
to iron **bügeln**
ironmonger's **die Eisen- und Haushaltswarenhandlung**
is (*see 'to be'*) **ist**
is there . . . ? **gibt es . . . ?**
island **die Insel**
it **es**
itch **das Jucken**

J

jacket **die Jacke**
jam **die Konfitüre**
jar **das Gefäß**
jaw **der Kiefer**
jazz **der Jazz**
jeans **die Jeans**
jelly **das Gelee**
(*pudding*) **die Götterspeise**
jellyfish **die Qualle**
Jesus Christ **Jesus Christus**
jetty **der Pier, die Anlegestell**
jeweller's **der Juwelier**
Jewish **jüdisch**
job **die Arbeit**
to jog **joggen**
jogging **das Joggen**
joke **der Witz**
journalist **der Journalist/die Journalistin**
journey **die Reise**
judge **der Richter**
jug **die Kanne**
juice **der Saft**
to jump **springen**
jump leads **die Starthilfekab**
jumper **der Pullover**
junction (*rail*) **der Gleisanschluß**
(*road*) **die Kreuzung**
just (*only*) **nur**

K

kaolin mixture **der Kaolin**
to keep **behalten**
(*to put by*) **zurücklegen**
kettle **der Kessel**
key **der Schlüssel**
key ring **der Schlüsselring**

kidney **die Niere**
to kill **töten**
kilo(gram) **das Kilogramm**
kilometre **der Kilometer**
kind (*sort*) **die Art**
(*generous*) **nett**
king **der König**
kiss **der Kuß**
to kiss **küssen**
kitchen **die Küche**
knee **das Knie**
knickers **der Slip**
knife **das Messer**
to knit **stricken**
knitting **das Stricken**
knitting needle **die Stricknadel**
to knock **klopfen**
knot **der Knoten**
to know (*someone*) **kennen**
(*something*) **wissen**
I don't know **Ich weiß nicht**

L

label **das Etikett**
lace **die Spitze**
ladder **die Leiter**
lady **die Dame**
ladies **Damen**
lager **das helle Bier**
lake **der See**
lamb (*meat*) **das Lammfleisch**
lamp **die Lampe**
lamp post **der Laternenpfahl**
land **das Land**
to land **landen**
landing (*aeroplane*) **die Landung**
(*house*) **der Flur**
(*ship*) **das Anlegen**
landlady **die Wirtin**
landlord **der Wirt**
language **die Sprache**
large **groß**
last **letzte/r/s**
to last **dauern**
late **spät**
later **später**
laugh **das Lachen**
to laugh **lachen**
launderette **der Waschsalon**
laundry **die Wäsche**
law (*study subject*) **die Jura**
lawyer **der Rechtsanwalt/die Rechtsanwältin**
laxative **das Abführmittel**
lazy **faul**
lead **das Blei**
lead-free **bleifrei**
leaf **das Blatt**
leaflet **der Prospekt**
to lean out **hinauslehnen**
to learn **lernen**
learner **der Anfänger**
least: at least **wenigstens, mindestens**
leather **das Leder**
to leave **lassen**
(*to go away*) **verlassen, weggehen**
lecturer **der Dozent/die Dozentin**
left **links**
left luggage (*office*) **die Gepäckaufbewahrung**
left-handed **linkshändig**
leg **das Bein**
legal **legal**
lemon **die Zitrone**
lemonade **die Limonade**

to lend **verleihen**
length **die Länge**
lens (*camera*) **die Linse**
less **weniger**
lesson (*instruction*) **der Unterricht**
to let (*allow*) **erlauben**
(*rent*) **vermieten**
letter **der Brief**
(*of alphabet*) **der Buchstabe**
letterbox **der Briekfasten**
lettuce **der Kopfsalat**
leukemia **die Leukämie**
level (*height, standard*) **das Niveau**
level (*flat*) **flach**
level crossing **der Bahnübergang**
library **die Bibliothek**
licence (*driving*) **der Führerschein**
(*fishing etc.*) **die Lizenz**
lid **der Deckel**
to lie down **sich hinlegen**
life **das Leben**
lifebelt **der Rettungsgürtel**
lifeboat **das Rettungsboot**
lifeguard (*swimming pool*) **der Bademeister**
lifejacket **die Schwimmweste**
lift **der Fahrstuhl**
light **das Licht**
light bulb **die Glühbirne**
light (*coloured*) **hell**
(*weight*) **leicht**
to light (*fire*) **anzünden**
lighter (*cigarette*) **das Feuerzeug**
lighter fuel **das Gas für's Feuerzeug**
lightning **der Blitz**

like (*similar to*) **wie**
like this/that **wie das**
what is . . like? **wie ist . ?**
what are . . like? **wie sind . ?**
to like (*food, people*) **mögen**
I like **ich mag**
to like doing something **etwas gern tun**
I like doing that **ich tue das gern**
likely **wahrscheinlich**
limited **beschränkt**
line **die Linie**
lion **der Löwe**
lip **die Lippe**
lipstick **der Lippenstift**
liqueur **der Likör**
liquid **die Flüssigkeit**
list **die Liste**
to listen (*to*) **zuhören + dat.**
(*see grammar, p. 179*)
litre **der Liter**
litter **der Abfall**
little **klein**
a little **ein bißchen**
to live **leben**
(*dwell*) **wohnen**
liver **die Leber**
living-room **das Wohnzimmer**
local **örtlich**
lock **das Schloß**
to lock **abschließen**
locker **das Schließfach**
London **London**
lonely **einsam**
long (*ing. hair*) **lang**
long-distance **Fern-**
long-distance call **das Ferngespräch**
look **der Blick**
to look (*at*) **sich ansehen**

to look for **suchen**
loose **los**
lorry **der LKW (Lastkraftwagen)**
lorry-driver **der LKW-Fahrer**
to lose **verlieren**
lost property (*office*) **das Fundbüro**
a lot (*of*) **viel (von)**
lotion **die Lotion**
lottery **die Lotterie**
loud **laut**
lounge **das Wohnzimmer**
(*in ship etc.*) **der Salon**
love **die Liebe**
to love **lieben**
low **niedrig**
low-fat **fettarm**
lower **niedriger**
lozenge **die Pastille**
LP **die LP**
lucky: to be lucky **Glück haben**
luggage **das Gepäck**
lump (*swelling*) **die Beule**
lunch **das Mittagessen**

M

machine **die Maschine**
machinist **der Machinist**
mad **verrückt**
madam **gnädige Frau**
magazine **die Zeitschrift**
mail **die Post**
main **Haupt-**
to make **machen**
make-up **der Schminkstoff**
male **männlich**
man **der Mann**
to manage (*cope*) **schaffen**
manager **der Manager**
managing director **der Geschäftsführer/die Geschäftsführerin**
many **viele**
not many **nicht viele**
map **die Karte**
marble **der Marmor**
margarine **die Margarine**
market **der Markt**
married **verheiratet**
to get married **heiraten**
mascara **die Maskara**
masculine **männlich**
mask (*diving*) **die Maske**
mass (*church*) **die Messe**
match **das Streichholz**
(*game*) **das Spiel**
material **der Stoff**
mathematics **die Mathematik**
matter: it doesn't matter **es macht nichts**
what's the matter? **was ist los?**
mattress **die Matratze**
air mattress **die Luftmatratze**
mature (*cheese*) **reif**
mayonnaise **die Mayonnaise**
me **mich**
meadow **die Wiese**
meal **das Essen**
mean: what does this mean? **was bedeutet das?**
was heißt das?
meanwhile **in der Zwischenzeit**
measles **die Masern**
German measles **die Röteln**
to measure **messen**
measurement **das Maß**
meat **das Fleisch**
cold meats **der Aufschnitt**
mechanic **der Mechaniker**

medical **medizinisch**
medicine (*subject*) **die Medizin**
(*drug*) **das Medikament**
medieval **mittelalterlich**
Mediterranean **das Mittelmeer**
medium (*size*) **mittelgroß**
(*steak*) **medium**
(*wine*) **halbtrocken**
meeting **das Treffen**
melon **die Melone**
member **das Mitglied**
men **die Männer**
to mend **reparieren**
menu (*à la carte*) **die Speisekarte**
(*set*) **das Menü**
message **die Mitteilung**
metal **das Metall**
meter **der Zähler**
metre **der Meter**
microwave oven **der Mikrowellenherd**
midday **der Mittag**
middle **die Mitte**
middle-aged **in den mittleren Jahren**
midnight **die Mitternacht**
migraine **die Migräne**
mild **mild**
mile **die Meile**
milk **die Milch**
milkshake **das Milchmixgetränk**
mill **die Mühle**
mince **das Hackfleisch**
mind: do you mind if . . . ? **macht das Ihnen etwas aus, wenn . . . ?**
I don't mind **es ist mir egal**
mine (*of me*) **mein/e/s**
minibus **der Kleinbus**
minister **der Minister**

minute (*time*) **der Augenblick/die Minute**
mirror **der Spiegel**
Miss **Fräulein**
to miss (*bus etc.*) **verpassen**
(*nostalgia*) **vermissen**
mist **der Nebel**
mistake **der Fehler**
to make a mistake **einen Fehler machen**
mixed **gemischt**
mixture **die Mischung**
model **das Modell**
modern **modern**
moisturiser **die Feuchtigskeitscreme**
monastery **das Kloster**
money **das Geld**
month **der Monat**
monthly **monatlich**
monument **das Denkmal**
moon **der Mond**
moped **das Moped**
more **mehr**
no more **nicht mehr**
morning **der Morgen**
mortgage **die Hypothek**
mosquito **die Stechmücke**
mosquito net **das Moskitonetz**
most (of) **die meisten (von)**
mother **die Mutter**
mother-in-law **die Schwiegermutter**
motor **der Motor**
motorbike **das Motorrad**
motorboat **das Motorboot**
motor racing **der Rennsport**
motorway **die Autobahn**
mountain **der Berg**
mountaineering **das Bergsteigen**
moustache **der Schnurrbart**

mouth **der Mund**
to move **bewegen**
to move house **umziehen**
Mr **Herr**
Mrs, Ms **Frau**
much **viel**
not much **nicht viel**
mug **der Becher**
to murder **ermorden**
museum **das Museum**
mushroom **der Pilz**
(*button*) **der Champignon**
music **die Musik**
musical **das Musical**
musician **der Musiker/die Musikerin**
must: you must ... **Sie müssen . . .**
mustard **der Senf**
my **mein**
mystery **das Rätsel**

N

nail **der Nagel**
nail clippers/scissors **der Nagelzwicker**
nail file **die Nagelfeile**
nail polish **der Nagellack**
nail polish remover **der Nagellackentferner**
naked **nackt**
name **der Name**
my name is . . . **ich heiße . . .**
what is your name? **wie heißen Sie?**
napkin **die Serviette**
nappy **die Windel**
disposable nappy **die Papierwindel**
nappy liner **die Einlegewindel**
national **national**
nationality **die Nationalität**
natural(ly) **natürlich**
naughty **bös**
navy **die Marine**
navy blue **marineblau**
near **nah**
nearby **in der Nähe**
nearest **der/die/das nächste**
nearly **fast**
necessary **nötig**
necklace **die Halskette**
to need **brauchen**
needle **die Nadel**
negative (*photo*) **das Negativ**
neighbour **der Nachbar/die Nachbarin**
neither . . . nor . . . **weder . . . noch . . .**
nephew **der Neffe**
nervous **nervös**
net **das Netz**
never **nie**
new **neu**
New Year's Day **der Neujahrstag**
New Year's Eve **das Silvester**
news **die Nachrichten**
newspaper **die Zeitung**
newspaper kiosk **der Kiosk**
next **nächste/r/s**
week/month/year (*see page 191*)
next to **neben + dat. or acc.** (*see grammar, p. 182*)
nice **nett**
niece **die Nichte**
night **die Nacht**
nightclub **der Nachtklub**
nightdress **das Nachthemd**
no **nein**
nobody **niemand**
noise **der Lärm**

noisy **laut**
non-alcoholic **alkoholfrei**
none **kein/e/r**
non-smoking **Nichtraucher**
normal **normal**
normally **normalerweise**
north **der Norden**
nose **die Nase**
nosebleed **das Nasenbluten**
nostril **das Nasenloch**
not **nicht**
note (*bank*) **der Schein**
notepad **der Notizblock**
nothing **nichts**
nothing else **sonst nichts**
now **jetzt**
nowhere **nirgendwo**
nuclear power **die Kernkraft**
number **die Nummer**
nurse **der Krankenpfleger/die Krankenschwester**
nursery slope **der Anfängerhügel**
nut **die Nuß**
(*DIY*) **die Schraubenmutter**
nylon **das Nylon**

O

oar **das Ruder**
object (*thing*) **der Gegenstand**
obvious **offensichtlich**
occasionally **hin und wieder**
occupied (*seat*) **besetzt**
odd **merkwürdig**
(*not even*) **ungerade**
of **von + dat.** (*see grammar, p. 182*)
of course **natürlich**
off (*TV, light*) **aus**
(*milk*) **alt**
offended **beleidigt**
offer **das Angebot**
special offer **das Sonderangebot**
office **das Büro**
officer **der Offizier**
official **der Beamte/die Beamtin**
often **oft**
how often? **wie oft?**
oil **das Öl**
OK **OK**
old **alt**
how old are you? **wie alt sind Sie?/wie alt bist du?**
how old is he/she? **wie alt ist er/sie?**
I am . . . years old **Ich bin . . . Jahre alt**
old-fashioned **altmodisch**
olive **die Olive**
olive oil **das Olivenöl**
on **auf + acc. or dat.** (*see grammar, p. 182*)
once **einmal**
onion **die Zwiebel**
only **nur**
open **geöffnet**
to open **öffnen**
opera **die Oper**
operation **die Operation**
opinion **die Meinung**
in my opinion **meiner Meinung nach**
opposite **gegenüber + dat.** (*see grammar, p. 182*)
optician **der Optiker/die Optikerin**
or **oder**
orange (*fruit*) **die Orange, die Apfelsine**
(*colour*) **orange**
order **die Bestellung**

to order **bestellen**
ordinary **gewöhnlich**
to organise **organisieren**
original **ursprünglich**
other **andere**
others **die anderen**
our **unser**
ours **unsere/r/s**
out (of) **aus + dat.** (*see grammar, p. 182*)
outdoor(s), outside **draußen**
over **über + acc. or dat.** (*see grammar, p. 182*)
overcast **bedeckt**
to overtake **überholen**
to owe **schuldig sein**
how much do I owe? **was bin ich schuldig?**
owner **der Besitzer/die Besitzerin**
ozone-friendly **ozonfreundlich**

P

package tour **die Pauschalreise**
packet **das Paket**
paddle (*canoeing*) **das Paddel**
padlock **das Vorhängeschloß**
page **die Seite**
pain **der Schmerz**
painful **schmerzhaft**
painkiller **das Schmerzmittel**
paint **die Farbe**
to paint **streichen**
(*picture*) **malen**
painter **der Maler/die Malerin**
painting **das Gemälde**
pair **das Paar**
palace **der Palast**
pale **blaß**
panties, pants **der Slip**
paper **das Papier**
paper clip **die Büroklammer**
paraffin **das Paraffin**
paralysed **gelähmt**
parcel **das Paket**
pardon? **wie bitte?**
parents **die Eltern**
park **der Park**
to park **parken**
parking **das Parken**
parking disc **die Parkscheibe**
parking meter **die Parkuhr**
parliament **das Parlament**
part **der Teil**
parting (*hair*) **der Scheitel**
partly **zum Teil, teilweise**
partner **der Partner/die Partnerin**
party **die Party**
(*political*) **die Partei**
to pass (*on road*) **überholen**
(*salt etc.*) **geben**
(*exam/test*) **bestehen**
passenger **der Passagier**
(*bus, taxi*) **der Fahrgast**
passion **die Leidenschaft**
passport **der Paß**
passport control **die Paßkontrolle**
past **die Vergangenheit**
in the past **in der Vergangenheit**
(*see Time, p. 193*) **nach . . .**
pasta **die Teigwaren, die Nudeln**
pastille **die Pastille**
pastry **der Teig**
path **der Weg**
patient (*hospital*) **der Pazient/die Pazientin**
pattern **das Muster**
pavement **der Gehsteig**
to pay **bezahlen**
to pay cash **bar bezahlen**

peas **die Erbsen**
peace **der Frieden**
peach **der Pfirsich**
peanut **die Erdnuß**
pear **die Birne**
pedal **das Pedal**
pedal-boat (*pedalo*) **das Tretboot**
pedestrian **der Fußgänger**
pedestrian crossing **der Zebrastreifen, der Fußgängerüberweg**
to peel **schälen**
peg **die Wäscheklammer**
pen **der Stift**
pencil **der Bleistift**
pencil sharpener **der Spitzer**
penfriend **der Brieffreund/die Brieffreundin**
penknife **das Taschenmesser**
penicillin **das Penizillin**
pension **die Rente**
pensioner **der Rentner/die Rentnerin**
people **die Leute**
pepper **der Pfeffer**
(*sweet/green/red*) **der Paprika**
peppermint **der Pfefferminz**
per **pro**
perfect **perfekt**
performance **die Vorstellung**
perfume **das Parfüm**
perhaps **vielleicht**
period (*menstrual*) **die Tage**
period pains **die Regelschmerzen**
perm **die Dauerwelle**
permit **die Erlaubnis**
to permit **erlauben**
person **die Person**
personal **persönlich**
personal stereo **der Walkman**
petrol **das Benzin**
petrol can **der Kanister**
petrol station **die Tankstelle**
petticoat **der Unterrock**
philosophy **die Philosophie**
photocopy **die Fotokopie**
to photocopy **fotokopieren**
photo(graph) **die Foto(grafie)**
photographer **der Fotograf/die Fotografin**
photography **die Fotografie**
phrase book **der Sprachführer**
physics **die Physik**
piano **das Klavier**
to pick (*choose*) **wählen**
(*flowers etc.*) **pflücken**
picnic **das Picknick**
picture **das Bild**
piece **das Stück**
pier **die Anlegestelle**
pig **das Schwein**
pill **die Tablette**
the pill **die Pille**
pillow **das Kissen**
pillowcase **der Kopfkissenbezug**
pilot **der Pilot/die Pilotin**
pilot light **die Zündflamme**
pin **die Stecknadel**
pineapple **die Ananas**
pink **rosa**
pipe (*smoking*) **die Pfeife**
(*drain*) **das Rohr**
place **der Ort**
(*seat*) **der Platz**
plain **einfach**
plan (*of town*) **der Stadtplan**
plane **das Flugzeug**
plant **die Pflanze**
plaster (*sticking*) **das Pflaster**

plastic **plastik**
plastic bag **die Plastiktüte**
plate **der Teller**
platform **der Bahnsteig**
play (*theatre*) **das Theaterstück**
to play **spielen**
pleasant **angenehm**
please **bitte**
pleased **erfreut**
plenty (of) **eine Menge (von) + dat.** (*see grammar, p. 182*)
pliers **die Zange**
plimsolls **die Turnschuhe**
plug (*bath*) **der Stöpsel**
(*electrical*) **der Stecker**
plumber **der Klempner**
pneumonia **die Lungenentzündung**
pocket **die Tasche**
point **der Punkt**
(*needle, pin*) **die Spitze**
poison **das Gift**
poisonous **giftig**
pole **der Pfahl**
police **die Polizei**
police car **das Polizeiauto**
police station **die Polizeiwache**
polish **die Politur**
polite **höflich**
politician **der Politker/die Politikerin**
political **politisch**
politics **die Politik**
polluted **verschmutzt**
pollution **die Verschmutzung**
pool (*swimming*) **das Schwimmbecken**
poor **arm**
pop (*music*) **die Popmusik**
Pope **der Papst**
popular **beliebt**
pork **das Schweinefleisch**
port (*harbour*) **der Hafen**
(*wine*) **der Portwein**
portable **tragbar**
porter **der Gepäckträger**
porthole **das Bullauge**
portion **die Portion**
portrait **das Porträt**
positive (*sure*) **sicher**
possible **möglich**
as . . . as possible **so . . . wie möglich**
possibly **möglicherweise**
post (*mail*) **die Post**
to post **abschicken**
postbox **der Briefkasten**
postcard **die Postkarte**
postcode **die Postleitzahl**
poster **das Poster**
(*billboard*) **das Plakat**
postman **der Briefträger**
post office **das Postamt**
to postpone **aufschieben**
pot **der Topf**
potato **die Kartoffel**
pottery **die Töpferei**
potty (*child's*) **das Töpfchen**
pound (*sterling*) **das Pfund Sterling**
to pour **gießen**
powder **das Pulver**
(*talcum*) **der Puder**
powdered milk **das Milchpulver**
powdery **pulvrig**
power **die Macht**
(*physical strength*) **die Kraft**
power cut **die Stromsperre**
pram **der Kinderwagen**
to prefer **vorziehen**
pregnant **schwanger**
to prepare **vorbereiten**

prescription **das Rezept**
present (*gift*) **das Geschenk**
press (newspapers) **die Presse**
to press **drücken**
pretty **hübsch**
price **der Preis**
priest **der Geistliche**
prime minister **der Ministerpräsident/die Ministerpräsidentin**
prince **der Prinz**
princess **die Prinzessin**
print (*photo*) **der Abzug**
to print **drucken**
prison **das Gefängnis**
private **privat**
prize **der Preis**
probably **wahrscheinlich**
problem **das Problem**
producer (*radio/TV/film*) **der Produzent/die Produzentin**
profession **der Beruf**
professor **der Professor/die Professorin**
profit **der Gewinn**
programme **das Programm**
prohibited **verboten**
to promise **versprechen**
to pronounce **aussprechen**
properly **richtig**
property **das Eigentum**
protestant **protestantisch**
public (*noun*) **die Öffentlichkeit** (*adj.*) **öffentlich**
public holiday **der gesetzliche Feiertag**
public relations officer **der Pressesprecher/die Pressesprecherin**
to pull **ziehen**
to pump up **aufpumpen**
puncture **die Platte**
pure **rein**
purple **purpur**
purse **der Geldbeutel**
to push **schieben**
push-chair **der Sportwagen**
to put down **hinstellen**
to put on (*clothes*) **anziehen**
pyjamas **der Pyjama**

Q

quality **die Qualität**
quarter **das Viertel**
quay **der Kai**
queen **die Königin**
question **die Frage**
queue **die Schlange**
quick(ly) **schnell**
quiet **still**
quite **ziemlich**

R

rabbi **der Rabbiner**
rabbit **das Kaninchen**
rabies **die Tollwut**
racecourse **die Rennbahn**
racing (*horse*) **der Pferderennsport** (*motor*) **das Motorrennen**
racket (*tennis*) **der Schläger**
radiator (*heating*) **der Radiator**
radio **das Radio**
radioactive **radioaktiv**
radio station **die Rundfunkstation**
raft **das Floß**
railway **die Eisenbahn**
railway station **der Bahnhof**

rain **der Regen**
it's raining **es regnet**
raincoat **der Regenmantel**
to rape **vergewaltigen**
rare **selten**
(*steak*) **blutig**
rash (*spots*) **der Ausschlag**
raspberries **die Himbeeren**
rate (*speed*) **das Tempo**
(*tariff*) **der Satz**
rather (*quite*) **ziemlich**
raw **roh**
razor **der Rasierer**
razor blade **die Rasierklinge**
to reach **erreichen**
to read **lesen**
reading **das Lesen**
ready **fertig**
real (*authentic*) **echt**
really **wirklich**
rear **der hintere Teil**
reason **der Grund**
receipt **die Quittung**
receiver (*telephone*) **der Hörer**
reception **der Empfang**
receptionist **die Rezeptionistin**
recipe **das Rezept**
to recognise **erkennen**
to recommend **empfehlen**
record **die Schallplatte**
to record **aufnehmen**
record-player **der Plattenspieler**
to recover (*from an illness*) **sich erholen**
red **rot**
Red Cross **das Rote Kreuz**
reduction **die Ermäßigung**
to refill **nachfüllen**
refrigerator **der Kühlschrank**
refugee **der Flüchtling**
refund **die Rückerstattung**
to refund **zurückerstatten**
region **das Gebiet**
to register (*luggage etc.*) **einschreiben**
registered (*letter*) **eingeschrieben**
registration number **das Kraftfahrzeugkennzeichen**
registration document (*car*) **der Kraftfahrzeugbrief**
relation **der/die Verwandte**
relatively **einigermaßen**
religion **die Religion**
to remain **bleiben**
to remember **sich erinnern an + acc.** (*see grammar, p. 182*)
to remove **wegnehmen**
(*tooth*) **herausnehmen**
rent **die Miete**
to rent **mieten**
to repair **reparieren**
to repeat **wiederholen**
reply **die Antwort**
to reply **antworten**
report **der Bericht**
to report **berichten**
to rescue **retten**
reservation (*hotel etc.*) **die Reservierung**
to reserve **buchen**
reserved **reserviert**
responsible **verantwortlich**
to rest **sich ausruhen**
restaurant **das Restaurant**
restaurant-car **der Speisewagen**
result **das Ergebnis**
retired **pensioniert**
return **die Rückkehr**
(*ticket*) **hin und zurück**

to return **wiederkommen**
to reverse (*car*) **rückwärts fahren**
reverse-charge call **das Rückgespräch**
rheumatism **das Rheuma**
ribbon **das Band**
(*typewriter*) **das Farbband**
rice **der Reis**
rich **reich**
to ride (*horse/bike*) **reiten, fahren**
right **rechts**
(*correct*) **richtig**
to be right **recht haben**
you're right **Sie haben recht**
right-hand **die rechte Seite**
ring (*jewellery*) **der Ring**
ripe **reif**
river **der Fluß**
road **die Straße**
(*main*) **die Hauptstraße**
roadworks **die Straßenbauarbeiten**
roast **der Braten**
to rob **berauben**
robbery **der Raub**
roof **das Dach**
roll (*bread*) **das Brötchen. die Semmel** (*Austria*)
roller (*hair*) **der Lockenwickler**
room **das Zimmer**
(*space*) **der Raum**
rope **das Seil**
rose **die Rose**
rosé **der Rosé**
rotten **faul**
rough (*surface*) **rauh**
(*sea*) **stürmisch**
round **rund**
roundabout **der Kreisverkehr**
row (*theatre etc.*) **die Reihe**
to row **rudern**
rowing boat **das Ruderboot**
royal **königlich**
rubber **der Gummi**
rubbish **der Abfall**
rucksack **der Rucksack**
rude **unhöflich**
ruins **die Ruinen**
ruler (*for measuring*) **das Lineal**
rum **der Rum**
to run **rennen**
rush hour **die Stoßzeit**
rusty **rostig**

S

sad **traurig**
safe (*strongbox*) **der Safe**
safe **sicher**
safety pin **die Sicherheitsnadel**
sail **das Segel**
to sail **segeln**
sailboard **das Surfbrett**
sailing **das Segeln**
sailing boat **das Segelboot**
sailor **der Matrose**
saint **der/die Heilige**
salad **der Salat**
sale (*bargains*) **der Ausverkauf**
sales representative **der Verkaufsvertreter/die Verkaufsvertreterin**
salmon **der Lachs**
salt **das Salz**
salty **salzig**
same **der-/die-/dasselbe**
sample **das Muster**
sand **der Sand**
sandals **die Sandalen**

sandwich **das Sandwich**
open sandwich **das belegte Brot**
sandy **sandig**
sanitary towel **die Damenbinde**
sauce **die Soße**
saucepan **der Kochtopf**
saucer **die Untertasse**
sauna **die Sauna**
sausage **die Wurst**
to save (*money*) **sparen**
to say **sagen**
scald **verbrühen**
scales **die Waage**
scarf **das Halstuch**
(*head*) **das Kopftuch**
scene **die Szene**
scenery **die Landschaft**
scent **der Duft**
school **die Schule**
science **die Wissenschaft**
scientist **der Wissenschaftler**
scissors **die Schere**
scooter **der Motorroller**
score: what's the score? **wie steht es?**
Scotland **Schottland (das)**
Scottish **schottisch**
scratch **der Kratzer**
to scratch **kratzen**
screen **der Bildschirm**
screw **die Schraube**
screwdriver **der Schraubenzieher**
sculpture **die Skulptur**
sea **das Meer, die See**
seafood **die Meeresfrüchte**
seasick **seekrank**
season **die Jahreszeit**
season ticket **die Zeitkarte**
seat **der Sitz**
seatbelt **der Sicherheitsgurt**
second **der/die/das zweite**
(*adj.*) **zweite/r/s**
second (*time period*) **die Sekunde**
secret **das Geheimnis**
secretary **die Sekretärin**
section **der Teil**
sedative **das Beruhigungsmittel**
to see **sehen**
to seem **scheinen**
self-catering **für Selbstversorger**
self-service **die Selbstbedienung**
to sell **verkaufen**
to send **schicken, senden**
senior citizen **der Rentner/die Rentnerin**
sensible **vernünftig**
sentence **der Satz**
separate(d) **getrennt**
septic tank **die Sickergrube**
serious **ernst(haft)**
(*grave*) **schlimm**
(*important*) **wichtig**
to serve **bedienen**
service (*charge*) **die Bedienung**
(*church*) **der Gottesdienst**
set (*collection*) **der Satz**
setting lotion **der Haarfestiger**
several **mehrere**
to sew **nähen**
sewing **das Nähen**
sex (*gender*) **das Geschlecht**
(*intercourse*) **der Sex**
shade (*not sunny*), shadow **der Schatten**
shampoo **das Shampoo**
shampoo and set **das Waschen und Legen**
sharp **scharf**
shave **die Rasur**
to shave **rasieren**

shaving cream/foam **die Rasiercreme**
she **sie**
sheep **das Schaf**
sheet **das Bettuch**
shelf **das Regal**
shell (*egg, nut*) **die Schale**
shellfish **die Schaltiere**
shelter **der Schutz**
sherry **der Sherry**
shiny **glänzend**
ship **das Schiff**
shirt **das Hemd**
shock (*electrical*) **der Schlag**
(*emotional*) **der Schock**
shocked **geschockt**
shoe(s) **der Schuh. die Schuhe**
shoelace **der Schnursenkel**
shoe polish **die Schuhcreme**
shoe repairer's **der Schuster**
shoe shop **das Schuhgeschäft**
shop **der Laden, das Geschäft**
shop assistant **der Verkäufer/ die Verkäuferin**
shopping: to go shopping **einkaufen gehen**
shopping centre **das Einkaufszentrum**
short **kurz**
shorts **die Shorts**
shout **der Ruf**
show **die Aufführung**
to show **zeigen**
shower **die Dusche**
to shrink **einlaufen**
shrunk **eingelaufen**
shut **geschlossen**
shutter **der Fensterladen**
sick **krank**
to be sick **sich übergeben**
to feel sick **sich schlecht fühlen**

sick bag **die Spucktüte**
side **die Seite**
sieve **das Sieb**
sight (*vision*) **das Sehvermögen**
(*tourist*) **die Sehenswürdigkeit**
sightseeing **die Besichtigungen**
sign **das Schild**
to sign **unterschreiben**
signal **das Zeichen**
signature **die Unterschrift**
silent **still**
silk **die Seide**
silver **das Silber**
similar **ähnlich**
simple **einfach**
since **seit + dat.** (*see grammar, p. 182*)
to sing **singen**
single (*room, ticket*) **Einzel-**
(*unmarried*) **ledig**
sink **das Spülbecken**
sir **mein Herr**
sister **die Schwester**
sister-in-law **die Schwägerin**
to sit (*down*) **sich hinsetzen**
size (*clothes, shoes*) **die Größe**
skates (*ice*) **die Schlittschuhe**
(*roller*) **die Rollschuhe**
to skate **Schlittschuh laufen**
ski **der Ski**
to ski **Ski laufen**
ski boots **die Skistiefel, die Skischuhe**
skiing **das Skilaufen**
downhill skiing **der Abfahrtslauf**
cross-country skiing **der Langlauf**
ski-lift **der Skilift**
skimmed milk **die Magermilch**
skin **die Haut**

skindiving **das Tauchen**
ski pole **der Skistock**
skirt **der Rock**
ski-run/slope **die Piste**
sky **der Himmel**
to sleep **schlafen**
sleeper/sleeping-car **der Schlafwagen**
sleeping bag **der Schlafsack**
sleeve **der Ärmel**
slice **die Scheibe**
sliced **geschnitten**
slide film **der Diafilm**
slim **schlank**
slip (*petticoat*) **der Unterrock**
slippery **rutschig**
slow(ly) **langsam**
small **klein**
smell **der Geruch**
to smell **riechen**
(*of . . .*) **nach + dat.** (*see grammar, p. 182*)
(*bad/good*) **schlecht/gut**
smile **das Lächeln**
to smile **lächeln**
smoke **der Rauch**
to smoke **rauchen**
smooth **glatt**
to sneeze **niesen**
snorkel **der Schnorchel**
snow **der Schnee**
snow chains **die Schneeketten**
to snow **schneien**
it's snowing **es schneit**
so **so**
(*therefore*) **also**
so much **so viel**
soap **die Seife**
sober **nüchtern**
socialism **der Sozialismus**
socialist **sozialistisch**
social worker **der Sozialarbeiter/die Sozialarbeiterin**
sociology **die Soziologie**
sock **die Socke**
socket **die Steckdose**
soda (*water*) **das Soda**
soft **weich**
soft drink **das alkoholfreie Getränk**
soldier **der Soldat**
sold out **ausverkauft**
solicitor **der Rechtsanwalt/die Rechtsanwältin**
solid **fest**
some **einige**
somehow **irgendwie**
someone **jemand**
something **etwas**
sometimes **manchmal**
somewhere **irgendwo**
son **der Sohn**
song **das Lied**
son-in-law **der Schwiegersohn**
soon **bald**
as soon as possible **so bald wie möglich**
sore (*inc. throat*) **weh**
sorry: I'm sorry **es tut mir leid**
sort **die Sorte**
sound **der Ton**
soup **die Suppe**
sour **sauer**
south **der Süden**
souvenir **das Souvenir**
space **der Raum**
spade **der Spaten**
spanner **der Schraubenschlüssel**
spare **übrig**

spare time **die Freizeit**
spare tyre **der Ersatzreifen**
sparkling wine **der Schaumwein**
to speak **sprechen**
special **besondere**
special offer **das Sonderangebot**
specialist **der Spezialist/die Spezialistin**
speciality **die Spezialität**
spectacles **die Brille**
speed **die Geschwindigkeit**
speed limit **die Geschwindigkeitsbegrenzung**
to spend (*money*) **ausgeben**
(*time*) **verbringen**
spice **das Gewürz**
spicy **würzig**
spinach **der Spinat**
spirits **die Spirituosen**
splinter **der Splitter**
to spoil **verderben**
sponge (*bath*) **der Schwamm**
spoon **der Löffel**
sport **der Sport**
spot **der Punkt**
(*place*) **die Stelle**
to sprain **verstauchen**
sprained **verstaucht**
spray **der Spray**
spring (*season*) **der Frühling**
square **der Platz**
(*shape*) **das Quadrat**
stadium **das Stadion**
stain **der Fleck**
stainless steel **der rostfreie Edelstahl**
stairs **die Treppe**
stalls (*theatre*) **das Parkett**
stamp (*postage*) **die Briefmarke**

stand (*stadium*) **dieTribüne**
to stand **stehen**
to stand up **aufstehen**
stapler **die Heftmaschine**
star **der Stern**
start **der Beginn**
to start **anfangen**
starter (*food*) **die Vorspeise**
state **der Staat**
station **der Bahnhof**
station master **der Bahnhofsvorsteher**
stationer's **die Schreibwarenhandlung**
statue **die Statue**
to stay (*live*) **wohnen**
(*remain*) **bleiben**
steak **das Steak**
to steal **stehlen**
steam **der Dampf**
steamer **der Dampfer**
steel **der Stahl**
steep **steil**
step (*footstep*) **der Schritt**
step-brother **der Stiefbruder**
step-children **die Stiefkinder**
step-father **der Stiefvater**
step-mother **die Stiefmutter**
step-sister **die Stiefschwester**
stereo **das Stereo**
sterling: pound sterling **das Pfund Sterling**
steward (*air*) **der Steward**
stewardess (*air*) **die Stewardess**
stick **der Stock**
sticking plaster **das Heftpflaster**
sticky **klebrig**
sticky tape **das Klebeband**
stiff **steif**
still (*yet*) **noch**

still (*non-fizzy*) **ohne Kohlensäure**
sting **der Stich**
to sting **stechen**
stock cube **der Suppenwürfel**
stock exchange **die Börse**
stockings **die Strümpfe**
stolen **gestohlen**
stomach **der Magen**
stomach ache **die Magenschmerzen**
stomach upset **der verdorbene Magen**
stone **der Stein**
stop (*bus*) **die Haltestelle**
to stop **halten**
stop! **halt!**
stopcock **der Abstellhahn**
story **die Geschichte**
stove **der Herd**
straight **gerade**
straight on **immer geradeaus**
strange **seltsam**
stranger **der/die Fremde**
strap **der Riemen**
straw (*drinking*) **der Strohhalm**
strawberries **die Erdbeeren**
stream **der Fluß**
street **die Straße**
streetlight **die Straßenlampe**
stretcher **die Bahre**
strike **der Streik**
string **die Schnur**
stripe **der Streifen**
striped **gestreift**
strong **stark**
to stick: it's stuck **es klemmt**
student **der Student/die Studentin**
studio (*radio/TV*) **das Studio**
to study **studieren**
stupid **dumm**
style **der Stil**
styling mousse **der Schaumfestiger**
subtitles **die Untertitel**
suburb **der Vorort**
to succeed **Erfolg haben**
success **der Erfolg**
such **solche/r/s**
suddenly **plötzlich**
sugar **der Zucker**
sugar lump **der Zuckerwürfel**
suit (*man's*) **der Anzug**
(*woman's*) **das Kostüm**
suitcase **der Koffer**
summer **der Sommer**
sun **die Sonne**
to sunbathe **sonnenbaden**
sunburn **der Sonnenbrand**
sunglasses **die Sonnenbrille**
sunny **sonnig**
sunshade **der Sonnenschirm**
sunstroke **der Sonnenstich**
suntan cream **die Sonnencreme**
suntan oil **das Sonnenöl**
supermarket **der Supermarkt**
supper **das Abendbrot**
supplement **der Zuschlag**
suppose: I suppose so **ich nehme es wohl an**
suppository **das Zäpfchen**
sure **sicher**
surface **die Oberfläche**
surname **der Nachname**
surprise **die Überraschung**
surprised **überrascht**
surrounded by **umgeben von + dat.** (*see grammar, p. 182*)
to sweat **schwitzen**
sweater **der Pullover**
sweatshirt **das Sweatshirt**

to sweep **fegen**
sweet **süß**
sweetener **der Süßstoff**
sweets **die Süßigkeiten**
swelling **die Schwellung**
to swim **schwimmen**
swimming **das Schwimmen**
swimming pool **das Schwimmbad**
swimming trunks **die Badehose**
swimsuit **der Badeanzug**
switch **der Schalter**
to switch off **ausschalten**
to switch on **einschalten**
swollen **geschwollen**
symptom **das Symptom**
synagogue **die Synagoge**
synthetic **synthetisch**
system **das System**

T

table **der Tisch**
tablet **die Tablette**
table tennis **der Tischtennis**
tailor **der Schneider**
to take **nehmen**
(*photo, exam*) **machen**
(*time*) **dauern**
taken (*seat*) **besetzt**
to take off (*clothes*) **sich ausziehen**
(*plane*) **abfliegen**
talcum powder **der Körperpuder**
to talk **sprechen**
tall **groß**
tampons **die Tampons**
tap **der Hahn**
tape (*adhesive*) **das Klebeband**
(*cassette*) **die Kassette**
tape measure **das Bandmaß**
tape recorder **das Tonbandgerät**
taste **der Geschmack**
to taste **schmecken**
it tastes good **es schmeckt gut**
tax **die Steuer**
taxi **das Taxi**
taxi rank **der Taxistand**
tea **der Tee**
teabag **der Teebeutel**
to teach **unterrichten**
teacher **der Lehrer/die Lehrerin**
team **das Team**
teapot **die Teekanne**
tear (*rip*) **der Riß**
teaspoon **der Teelöffel**
teat (*for baby's bottle*) **der Sauger**
tea-towel **das Geschirrtuch**
technical **technisch**
technology **die Technologie**
teenager **der Teenager**
telegram **das Telegramm**
telephone **das Telefon**
telephone card **die Telefonkarte**
telephone directory **das Telefonbuch**
telephone kiosk **die Telefonzelle**
to telephone **anrufen**
television **das Fernsehen**
telex **das Telex**
to tell **erzählen**
temperature **die Temperatur**
to have a temperature **Fieber haben**
temporary **provisorisch**
tender **zart**
tennis **das Tennis**
tennis court **der Tennisplatz**
tennis shoes/trainers **die Turnschuhe**
tent **das Zelt**
tent peg **der Hering**

tent pole **die Zeltstange**
terminal (*airport*) **der Terminal**
terminus **die Endstation**
terrace **die Terrasse**
terrible **schrecklich**
terrorist **der Terrorist/die Terroristin**
thank you **danke**
thank you very much **vielen Dank**
that (one) **das (da)**
the **der, die, das**
theatre **das Theater**
their **ihr**
theirs **ihre/r/s**
them **sie**
(to) them **ihnen**
then **dann**
there **dort, da**
there is/are **es gibt**
therefore **deshalb**
thermometer **das Thermometer**
these **diese**
they **sie**
thick **dick**
thief **der Dieb**
thin **dünn**
thing **die Sache, das Ding**
to think **denken**
(*believe*) **glauben**
I (don't) think so **ich glaube (nicht)**
third **dritte/r/s**
thirsty **durstig**
this (one) **das (hier)**
those **jene**
thread **der Faden**
throat lozenges/pastilles **die Halspastillen**
through **durch + acc.** (*see grammar, p. 182*)
to throw **werfen**
to throw away **wegwerfen**
thumb **der Daumen**
thunder **der Donner**
ticket (*travel*) **die Fahrkarte**
(*theatre etc.*) **die Eintrittskarte**
ticket office **der Fahrkartenschalter**
tide (*high/low*) **das Hochwasser/ das Niedrigwasser**
tidy **ordentlich**
tie **der Schlips**
to tie **befestigen**
tight (*clothes*) **eng**
tights **die Strumpfhose**
till (*until*) **bis**
time **die Zeit**
(*once etc.*) **das Mal**
(*on clock, see p. 193*) **die Uhr**
timetable (*trains*) **der Fahrplan**
tin **die Dose**
tin foil **die Alufolie**
tinned **Dosen-**
tinned milk **die Dosenmilch**
tin opener **der Dosenöffner**
tip (*in restaurant etc.*) **das Trinkgeld**
tired **müde**
tissues **die Papiertaschentücher**
to **zu + dat.** (*see grammar, p. 182*)
(*with named places*) **nach + dat.** (*see grammar, p. 182*)
toast **der Toast**
tobacco **der Tabak**
tobacconists **der Tabakladen**
toboggan **der Schlitten**
today **heute**
toiletries **die Toilettenartikel**
toilets **die Toiletten**
toilet paper **das Toilettenpapier**
toilet water **das Eau de Toilette**
toll **die Maut**

tomato **die Tomate**
tomorrow **morgen**
tongue **die Zunge**
tonic water **das Tonic**
tonight **heute abend**
too **zu**
(*as well*) **auch**
tool **das Werkzeug**
tooth **der Zahn**
toothache **die Zahnschmerzen**
toothbrush **die Zahnbürste**
toothpaste **die Zahnpasta**
toothpick **der Zahnstocher**
top (*mountain*) **der Gipfel**
on top of **oben auf + acc. or dat.** (*see grammar, p. 182*)
torch **die Taschenlampe**
torn **zerrissen**
total **die Endsumme**
totally **total**
to touch **berühren**
tough (*meat*) **zäh**
tour **die Fahrt**
to tour **eine Reise machen**
tourism **der Tourismus**
tourist **der Tourist**
tourist office **das Fremdenverkehrsbüro**
to tow **abschleppen**
towards **nach + dat.** (*see grammar, p. 182*)
towel **das Handtuch**
tower **der Turm**
town **die Stadt**
town centre **das Stadtzentrum**
town hall **das Rathaus**
town plan **der Stadtplan**
tow rope **das Abschleppseil**
toy **das Spielzeug**
track **die Bahn**
tracksuit **der Trainingsanzug**
trade union **die Gewerkschaft**
traditional **traditionell**
traffic **der Verkehr**
traffic jam **der Verkehrsstau**
traffic lights **die Verkehrsampel**
trailer **der Anhänger**
train **der Zug**
by train **mit dem Zug**
training shoes (*trainers*) **die Trainingschuhe**
tram **die Straßenbahn**
tranquilliser **das Beruhigungsmittel**
to translate **übersetzen**
translation **die Übersetzung**
to travel **reisen**
travel agency **das Reisebüro**
traveller's cheques **die Reiseschecks**
travel sickness **reisekrank**
tray **das Tablett**
treatment **die Behandlung**
tree **der Baum**
trip **der Ausflug**
trousers **die Hose**
trout **die Forelle**
true **wahr**
that's true **das stimmt/das ist wahr**
to try (*attempt*) **versuchen**
to try on **anprobieren**
T-shirt **das T-Shirt**
tube (*pipe*) **das Rohr**
(*underground*) **die U-Bahn**
tuna **der Thunfisch**
tunnel **der Tunnel**
turn: it's my turn **ich bin daran**
to turn **drehen**
to turn off **abbiegen**
turning (*side road*) **die Abfahrt**

twice **zweimal**
twin beds **zwei Einzelbetten**
twins **die Zwillinge**
twisted (*ankle*) **verrenkt**
type (*sort*) **der Typ**
to type **tippen**
typewriter **die Schreibmaschine**
typical **typisch**

U

ugly **häßlich**
ulcer **das Geschwür**
umbrella **der Regenschirm**
uncle **der Onkel**
uncomfortable **unbequem**
under **unter + acc. or dat.** (*see grammar, p. 182*)
underground (*tube*) **die U-Bahn**
underpants **die Unterhose**
underpass **die Unterführung**
to understand **verstehen**
underwater **Unterwasser-**
underwear **die Unterwäsche**
to undress **sich ausziehen**
unemployed **arbeitslos**
unfortunately **leider**
unhappy **unglücklich**
uniform **die Uniform**
university **die Universität**
unleaded petrol **das bleifreie Benzin**
unless **es sei denn**
unless they arrive **es sei denn, sie kommen an**
unpack **auspacken**
unpleasant **unangenehm**
to unscrew **aufschrauben**
until **bis**
unusual **ungewöhnlich**
unwell **unwohl**
up **auf**
up the hill **bergauf**
up the road **die Straße hoch**
upper **obere/r/s**
upstairs **oben**
urgent **dringend**
urine **der Urin**
us **uns**
to use **benutzen**
useful **nützlich**
useless **nutzlos**
usually **gewöhnlich**

V

vacant **frei**
vacuum cleaner **der Staubsauger**
vacuum flask **die Thermosflasche**
valid **gültig**
valley **das Tal**
valuable **wertvoll**
valuables **die Wertsachen**
van **der Lieferwagen**
vanilla **die Vanille**
vase **die Vase**
VAT **die Mehrwertsteuer**
veal **das Kalbfleisch**
vegan **der Vegetarier/die Vegetarierin**
vegetables **das Gemüse**
vegetarian **der Vegetarier/die Vegetarierin**
(*adj.*) **vegetarisch**
vehicle **das Fahrzeug**
vermouth **der Wermut**
very **sehr**
vest **das Unterhemd**
vet **der Tierarzt/die Tierärztin**

via **über**
video **das Video**
view **die Aussicht**
villa **die Villa**
village **das Dorf**
vinegar **der Essig**
vineyard **der Weinberg**
virgin **die Jungfrau**
Virgin Mary **die Jungfrau Maria**
visa **das Visum**
visit **der Besuch**
to visit **besuchen**
(*tourist sites*) **besichtigen**
visitor **der Besucher/die Besucherin**
vitamin **das Vitamin**
vodka **der Wodka**
voice **die Stimme**
volleyball **der Volleyball**
voltage **das Volt**
to vote **wählen**

W

wage **der Lohn**
waist **die Taille**
waistcoat **die Weste**
to wait (*for*) **warten (auf) + acc.**
waiter **der Ober**
waiting room **der Warteraum**
waitress **die Kellnerin**
Wales **Wales**
walk **der Spaziergang**
to walk, go for a walk **einen Spaziergang machen**
walking stick **der Spazierstock**
wall (*inside*) **die Wand**
(*outside*) **die Mauer**
wallet **die Brieftasche**
walnut **die Walnuß**
to want **wollen**
would like **möchte**
war **der Krieg**
warm **warm**
to wash **waschen**
washable **waschbar**
wash-basin **das Waschbecken**
washing **die Wäsche**
washing machine **die Waschmaschine**
washing powder **das Waschpulver**
washing-up **der Abwasch**
washing-up liquid **das Spülmittel**
wastepaper basket **der Papierkorb**
watch (*clock*) **die Armbanduhr**
to watch **zuschauen**
to watch TV **fernsehen**
watchstrap **das Uhrarmband**
water **das Wasser**
water heater **der Warmwasserbereiter**
water melon **die Wassermelone**
waterfall **der Wasserfall**
waterproof **wasserdicht**
water-skiing **das Wasserskilaufen**
water-skis **die Wasserskis**
wave **die Welle**
way (*path*) **der Weg**
that way **in der Richtung**
this way **in dieser Richtung**
way in **der Eingang**
way out **der Ausgang**

wax **das Wachs**
we **wir**
weather **das Wetter**
what's the weather like? **wie ist das Wetter?**
weather forecast **die Wettervorhersage**
wedding **die Hochzeit**
week **die Woche**
weekday **der Werktag**
weekend **das Wochenende**
weekly **wöchentlich**
to weigh **wiegen**
weight **das Gewicht**
well **gut**
as well **auch**
well done (*steak*) **durch**
Welsh **walisisch**
west **der Westen**
western **westlich**
(*film*) **der Western**
wet **naß**
wetsuit **der Taucheranzug**
what **was, das**
what? **was?**
what is . . . ? **was ist . . . ?**
wheel **das Rad**
wheelchair **der Rollstuhl**
when (*whenever*) **wenn**
(*with past tense*) **als**
when? **wann?**
where **wo**
where? **wo?**
where is/are . . . ?
wo ist . . . ?/wo sind . . . ?
which **welche/r/s**
which? **welche?**
while **während + gen.**
whisky **der Whisky**
on the rocks **mit Eis**
neat **pur**
white **weiß**
(*with milk*) **mit Milch**
who (*relative*) **der, die, das**
who? **wer?**
who is it? **wer ist das?**
whole **vollständig**
wholemeal bread **das Vollkornbrot**
why **warum, weshalb**
why? **warum?**
why not? **warum nicht?**
wide **breit**
widow **die Witwe**
widower **der Witwer**
wife **die Frau**
wild **wild**
to win **gewinnen**
who won? **wer hat gewonnen?**
wind **der Wind**
windmill **die Windmühle**
window **das Fenster**
(*shop*) **das Schaufenster**
to windsurf **windsurfen**
windy: it's windy **es ist windig**
wine **der Wein**
wine merchant/shop **die Weinhandlung**
wing **der Flügel**
winter **der Winter**
with **mit + dat.** (*see grammar, p. 182*)
without **ohne + acc.** (*see grammar, p. 182*)
woman **die Frau**
wonderful **wunderbar**
wood **das Holz**
wool **die Wolle**
word **das Wort**
work **die Arbeit**
to work (*job*) **arbeiten**
(*function*) **funktionieren**

world (*noun*) **die Welt**
(*adj.*) **Welt-**
World War One **der erste Weltkrieg**
World War Two **der zweite Weltkrieg**
worried **besorgt**
worse **schlimmer**
worth: it's worth . . . **es ist . . . wert**
it's not worth it **es lohnt sich nicht**
would like (*see 'to want'*) **möchte**
wound **die Wunde**
to wrap (*up*) **verpacken**
wrong (*incorrect*) **falsch**
to write **schreiben**
writer **der Schriftsteller/die Schriftstellerin**
writing pad **der Notizblock**
writing paper **das Briefpapier**

X

X-ray **die Röntgenaufnahme**

Y

yacht **die Yacht**
to yawn **gähnen**
year **das Jahr**
leap year **das Schaltjahr**
yellow **gelb**
yes **ja**
yesterday **gestern**
yet **noch**
yoghurt **der Joghurt**
you **Sie** (*formal*)
du (*informal singular*)
ihr (*informal plural*)
young **jung**
your **Ihr, dein, euer** (*see grammar, p. 180*)
yours **Ihre/r/s, deine/r/s, eure/r/s**
youth **die Jugend**
youth hostel **die Jugendherberge**

Z

zip **der Reißverschluß**
zoo **der Zoo, der Tiergarten**
zoology **die Zoologie**

EMERGENCIES

You may want to say

See also Problems and complaints, *page 170*; Health, *page 158*)

Phoning the emergency services

(Emergency telephone numbers, *page 289*)

(I need) the police
(Ich brauche) die Polizei
*(ish **browke**) die polit**siy***

(I need) the fire brigade
(Ich brauche) die Feuerwehr
*(ish **browke**) dee **foyervayr***

(I need) an ambulance
(Ich brauche) eine Ambulanz
*(ish **browke**) **iyne amboolants***

I've been attacked (mugged)
Ich bin überfallen worden
*ish bin ewber**fallen** **vorden***

I've been raped
Ich bin vergewaltigt worden
*ish bin fergay**valtigt** **vorden***

There's been an accident
Es ist ein Unfall passiert
*es ist iyn **oonfall** pas**seert***

There's a fire
Es brennt
es brennt

There's someone injured/ill
Jemand ist verletzt/krank
*yay**mant** ist fer**letst**/krank*

It's my husband/son/boyfriend
Es ist mein Mann/Sohn/Freund
es ist miyn mann/zohn/froynd

It's my wife/daughter/girlfriend
Es ist meine Frau/Tochter/Freundin
*es ist **miyne** frow/**toshter**/froyn**din***

Please come immediately
Kommen Sie sofort
kommen** zee zoh**fort

Come to . . .
Kommen Sie zu . . .
***kommen** zee tsoo . . .*

My name is . . .
Mein Name ist . . .
*miyn **naame** ist . . .*

The number of this telephone is . . .
Die Telefonnummer hier ist . . .
*dee tele**fohn**noommer heer ist . . .*

Where is the police station?
Wo ist das Polizeiamt?
*voh ist das polit**siyamt***

Where is the hospital?
Wo ist das Krankenhaus?
*voh ist das **krank**enhows*

Can anyone speak English?
Kann jemand Englisch sprechen?
*kan **yay**mant **en**glish shprecken*

Please call the British Embassy
Bitte rufen Sie die britische Botschaft an
*bitte **roo**fen zee dee **brit**ishe **boht**shaaft an*

I want to see a lawyer
Ich möchte einen Anwalt sehen
*ish **mersh**te **iy**nen **an**valt zayen*

I want to speak to a woman
Ich möchte eine Frau sprechen
*ish **mersh**te **iy**ne frow **shpre**ken*

You may hear

When you phone the emergency services

Kann ich helfen?
*kann ish **helf**en*
Can I help?

Was ist passiert?
*vas ist pas**seert***
What's happened?

Wie heißen Sie?
*vee **hiy**ssen zee*
What is your name?

Was ist Ihre Adresse?
*vas ist **eere** a**dresse***
What is your address?

Was ist passiert?
*vas ist pas**seert***
What happened?

Wo ist es passiert?
*voh ist es pas**seert***
Where did it happen?

Wann ist es passiert?
van ist es passeert
When did it happen?

Können Sie beschreiben . . . ?
kernnen zee beshriyben
Can you describe . . . ?

The police

Kommen Sie mit zur Polizei
kommen zee mit tsoor politsiy
Come with me/us to the police station

Sie sind verhaftet
zee zint ferhaftet
You are under arrest

The doctor

Sie müssen ins Krankenhaus
zee mewssen ins krankenhows
You have to go to hospital

Er/Sie muß ins Krankenhaus
er/zee moos ins krankenhows
He/She has to go to hospital

Wo tut es weh
voh toot es vay
Where does it hurt?

Tut das weh?
toot das vay
Does that hurt?

Wie lange haben Sie das schon?
vee lange haaben zee das shon
How long have you been like this?

Wie lange hat er/sie das schon?
vee lange hat er/zee das shon
How long has he/she been like this?

You may want to say

Quickly!	**Schnell!** *schnell*
Call the police	**Rufen Sie die Polizei** *roofen zee dee politsiy*
Call the fire brigade	**Rufen Sie die Feuerwehr** *roofen zee dee foyervayr*
Call an ambulance	**Rufen Sie eine Ambulanz** *roofen zee iyne amboolants*
Get a doctor	**Rufen Sie einen Arzt** *roofen zee iynen artst*
Help	**Hilfe!** *hilfe*
Police!	**Polizei!** *politsiy*
Stop!	**Halt!** *halt*
Stop thief!	**Haltet den Dieb!** *haltet dayn deep*
Fire!	**Feuer!** *foyer*
Look out!	**Paß auf!** *pass owf*
Be careful!	**Vorsicht!** *forzisht*
Danger! Gas!	**Gefahr! Gas!** *gayfaar gas*
Get help quickly	**Wir brauchen schnell Hilfe** *veer browken shnell hilfe*
It's very urgent	**Es ist sehr dringend** *es ist zayr dringent*
It's an emergency	**Es ist ein Notfall** *es ist iyn nohtfall*

POLICE	**110**
FIRE	**112**
AMBULANCE	**112**